Introduction to Natural and Man-made Disasters and their Effects on Buildings

Roxanna McDonald

AMSTERDAM BOSTON HEIDELBERG LONDON
NEW YORK OXFORD PARIS SAN DIEGO
SAN FRANCISCO SINGAPORE SYDNEY TOKYO

Architectural Press
An imprint of Elsevier
Linacre House, Jordan Hill, Oxford OX2 8DP
200 Wheeler Road, Burlington, MA 01803

First published 2003

British Library Cataloguing in Publication Data
A catalogue record for this book is available from the British Library

Library of Congress Cataloguing in Publication Data
A catalogue record for this book is available from the Library of Congress

ISBN 0 7506 56700

For information on all Architectural Press publications
visit our website at www.architecturalpress.com

Typeset by Newgen Imaging Systems (P) Ltd, Chennai, India
Printed and bound in Great Britain

Contents

Foreword

While it has become an accepted fact that the escalation of severe disaster events triggered by natural hazards and related technological and environmental disasters is increasingly threatening communities worldwide, the journey towards integrated disaster reduction in light of these threats is far from being achieved. The loss of human lives, livelihoods and property – often due to human activities that lead to increasing poverty, population growth and density, environmental degradation and climate change – has forced the issue of disaster reduction and risk management higher on the policy agenda of affected governments as well as multilateral and bilateral agencies and non-governmental organizations (NGOs), and it is time to take action to incorporate disaster reduction at all levels of society.

Losses from disasters caused by natural hazards will continue to increase unless there is a shift towards proactive solutions, with due recognition given to the reality that risk and vulnerability are indeed cross-cutting concerns relating to the social, economic, environmental and humanitarian sectors, with disaster reduction playing a fundamental role in the agenda of sustainable development.

The increasing pressure of growing urban populations is a key consideration in the planning and implementation of disaster reduction initiatives. Protecting critical facilities and infrastructure is necessary for the effective and sustainable functioning of any society in order to avoid disruption or compromise in the event of a natural disaster. The planet cannot afford the increasing costs and losses due to disasters, and while we cannot always anticipate natural hazards, we can at least ensure that we build our communities to be as resilient as possible by way of protecting urban infrastructure and implementing the appropriate codes, policies and procedures to protect public safety.

Earthquakes in India, El Salvador and Turkey brought enormous loss of life and widespread destruction across local affected communities, largely attributable to the collapse of buildings. Contrary to the wider perception that disasters only occur in developing countries suffering from socio-economic constraints, the European floods in 2002 devastated historic landmarks and urban constructions, demonstrating that even developed countries are not immune to the threat of natural hazards.

The magnitude and destructive consequences of disaster have serious implications for communities' risk and vulnerability to disasters across the planet. By learning more about disasters and their potential impacts, we are able to put into practice our knowledge towards global disaster reduction. *Introduction to Natural and Man-Made Disasters and their Effects on Buildings* is one such example of the value of analysing natural hazards and learning from case studies and experiences appropriate methodologies and best practices to enhance protection from hazard impact so that societies can remain functional at the time of crisis or following a major disaster. We welcome the work of Roxana McDonald, contributing to the advancement of disaster reduction efforts.

Sálvano Briceño
Director, UN/ISDR
United Nations Inter-Agency Secretariat for
the International Strategy for Disaster Reduction

Introduction

Introduction

We have all suffered from minor disasters, such as breaking a beautiful vase – or possibly a major disaster such as a motor accident, but this book deals with a wide variety of natural and man-made disasters. We don't like to think of disasters, hoping that they won't happen in our lifetime. This book is, however, a useful reminder. It shows the incredibly large range of possible disasters.

Curiously, floods are the most damaging, and with 'greenhouse warming', these are likely to increase. The most awful scenario that I can imagine is if either the Aswan High Dam or the Yangtze Dam were to break, and both are in seismic regions. If this disaster were to happen, would it be 'natural' or 'man-made' – or both? The new 100-year flood maps issued by the Environment Agency in the UK are not particularly accurate, and cause insurance problems for householders. It is worth a house purchaser's while to assess the risk from flood, soil subsidence and settlements.

Earthquakes immediately come to mind as the most lethal, because their effect is almost instantaneous, whereas one should get some warning of flood. People living in seismic zones can do a great deal to mitigate the next earthquake, but are reluctant to do this, because they hope it won't happen in their lifetime. The trouble is that although earthquakes may be probable, the exact timing of their arrival cannot yet be predicted. House owners can do a good deal to mitigate damage by good maintenance of their property, and adding strength to possible weak points. Studies after earthquake shows weaknesses in traditional construction, which should be rectified. A great deal can be done to protect the infrastructure of services, and to plan ahead of a possible earthquake. After earthquakes, delays in protecting buildings from the weather, and repairing damaged buildings, increase the cost of repairs and cause unnecessary hardship.

Unsurprisingly, Fire causes greatest loss of life in North America, because of the use of softwood in domestic buildings. Fire is something we must all guard against, and the causes are common. Unattended cooking, cigarettes and arson are frequent causes of fire. Historic buildings are often subject to arson, and their security needs special care.

Whereas most disasters are relatively local some, such as the Chernobyl atomic meltdown or the release of cyanide into a tributary of the Danube can affect many countries. Wild-fire can also extend over vast areas, and severe storms can wreak widespread havoc to buildings, trees and communications.

This book ranges over the whole spectrum of disasters, ending with Appendices giving emergency action checklists and fact sheets for earthquakes, floods, hurricanes and tornadoes, extreme heat, landslides and mudflows, terrorism, wildfire emergencies, and nuclear accident mitigation. Wars are man-made disasters, made even worse by ethnic cleansing as in the former Yugoslavia, and collateral damage as in Afghanistan.

The author has had first hand experience with buildings affected by natural and man made disasters. She stresses the effect of good design and planning can have in limiting the impact of disasters on the built environment. Legislation for good standards of construction reduces vulnerability only if implemented.

National Governments, the United Nations Agencies and non-governmental organisations face the urgent need to find solutions to the escalating threat of macro disasters to mankind. Unfortunately, they meet the reluctance of human nature to face potential disasters.

The author defines the purpose of her book – 'to make a small step towards providing a general understanding of the principal types of disaster, and in particular, how they can affect buildings. By understanding how these natural and man-made events take place, how they evolve, and how they affect us, we stand a better chance to build and live safely in stronger communities resilient to disaster.' I believe the author has succeeded.

B. M. Feilden, May 2003

Acknowledgements

Many people and organizations have been helpful in the process of assembling information and writing this book. Amongst them, I am especially grateful to the following, whose assistance and support have made it possible for me to successfully complete what at times has been daunting task:

First, I am indebted to my Contributors, for generously agreeing to share their experiences and particular insight:

Professor Engineer Alexandru Cismigiu – Romania

Bertrand Penneron – architect – France

Miro Group – structural engineers – Romania and France

Jonathan P. Kumin – architect – Alaska

Christine Theodoropoulos – Associate Professor at the University of Oregon, and students Anne Deutch and John Glavin

Rena Pitsilli-Graham – architect – UK

I am also grateful to:

Debbie and Rick Haller for introducing me to the American point of view.

Linda Millard – architect – for the Alaskan connection.

Patrick Cherouette – Editor of *Les Cahiers Techniques du Batiment*, Group Moniteur, France, for assisting with earthquake information and images.

Loic Babary – Mayor of Reignac sur Indre, for providing the village archive flood images.

Andrew Beattie-Grant – for help with the research and the Irish connection.

Ing. Vlastar Apostolescu – for help with the finer points of earthquake details.

Bogdan Goilav – structural engineer – Everest Engineering, France, for the Romanian connection

I am especially grateful to Jane Fawcett for her generous encouragement and advice.

Of the many organizations addressing the problems of coping with disasters, I am particularly grateful to the following, which have provided indispensable information:

United Nations International Strategy for Disaster Reduction (ISDR)

United Nations Environment Programme (UNEP)

FEMA (US Federal Emergency Management Agency)

EERI (The Earthquake Engineering Research Institute)

A non-profit, technical society of engineers, geo-scientists, architects, planners, public officials, and social scientists. EERI members include researchers, practicing professionals, educators, government officials, and building code regulators.

Grateful thanks to my editors:

Katherine MacInnes, for not giving up on the idea of this book, Alison Yates for her supportive advice and Liz Whiting for helping it come into being.

1 Introduction

Definition

The Oxford Dictionary defines disaster as a: *Sudden or great misfortune, calamity, great failure, ill starred event – (DIS + GK ASTRON star)*, which gives an indication of how we perceive disaster: unpredictable, outside our control, and overpowering; an event, controlled by the stars and gods!

From antiquity to modern times, human existence has been marked by the dramatic effects of nature's hazardous power. Despite catastrophic events, man did not give up, he tried to fight it, tried to coexist with it, and tried to control it.

Most disaster sites have remained populated; sometimes through faith in tradition and continuity, more often due to increased poverty and inability to travel to a better place. Archaeological excavations have revealed that at the time the city of Pompeii was destroyed by the eruption of Mount Vesuvius, many buildings had just been repaired following damage from an earthquake. All the same, the village of Pompeii and surrounding settlements continue to be populated to this day. The wine from the vines planted on the warm mountain slopes is just as sought after now as it was in Roman times, and tourists watch happily the guides frying eggs on the hot bare ground near the volcano's crater.

In building terms, man's best efforts, like the seven wonders of the ancient world, were time and time again defeated by nature. The Colossus of Rhodes was destroyed by an earthquake in 224 BC, as was the Mausoleum of Halicarnasus in 1402. The Alexandria Lighthouse survived a first earthquake in 500, as well as deliberate Arab attempts to demolish it in the ninth century. Having escaped further earthquakes in 1182 and 1303, it was finally destroyed, in 1375, by yet another earthquake.

With the advance of science and technology, man has significantly improved his ability to cope with nature's might, but at the same time, he has also brought onto himself a new set of problems: global warming, ecological disasters, mutating life forms.

When talking of disasters, most people tend to think of natural hazard events, but this is no longer the case. There are *natural disasters*: such as earthquakes, floods, tornadoes, hurricanes, droughts, volcanic eruptions etc. *man-made disasters* such as war, terrorism, or industrial accidents, and also disasters such as wild fires, which can be both, or man-made disasters that can trigger natural ones and vice versa.

Whether we regard nature as a mysterious force to be feared and placated with offerings or as a generous 'Mother Earth' in need of our protection, Nature cannot be ignored and man is constantly learning how to coexist with its unpredictable behaviour.

But when do Nature's actions change from spectacular displays into disasters? When does man's scientific and social progress become calamity?

From the safety of home, remoteness of satellites or TV we are amazed to see that extreme weather such as hurricanes and tornadoes can be so powerful as to leave a trail visible from space (see Fig. 1.1). We are mesmerized by the flowing lava of an active volcano and astonished at the effect an earthquake can have on the landscape. We feel inspired and scientists use these phenomenon to advance man's ability to survive adversity.

The same phenomena cease to be fascinating and are no longer just scientific data when they happen in densely populated areas causing major loss of human lives and livelihoods, as well as the destruction of economic and social infrastructures, or environmental damage. They become disasters.

During the past four decades, natural hazards such as earthquakes, droughts, floods, storms and tropical cyclones, wild land fires, and

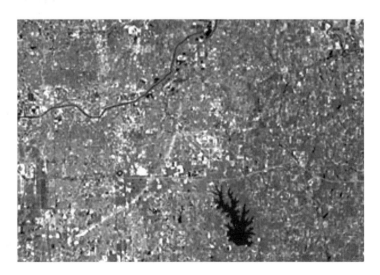

Fig. 1.1
Satellite view of tornado path over Oklahoma. © USDA United States Department of Agriculture.

volcanic eruptions have caused substantial devastation. Economic losses have increased almost 10 times during this period.

Although recent natural disasters have not been the century's worst, their cost in human lives, homelessness, and economic disruption has escalated. The reasons for this are being put down to:

- An increase in frequency of natural phenomena. The explanations for this vary and have been subject to considerable ongoing debate: global warming, climate change, the destruction of the ecological balance through unscrupulous depletion of natural resources by man, deforestation, planetary evolution influencing the Earth's structure and behaviour.
- An increase in world's population moving into areas vulnerable to earthquakes, landslides, flooding, and other natural hazards. Poverty and population increase mean that a growing number of people have no other choice but to move to vulnerable or unsafe areas where housing is cheaper or easily available whilst the better off are able to move to safer buildings and locations.
- Economic conditions in the developing world. Poverty and social economic pressure often make people more vulnerable as they often have to move to unsafe land because there are no alternative at reasonable cost close to employment opportunities. Also, economic factors create an increasing infrastructure vulnerability either through lack of understanding by decision makers or by tendency by some builders to use the cheapest design and materials for increased short-term returns on their investments.

A United Nations evaluation assesses that in addition to the projected estimation of 100 000 lives lost each year due to natural hazards alone, the anticipated global cost of natural disasters will top US$ 300 billion annually by the year 2050. (*Source*: United Nations background Paper No. 5 for WSSD – World Summit on Sustainable Development.)

The compounded effects of natural and man-made catastrophes pose escalating threats to humankind on a multitude of inter-related levels. Governments, multilateral agencies, and non-governmental organizations (NGOs) facing the urgent need to find solutions, are uniting their efforts to find an international strategy for disaster reduction and risk management, but despite general good intentions it is proving a difficult task, as economic and political priorities have continued to prevent conclusive action.

At the 1992 Earth Summit in Rio, 172 governments took part at the conference, which examined the link between sustainable development and the environment. The subsequent climate conference, leading to the Kyoto agreement, created the framework to reduce global warming through reducing carbon dioxide emissions, but the withdrawal of the United States has been a serious setback.

In September 2002, at the Johannesburg Summit, participants discussed ways of creating a solid basis for implementing sustainable development but progress on firm commitment has been disappointing. In the context of a number of United Nations actions, a concerted effort is evolving towards developing policies and measures to enable societies to: (a) be more resilient to hazards; (b) undertake developments that do not increase vulnerability to hazards.

While no country in the world is entirely safe, developing countries are most exposed due to their inability to limit the impact of hazards. An estimated 97% of natural disaster related deaths each year occur in developing countries and the percentage of economic loss in relation to the gross national product (GNP) far exceeds the one in developed countries. (*Source*: UN International Strategy for Disaster Reduction – background document to WSSD.)

The need to reverse trends in vulnerability is also highlighted by the fact that the emphasis on disaster response and humanitarian assistance has absorbed significant resources which would have been directed in development and risk reduction.

The subject of natural and man-made disasters is vast and the world is becoming more and more concerned with analysing, reviewing, and finding solutions.

The purpose of this book is to make a small step towards providing a general understanding of the principal types of disaster and, in particular, of the way in which they can affect buildings. By understanding how these natural and man-made events take place, how they evolve, and how they affect us, we stand a better chance to build and live safely in stronger communities resilient to disaster.

Disasters and buildings

In coping with disaster, man-made structures often constitute the weakest link. Buildings, roads, bridges, and dams – structures that normally serve and protect us become the most dangerous places to be in when disaster strikes (Figs 1.2 and 1.3).

Whilst it is not possible or desirable to turn buildings into bunkers and war shelters, in the aftermath of recent disasters, a world traumatized by the World Trade Centre collapse is seeking ways of enabling buildings to better withstand such unforeseen threats.

The increased frequency of disasters and their cost in both human life and recovery terms, can be partly accounted for by the fact that modern society is more and more that of urban and suburban dwellers. When disasters hit unpopulated areas, they pass without much effect but when

they hit large concentrations of both people and property they create urban disasters.

The greatest proportion of these losses is taken by the destruction of housing which also affects the ability of the survivors to recover physically and financially. The impact of disasters such as earthquakes or storms on the building stock in general has exposed the extent to which, in many countries, little or no provisions were made in respect of setting building design standards to prevent, or at least minimize, hazard damage.

Whilst it would be impossible to anticipate random or freak events, it is possible to ensure a basic resistance which would enable the occupants of a building to escape to safety and that the building does not suffer major damage. The public may perceive these standards as guarantees of a building's safety but this cannot be the case.

The World Trade Centre in New York is a perfect example in this context: designed to withstand 30000 tonnes of wind pressure as well as impact from a jet aeroplane, (following a 1947 incident when the Empire State Building was hit by one) it survived relatively unscathed a terrorist attack in 1994 (see Chapter C, c, page 148). However, when hit by not one but two larger, fuel-loaded planes, events went beyond imaginable design parameters and as the fire protection was blown away by the immense impact force, the heat generated by the burning fuel caused the structure to fail. Nevertheless, the buildings stood long enough to allow thousands to escape.

Examining vulnerabilities of structures and exploring all available avenues with the help of technology in order to identify possible changes in design control mechanisms, improvements on building standards and control standards has become a priority. Building designers must ask themselves what are the greatest threats to the particular structure concerned and what can be done about it within available budgets. It is not just new buildings that are concerned but existing ones as well.

Older cities have the difficult task of finding solutions for deteriorating buildings and ageing bridges, constructed at a time when currently accepted hazard threats were not envisaged and which together with leaking tunnels, unreliable levees and pipelines may put them on the brink of catastrophe.

This book aims at giving a general idea about the way disasters can affect buildings. A better understanding of how buildings fail in these extreme conditions can enable research and technology to make buildings and other structures safer, more reliable and secure. Governments, architects, engineers, and other allied professions are joining efforts at all levels to examine vulnerabilities of structures, exploring all available avenues with the help of technology in order to identify possible changes in design control mechanisms, improvements on building standards and control standards.

What is a disaster?

A disaster can be defined as an event, either natural or man-made, which has the ability to destroy life, natural landscape and man-made infrastructure.

The same event, in different circumstances, could be a source of scientific data or a deadly catastrophe. It all depends on where it took place and how it was perceived.

From the safe distance of a satellite, an earthquake in a deserted area will provide a fascinating glimpse of earth's activity as a living planet, but in a densely populated area it will probably leave thousands dead, home-less, and displaced causing total devastation.

Disasters often develop in stages:

1. A hazard is being created or exists as a potential, direct or indirect, threat to human life, property, and the environment. For example, the danger of a landslide can be created by extensive deforestation or mining. When new buildings are to be located in an earthquake or flood-prone area, the potential danger is there. Similarly, when nuclear waste disposal or CO_2 pollution are present, the environment is under threat, sometimes with catastrophic consequences.
2. When a hazard becomes active reality and when damage relevant to man is inflicted, it becomes a disaster. This is usually as a result of:
   • failure to recognize in time the existence and extent of a potential danger, such as continuing to build on in-fill or flood zones; or
   • inadequate prevention measures when awareness exists but the extent is underestimated, for example, not consolidating buildings in earthquake zones or not providing lightning conductors in storm areas.
3. In the aftermath, chain effects occur, propagating further disasters and/or serious disruption to the social fabric and community. When disaster strikes, there is a often a complete breakdown of the main services and communications, which leads to panic, propagation of disease, fires, and further loss of life. The basic needs of the population such as food and shelter cannot be met as vital aid is slow to reach the affected areas. Earthquakes can bring on fires and land-slides as well as destruction of roads and services, industrial acci-dents or nuclear plumes can contaminate waterways and lands in countries far afield.

The response associated with the three stages is reflected in relative measures:

(a) *Preparedness*: When the threat of a hazard is recognized, the response involves measures and activities that facilitate evaluating its danger and potential, in order to assess what action would be neces-sary to avoid, preempt or limit the damaging effect likely to result in loss of life and property. Limiting mining and deforestation, con-trolling development on dangerous land, raising awareness of the dangers, and applying lessons learned from similar events are possible preventive measures.
(b) *Mitigation*: Measures for coping with disaster and lessen its impact. Consolidating and upgrading building to a better seismic resistance or constructing levees to contain flooding, are some examples of suitable steps.
(c) *Loss assessment and management*: Larger-scale measures; these concern the wider scale proactive reaction, aimed at organizing and

using community resources for evaluating loss and preventing a serious disruption of its social and economic fabric taking place in the event of an other disaster occurring.

Minimizing risks and improving chances of fighting the effects of a disaster as well as ensuring that the community is able to be self-contained until the situation becomes more stable, are the main considerations of this stage.

Disaster impact

Impact can vary depending on its type and the economic conditions in the areas struck by a disaster.

(a) Relation between different types of disaster, death toll, and level of damage (Table 1.1). Statistics show that 90% of high death toll disasters (more than 100 deaths in a single event) tend to be natural disasters of which, 40% floods, 20% tropical storms, and 15% earthquakes and drought.

(b) Relation between the effect of disasters on developed and poorer countries. Analysis of the impact of disasters relative to their geographical location (Table 1.2) show that poorer countries suffer more life loss that more developed countries, where the impact is felt more in high costs. Table 1.2 covers a sample period between 1947 and 1980.

This can be explained by a number of factors:

- population growth;
- use of marginal land for settlement for cost reasons and shortage of suitable land due to environmental erosion;

Table 1.1
Types of disaster, death toll, and the level of damage.

Type of disaster	High death toll (in number of disasters)	Extensive damage caused (in number of disasters)
Floods	202	76
Tropical storms	153	73
Epidemics	133	
Earthquakes	102	24
Landslides	54	1
Storms	46	6
Droughts	21	53
Heat waves	20	
Fires	15	4
Cold waves	14	1
Volcanoes	12	2
Tsunamis	9	1
Famine	4	
Avalanches	2	

Source: Landau Forte School case studies.

Table 1.2
Impact of disasters relative to their geographical location for the period 1947–1980.

Location	Death toll (in number of lives)	Number of disasters	Average life loss per event
North America	11531	358	32
Central America and The Caribbean	50676	80	633
South America	49265	75	657
Europe	26694	119	224
Africa	25540	34	751
Asia	1054090	437	2412
Australasia	4502	16	282
Total	1222298	1119	1092

Source: Landau Forte Geography case studies.

- people forced by poverty to live in hazardous areas;
- new hazards being created as a result of economic considerations (radiation, chemical spills, etc.);
- technical solutions such as high-rise blocks or large dams;
- poor housing, building materials, and workmanship;
- vulnerability of population due to poor health and inadequate infrastructure.

Whilst it has been considered that more developed countries were less at risk thanks to their better built environment and support systems, recent sustained devastation in the United States and Japan, considered amongst the best equipped in the world, have made clear that other aspects have influenced events and consequently have to be considered when evaluating the effects of disasters.

Disaster characteristics
(a) *Magnitude* – The size of the particular event measured on an accepted scale and the extent of its destructiveness.
(b) *Frequency* – How often disasters happen? Whilst scientists do not agree whether the change of weather pattern or tectonic plates movement are the cause, there is no doubt that the frequency of natural disasters has increased in recent years.
(c) *Duration* – The length of time a disaster can take varies from a few seconds in the case of an earthquake, for example, to a few days as during floods, and up to decades in the case of droughts.
(d) *Area covered* – Can range from local to worldwide.
(e) *Distribution* – This can be coastal, at plate boundaries, fault lines, polar, etc.
(f) *Speed of onset* – This concerns the time elapsing between the start and the moment of peak.
(g) *Occurrence pattern* – This can be regular like cyclones, more random like earthquakes, in tandem with another like tsunamis, etc.

Disaster response

Whilst hazards will always exist, they do not have to become disasters.

Recent analysis of the more measurable hazards such as earthquakes, storms, or floods shows that even in cases of historically lower intensity, more hazards become disasters because they cause more loss of life and socioeconomic disruption than ever before.

As shown earlier, the increase in world population, urbanization, and poverty play a deciding role in the current situation, and international action is being focused accordingly. Led by the United Nations International Strategy for Disaster Reduction (ISDR) numerous initiatives are taken to address the problems at each disaster development stage: preparedness, mitigation, and management.

Preparedness

Having survived devastation and loss, the obvious priority is to prevent its recurrence, or if events are unavoidable, to be ready and able to use available resources for relief and rehabilitation.

Achieving this is a matter for constant review and organization within a number of main considerations:

- Obtaining reliable information about similar events and interfacing with other communities – This means analysing what actually happened, both in terms of scientific data and loss valuation. At the time of a crisis, when events are highly charged with emotion and human tragedy, the media's tendency to sensationalize and politicize events can distort the facts. Data from humanitarian organizations can prove invaluable in estimating the nature, quantities, and priorities of aid required in any particular situation.
- Increasing public awareness of natural hazards and their causes – Explaining to people what happened and what could happen again, facilitating self-help as well as reducing the confusion that compounds the disaster effects in the immediate aftermath.
- Reducing risk through minimizing the potential for damage – For example, in an earthquake-prone area inspecting the remaining buildings and deciding on selective consolidations, setting design parameters for new buildings and restricting development in areas at risk will help the community to survive in the long term.
- Recognizing the need to reverse trends in vulnerability to natural and man-made disasters – Poverty, population growth, and social pressure force people to live in dangerous locations and in low-cost unsafe shelters because no other reasonable alternatives are available.
- Improving the ability to provide advance warning.

In the United States, the Federal Emergency Management Agency (FEMA) has developed *Project Impact* as a national strategy programme to be implemented by 2010. It has two main objectives: (a) to increase public awareness of natural hazard risks; and (b) to reduce the risk of loss of life, injury, economic cost, and destruction of natural and cultural resources. The five key elements of the programme are: (i) hazard identification and risk assessment; (ii) applied research and technology transfer; (iii) public awareness training; (iv) incentives and resources; and (v) leadership and coordination.

Many of the fact sheets provided in this book are based on, or adapted from FEMA information. The availability and common sense approach of this information makes raising the public self-awareness possible.

Mitigation

Mitigation includes any activity that prevents an emergency, reduces the chance of an emergency happening, or lessens the damaging effects of unavoidable emergencies. If disaster strikes, the immediate concern will be how to cope with its effects. There will be an urgent need to search for survivors and lead them to safety, provide relief and temporary shelter, stabilize the situation, and clear the debris.

Emergency services are usually first on the scene:

- fire-fighters;
- medical teams;
- engineering teams clearing dangerous areas.

Numerous governmental agencies and NGOs step in providing emergency food and water supplies, medical assistance, transport, and temporary shelter. Organizations such as FEMA in the United States, have the responsibility to coordinate all state agencies involved, provide assistance, temporary shelter, and general guidance.

Management

Once the crisis has passed, the main task is to plan ahead not only to prevent and be prepared should it happen again, but also to assimilate the long-term implications of potential hazards and ensure that the community has the necessary mechanisms in place to continue functioning during and after the recurrence of an event.

The main concern is to put in place the necessary support for undertaking the principal tasks: prevention, preparedness, response, rehabilitation, and recovery. Experts in post-disaster reconstruction issues such as Prof. Mary C. Comerio of the University of California, increasingly recognize the need for a type of *disaster recovery* that is capable of fine-tuning the input to differentiate the needs of public and private sectors, housing and commercial buildings, offices and industrial concerns.

A key element to disaster management is capacity building and strengthening of institutional arrangements at all levels to address risk reduction in the long term. This involves:

1. Creating legislation related to disaster reduction, such as:
   - land-use regulations to prevent the use of dangerous or flood-prone land for building;
   - building codes to ensure suitable standards for known hazards, such as earthquake;
   - environmental protection.
2. Facilitating cross-boundary harmonization in the management of natural hazards occurring in neighbouring countries.
3. Creating and implementing urban development strategies and land-use plans that identify suitable locations of facilities such as roads, power plants in vulnerable areas.
4. Creating early warning systems and maintaining an information system capable of building people's capacity to respond quickly at the local level when crisis occurs.

Loss assessment

The extent to which community is able to survive disaster impact depends a great deal on the ability to forecast losses, preparedness for acting in emergency, and anticipation of likely characteristics of the event. The increased frequency of disasters in the past decade has provided additional data, which is making it possible to re-evaluate past decisions. An examination of lessons learned and a better understanding of what happens when disaster strikes are essential in providing ways and means for survival.

The sequence of events in the aftermath of disaster are:

(a) *Emergency response.* People are taken out of immediate danger, fires put out, and victims taken to hospitals. Experts, volunteers, and emergency services begin searching for survivors, making buildings as safe as possible and assessing damage. Relief services direct people affected to temporary shelters, distribute humanitarian aid and comfort the shocked population. At this stage, chaos and panic are endemic and a clear and firm action is imperative if confusion is to be avoided.
(b) *Action to restore main services and provide temporary shelters.*
(c) *Fact-finding activities.* Governments, technical experts, and insurers, etc. move in to evaluate the situation, establish what medium- and long-term aid is needed. Volunteers and officials work round the clock to understand the implications, often under media pressure highlighting personal tragedy and politicizing what is seen as a lack of adequate support.
(d) *Assessing the damage and loss.* Escalating recovery costs have become a major concern not only for their immediate drain of resources but also for their likely medium- and long-term economic effects and indirect losses that are not immediately perceived.

Table 1.3 lists the 100 most expensive natural disasters of the twentieth, but it is difficult to judge to what extent it reflects the real costs and long-term effect.

Table 1.3
The 100 most expensive natural disasters of the twentieth century.

	Country	Year	Day	Month	Disaster	Region	Continent	Damage (US$)
1	Japan	1995	20	1	Earthquake	E. Asia	Asia	131 500 000 000
2	Soviet Union	1991	27	4	Flood	Russia. Fed.	Europe	60 000 000 000
3	Soviet Union	1988	7	12	Earthquake	Russia. Fed.	Europe	20 500 000 000
4	China, P Rep	1998	6	8	Flood	E. Asia	Asia	20 000 000 000
5	Italy	1980	23	11	Earthquake	Euro. Union	Europe	20 000 000 000
6	United States	1992	24	8	Cycl., Hurr., Typh.	N. America	Americas	20 000 000 000
7	United States	1994	17	1	Earthquake	N. America	Americas	20 000 000 000
8	Indonesia	1997	16	9	Wild fire	SE. Asia	Asia	17 000 000 000
9	Korea, Dem P Rep	1995	18	8	Flood	E. Asia	Asia	15 000 000 000
10	China, P Rep	1996		7	Flood	E. Asia	Asia	12 600 000 000
11	United States	1989	17	10	Earthquake	N. America	Americas	12 000 000 000
12	United States	1993	19	7	Flood	N. America	Americas	12 000 000 000
13	Japan	1994	4	10	Earthquake	E. Asia	Asia	11 700 000 000
14	Russia	1994	8	8	Flood	Russia. Fed.	Europe	11 200 000 000
15	United States	1995	16	5	Storm	N. America	Americas	10 000 000 000
16	India	1990	10	11	Cycl., Hurr., Typh.	S. Asia	Asia	8 000 000 000
17	Japan	1992	31	1	Storm	E. Asia	Asia	7 800 000 000
18	China, P Rep	1991	18	5	Flood	E. Asia	Asia	7 500 000 000
19	China, P Rep	1976	27	7	Earthquake	E. Asia	Asia	7 000 000 000
20	Iran, Islam Rep	1990	20	6	Earthquake	S. Asia	Asia	7 000 000 000
21	China, P Rep	1996		8	Flood	E. Asia	Asia	6 314 500 000
22	Australia	1982			Drought	Oceania	Oceania	6 000 000 000
23	Italy	1994	5	11	Flood	Euro. Union	Europe	6 000 000 000
24	China, P Rep	1994		6	Flood	E. Asia	Asia	5 460 000 000
25	Japan	1991	27	9	Cycl., Hurr., Typh.	E. Asia	Asia	5 200 000 000
26	United States	1992	11	9	Cycl., Hurr., Typh.	N. America	Americas	5 000 000 000
27	NA	1990	25	1	Storm	Euro. Union	Europe	4 600 000 000
28	Italy	1997	26	9	Earthquake	Euro. Union	Europe	4 524 900 000
29	Spain	1995			Drought	Euro. Union	Europe	4 500 000 000
30	China, P Rep	1995	4	7	Flood	E. Asia	Asia	4 450 000 000
31	Poland	1997	28	6	Flood	Rest. Europ	Europe	4 300 000 000
32	China, P Rep	1994	10	6	Cycl., Hurr., Typh.	E. Asia	Asia	4 000 000 000
33	Mexico	1985	19	9	Earthquake	C. America	Americas	4 000 000 000
34	Spain	1983	25	8	Flood	Euro. Union	Europe	3 900 000 000
35	United States	1998	16	7	Heat. wave	N. America	Americas	3 700 000 000
36	NA	1989	17	9	Cycl., Hurr., Typh.	Caribbean	Americas	3 579 000 000
37	United States	1996	5	9	Cycl., Hurr., Typh.	N. America	Americas	3 400 000 000
38	NA	1990	25	2	Storm	Euro. Union	Europe	3 200 000 000
39	India	1998	9	6	Cycl., Hurr., Typh.	S. Asia	Asia	3 010 000 000
40	Algeria	1980	10	10	Earthquake	N. Africa	Africa	3 000 000 000
41	China, P Rep	1997	8	1	Cold. wave	E. Asia	Asia	3 000 000 000
42	United States	1995	6	10	Cycl., Hurr., Typh.	N. America	Americas	3 000 000 000
43	Ecuador	1998		2	Flood	S. America	Americas	2 869 300 000
44	United States	1977			Cold. wave	N. America	Americas	2 800 000 000
45	China, P Rep	1989	14	7	Flood	E. Asia	Asia	2 789 000 000
46	Yugoslavia	1979	15	4	Earthquake	Rest. Europ	Europe	2 700 000 000

Table 1.3 *Continued*

	Country	Year	Day	Month	Disaster	Region	Continent	Damage (US$)
47	China, P Rep	1997	19	8	Cycl., Hurr., Typh.	E. Asia	Asia	2 675 000 000
48	Argentina	1998			Flood	S. America	Americas	2 500 000 000
49	Zimbabwe	1982			Drought	E. Africa	Africa	2 500 000 000
50	China, P Rep	1993		7	Flood	E. Asia	Asia	2 450 000 000
51	Brazil	1978			Drought	S. America	Americas	2 300 000 000
52	United States	1979	12	9	Cycl., Hurr., Typh.	N. America	Americas	2 300 000 000
53	India	1990	25	8	Storm	S. Asia	Asia	2 200 000 000
54	Dominican Rep	1998	15	9	Cycl., Hurr., Typh.	Caribbean	Americas	2 193 400 000
55	Bangladesh	1988		8	Flood	S. Asia	Asia	2 137 000 000
56	United States	1972	18	6	Cycl., Hurr., Typh.	N. America	Americas	2 100 000 000
57	Bangladesh	1998	8	7	Flood	S. Asia	Asia	2 000 000 000
58	Canada	1992		6	Cold. wave	N. America	Americas	2 000 000 000
59	Honduras	1998	26	10	Cycl., Hurr., Typh.	C. America	Americas	2 000 000 000
60	Italy	1966	4	11	Flood	Euro. Union	Europe	2 000 000 000
61	Soviet Union	1991		5	Flood	Russia. Fed.	Europe	2 000 000 000
62	United States	1995	9	3	Storm	N. America	Americas	2 000 000 000
63	United States	1997	11	1	Flood	N. America	Americas	2 000 000 000
64	China, P Rep	1994	29	8	Flood	E. Asia	Asia	1 810 000 000
65	NA	1993	10	3	Storm	NA	Americas	1 800 000 000
66	United States	1983	17	12	Storm	N. America	Americas	1 800 000 000
67	Bangladesh	1991	30	4	Cycl., Hurr., Typh.	S. Asia	Asia	1 780 000 000
68	Netherlands	1995	20	1	Flood	Euro. Union	Europe	1 760 000 000
69	United States	1994	9	1	Cold. wave	N. America	Americas	1 755 000 000
70	United States	1986	1	7	Heat. wave	N. America	Americas	1 750 000 000
71	Mongolia	1996	23	2	Wild fire	E. Asia	Asia	1 712 800 000
72	France	1987	15	10	Storm	Euro. Union	Europe	1 700 000 000
73	Georgia	1991	29	4	Earthquake	Russia. Fed.	Asia	1 700 000 000
74	Japan	1990	21	6	Flood	E. Asia	Asia	1 700 000 000
75	Korea, Dem P Rep	1996	15	7	Flood	E. Asia	Asia	1 700 000 000
76	United Kingdom	1987	15	10	Storm	Euro. Union	Europe	1 700 000 000
77	Mexico	1993	19	6	Storm	C. America	Americas	1 670 000 000
78	United States	1983	17	8	Cycl., Hurr., Typh.	N. America	Americas	1 650 000 000
79	China, P Rep	1980		7	Flood	E. Asia	Asia	1 600 000 000
80	Iran, Islam Rep	1986	31	12	Flood	S. Asia	Asia	1 560 000 000
81	India	1996	6	11	Cycl., Hurr., Typh.	S. Asia	Asia	1 500 300 000
82	Chile	1985	3	3	Earthquake	S. America	Americas	1 500 000 000
83	China, P Rep	1986		8	Flood	E. Asia	Asia	1 500 000 000
84	China, P Rep	1996	10	9	Cycl., Hurr., Typh.	E. Asia	Asia	1 500 000 000
85	El Salvador	1986	10	10	Earthquake	C. America	Americas	1 500 000 000
86	Spain	1981			Drought	Euro. Union	Europe	1 500 000 000
87	United States	1985	27	10	Cycl., Hurr., Typh.	N. America	Americas	1 500 000 000
88	United States	1991	20	10	Wild fire	N. America	Americas	1 500 000 000
89	United States	1996	30	12	Storm	N. America	Americas	1 500 000 000
90	United States	1997	4	1	Flood	N. America	Americas	1 500 000 000
91	Virgin Is (US)	1995	15	9	Cycl., Hurr., Typh.	Caribbean	Americas	1 500 000 000
92	United States	1965	7	9	Cycl., Hurr., Typh.	N. America	Americas	1 420 000 000
93	China, P Rep	1931		7	Flood	E. Asia	Asia	1 400 000 000
94	United States	1969	17	8	Cycl., Hurr., Typh.	N. America	Americas	1 420 000 000
95	Mexico	1988	14	9	Cycl., Hurr., Typh.	C. America	Americas	1 350 000 000
96	United States	1995	8	1	Flood	N. America	Americas	1 340 000 000
97	France	1985		1	Storm	Euro. Union	Europe	1 320 000 000
98	Argentina	1985		10	Flood	S. America	Americas	1 300 000 000
99	Germany, Fed Rep	1976	2	1	Storm	Euro. Union	Europe	1 300 000 000
100	India	1990	6	5	Storm	S. Asia	Asia	1 300 000 000

Source: The Disaster Center, EM-DAT: The OFDA/CRED, International Disaster Database; www.md.ucl.ac.be/cred

In the aftermath of a disaster, decisions are often made under pressure and sometimes based on inaccurate information. Aid and resources available are usually provisions made on the basis of the previous similar crisis, and, more often than not, it is found that circumstances have altered, sometimes to a degree which renders provisions available totally inappropriate or inadequate. A closer look at the factors involved may help in avoiding the repetition of past mistakes and errors of judgement.

- *Accuracy of assessment* – This is subject to how *reliable* is the data used. Damage evaluation is usually established on the basis of insurance claims and government aid or loans. This does not take into account undeclared business losses and privately funded repairs. Also, over-evaluation or inclusion of very minor damage in claims distorts the true situation. When based on past relief costs, it is not always sure that all the funds expended were necessary or appropriate to the damage sustained and there is a risk for inadvertently compounding management errors and bad decisions.
- *Measure of loss* – Primarily loss is measured in lives lost and value of built infrastructure. This is neither straightforward nor immediately available for logistic and technical reasons. Analysis of past events often shows substantial discrepancies between estimated losses and number of insurance and state aid claims. The US Board on Natural Disasters of the National Research Council has appointed a new Committee on Assessing the Costs of Natural Disasters. The losses from natural disasters are far reaching, including direct damage to buildings, infrastructure elements, inventory, and natural resources and indirect costs from lost productivity and wages. To understand the scope and magnitude of the costs before action can begin, a multidisciplinary group of experts will identify the cost components that will be most useful for accurate characterization of disaster events. The committees report will help FEMA in its efforts to develop successful mitigation policies for natural disasters.
- *Coordination between the emergency and relief activities and decisions about recovery aid* – Most experts and analysts have concluded that whilst financing the recovery of public infrastructure must be immediate, the distribution of funds for general private recovery assistance should commence only when sufficient reliable information is available to enable them to evaluate the true extent of the need.
- *Careful evaluation of past claims* – This must be part of the recovery policy to ensure that adequate provisions are made.

Strategy trends

It is now widely accepted that more effective disaster prevention policies would not only save millions of lives but would also release the substantial funds currently spent in intervention and relief for use in sustainable development initiatives which would reduce the risk of disasters in the long term.

In preparation for the Johannesburg World Summit on Sustainable Development in September 2002, United Nations ISDR looked into ways of understanding the link between development environment and natural disasters. The current conclusion is that policies have to counteract a number of present global trends, which enable exposure to natural hazards to turn into disasters.

Human and infrastructure vulnerability

Least developed countries have been subject to highest population growth. Poverty, AIDS, and socioeconomic pressures such as unemployment cause migration and force people to live in dangerous locations, on unsafe land and in low-cost, sub-standard dwellings simply because there is no other alternative available to them. People are made further vulnerable by political instability and lack of personal security. Exposure to disasters exacerbates their predicament into chronic poverty and total inability to cope.

Deficiencies highlighted by recent disasters have also exposed the poor understanding of decision makers of disaster risks, allowing the construction of poorly designed buildings with cheap materials and inadequate protection against potential risks such as seismic or storm damage.

The 'domino effect' where natural hazards trigger technological ones, which are followed by environmental and humanitarian disasters can have global repercussions. In the context of a globalized society, both urban and rural populations are dependent on services distribution at a national and international level to such an extent that failure of one sector can affect people in areas not directly hit, causing general chaos and infrastructure failure.

Environmental degradation

Environmental degradation is often a factor in transforming a natural hazard or climatic extreme into a disaster. For example, river and lake flooding is aggravated and even caused by deforestation, which causes erosion, clogging of rivers, and river bed mutation.

The catastrophic consequence of unchecked emissions of greenhouse gases on climate changes has remained an unresolved issue, countries and political opinions disputing the facts in pursuit of different socioeconomic agendas.

The overuse of natural resources causes pollution leading ultimately to global changes in the environment. The human-induced climate change, according to recent projections of the Intergovernmental Panel on Climate Change, is likely to result in more water-related disasters with changes in temperature and rainfall variations. These affect the environment through accelerated desertification and degradations damaging agriculture, water resources, and human health.

It follows that reversing the current trends of environmental degradation must be a strategic priority in reducing disaster risks.

Growing poverty in developing countries

Poverty and hazard push people into exploiting environmental resources for survival, which only compounds their exposure to disasters such as drought, floods, or landslides. Whilst it has been established that in developed countries, economic losses caused by natural disasters have risen, their cost has not exceeded the national gross domestic product (GDP) wealth. In developing countries, on the other hand, in the context of receding economies, disaster losses are steadily overtaking GDP growth.

The reversal of current trends of environmental degradation with sustainable management of natural resources such as reforestation, suitable use of land and good management of rivers and coastal areas would increase the resilience to disasters of vulnerable communities.

The UN strategy for development policies to reduce vulnerability to disasters is currently promoting the following activities:

1. Motivating societies at risk to become engaged in the conscious management of risk and reduction of vulnerability by:
   * obtaining the commitment of the public authorities;
   * increasing public awareness;
   * stimulating interdisciplinary and intersectional partnerships;
   * Encouraging and facilitating the transfer of relevant data and information.
2. Developing more effective methodologies for assessing the economic impact of natural disasters to secure investment and trade continuity.
3. Harmonizing management of disasters that spread over several countries at a time.
4. Developing comprehensive urban development strategies and land-use plans.
5. Ensuring that environmental impact reviews systematically cover the hazard proneness and consider reduction measures where appropriate.
6. Encouraging proactive solutions in disaster risk reduction development.

Part I
Natural Disasters

2 Earthquakes

What happens during an earthquake

An earthquake is a wave-like vibration, which travels through the earth's crust. The Earth is a living planet and forces under the surface layer (the *lithosphere*) are in constant turmoil affecting its surface.

Observation of a number of phenomena, such as the drift of continents, grouping of volcanic eruptions, or ridges on the ocean floors, has led to the development in mid-twentieth century of the theory of *plate tectonics*, based on the premise that the Earth's surface is made out of gigantic rigid plates of rock, 80 km thick, floating in slow motion on top of the earth's hot and malleable core (see Fig. 2.1). Tectonic

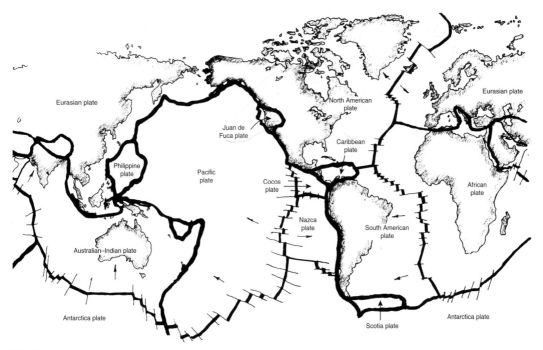

Fig. 2.1
Tectonic plates.

earthquakes occur when accumulated strain is suddenly released. Rocks break and brittle failure takes place.

Tectonic plates

There are seven major plates, sub-divided into smaller ones, and they change size and position moving relative to one another at speeds between 1 and 10 cm/year. As they move, intense geologic activity, such as earthquakes, formation of mountain ranges, or volcanic eruptions occurs (see Fig. 2.2).

Different types of seismic zones can be observed relative to the plate movement:

- When *plates move apart at divergent boundaries*, such as at the mid-Atlantic Ridge, hot magma flows up and, as it cools down, fills the gap forming new ridges, adding new material to the edges of oceanic plates. This process is known as *sea-floor spreading*. This seismicity is associated with volcanic activity along the axis of the ridges.
- Plates can *move towards each other at convergent boundaries*, and in doing so, they can either overlap (one side submerging the other), or push upwards against each other, forming major mountain systems such as the Himalayas. When the plates collide, and one plate becomes submerged by the collision, the hot temperatures it encounters deep in the earth's interior, melts the rocks creating new magma, which rises to the surface and erupts forming chains of volcanoes around the edges of the plates like in the case of *the Ring of Fire* (see Fig. 2.3), where earthquakes and volcanic eruptions are frequent. These narrow plates boundary areas, known as 'subduction zones', are associated with the creation of deep ocean trenches and big earthquakes.

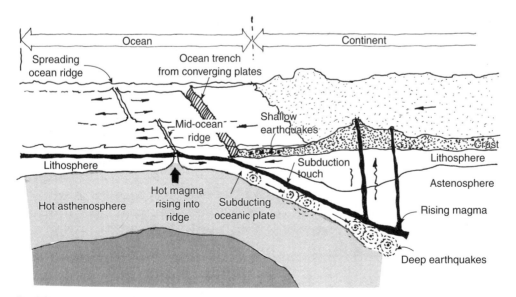

Fig. 2.2
Tectonic plate activity.

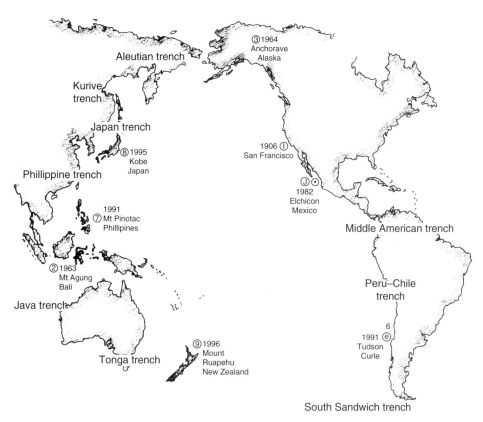

Fig. 2.3
The 'Ring of Fire'.

In the case of an earthquake under the sea, one side of the ocean floor drops suddenly, sliding under the other plate and in doing so, creates a vertical fault which generates a giant wave, a 'tsunami'. The tsunami travels at fantastic speeds, equalling that of commercial jetliners, but they can hardly be seen on the surface of the water. It is only when they reach the shore that they become destructive giants.

When oceanic plates collide with continental plates, the oceanic one slides beneath the continental plate forming a *deep ocean trench*, such as that which occurs at the boundary between the oceanic Nazca plate and the continental South American plate.

- Plates can also *slide past each other horizontally*, at transform fault boundaries. When the edges scrape each other tightly, they create tensions along the boundaries, which are associated with shallow-focus seismic events, unaccompanied by volcanic activity. San-Andreas Fault, or the Anatolian Fault in North Turkey are examples of this type of events.

Earthquake characteristics

The area of fault where a sudden rupture takes place, usually within the Earth, is called the *focus* or *hypocentre* of the earthquake. The point on

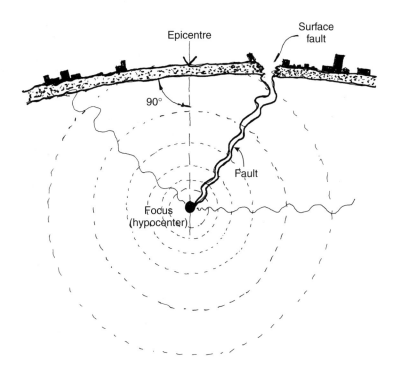

Fig. 2.4
Earthquake characteristics.

the Earth's surface situated above the focus is the *epicentre* of the earthquake (see Fig. 2.4).

Earthquakes are usually classified in terms of their depth:

- shallow – less than 70 km deep;
- intermediate – 70–300 km deep;
- deep – more than 300 km deep.

There are no earthquakes known to take place below a depth of 720 km.

Earthquake measurement

The severity of an earthquake can be assessed in different ways: either by quantifying its *magnitude* in terms of the energy released by measuring the amplitude, frequency, and location of the seismic waves, or by evaluating its *intensity*, by considering the destructiveness effect of the shaking ground on people, buildings and natural features.

Intensity is measured against key responses, ranging from people being woken up by movement, furniture moving, up to total destruction, subject to the distance between the place observed and the epicentre of the earthquake.

This is the principle of the Modified Mercalli (MM) Intensity scale, developed in 1931 by American seismologists. It has 12 increasing levels ranging from: I – hardly noticeable vibration, II – felt by most people at rest, through to VII – difficult for a person to remain standing, X – most structures destroyed, and XII – catastrophic devastation. It is not scientifically arrived at and is based on arbitrary ranking based on observation.

Magnitude quantifies the energy released at the hypocentre of an earthquake as expressed by the amplitude of the seismic wave measured by instruments, and is represented by a single value.

Magnitude is measured by seismographs on the Richter magnitude scale, which was developed by Charles F. Richter of the California Institute of Technology in 1935. Its value is determined from the logarithm of the amplitude of the strongest wave recorded with adjustments for variations of distance between the epicentre and the measuring instruments. A recording of 7, for example, indicates a disturbance with ground motion 10 times as large as a recording of 6. The energy released by an earthquake increases by a factor of 30 for every unit increase in the Richter scale. Table 2.1 gives the frequency of earthquakes and the effects of the earthquakes based on this scale.

To cause objects and buildings to be thrown into the air, the upward motion of the Earth's crust has to be greater than the accelerating effect of the gravitational pull on these objects. Table 2.2 gives an indication of how the two measuring scales compare against each other and relative to the corresponding gravity-induced acceleration.

Table 2.1

Frequency of earthquakes and their effects based on the Richter scale.

Richter scale magnitude	No. of earthquakes per year	Typical effects of magnitude
<3.4	800 000	Detected only by seismometers
3.5–4.2	30 000	Just about noticeable indoors
4.3–4.8	4800	Most people notice them, windows rattle
4.9–5.4	1400	Everyone notices them, dishes may break, open doors swing
5.5–6.1	500	Slight damage to buildings, plaster cracks, bricks fall
6.2–6.9	100	Much damage to buildings, chimneys fall, houses move on foundations
7.0–7.3	15	Serious damage, bridges twist, walls fracture, buildings may collapse
7.4–7.9	4	Great damage, most buildings collapse
>8	One every 5–10 years	Total damage, surface waves seen, objects thrown in the air

Source: UP Seis – Department of Geological Engineering and Sciences, Michigan Technological University, USA.

Table 2.2
Comparison of MM intensity scale and Richter scale.

Mercalli scale	Acceleration (cm/s^2)	Richter scale
I		
	1	
II		3.5–4.2
	2.5	
III		
	5	
IV		
	10	4.3–4.8
V		
	25	
VI		4.9–5.4
	50	
VII		5.5–6.1
	100	
VIII		
	250	6.2–6.9
IX		
	500	
X		7.0–7.3
	750	
XI		7.4–8.1
	980	
XII		> 8.1

Source: Zephryus.demon.co.uk/education

Geographic and historic evolution: statistics

Earthquake prediction

The shift of tectonic plates is a major consideration when attempting to predict earthquakes.

Many earthquakes occur at plate boundaries, such as the 'ring of fire' (see Fig. 2.3) along the margins of the Pacific, others take place in mid-plate. This knowledge enables us to locate those regions on the Earth's surface where it is likely that large earthquakes will occur, but whilst it tells us *where* 90% of Earth's major earthquakes will take place, we cannot tell accurately *when*. This is because, in the context of millions of years of plate tectonic process, it is difficult to tell exactly where a particular year fits in within the world cycle of stress build-up and stress release.

In a letter about a devastating Romanian earthquake in March 1977 (see Fig. 2.5) Charles Richter remarks:

> 'As yet, there is no way of forecasting such happenings in advance. It may be that observations made preceding the present disaster may lead to progress in that direction'

LRA\WW— LINDVALL, RICHTER & ASSOCIATES
EARTHQUAKE SCIENCES AND ENGINEERING

825 COLORADO BOULEVARD, LOS ANGELES, CALIFORNIA 90041 □ TELEPHONE (213) 254-5259

FREDERICK C. LINDVALL
RAY W. CLOUGH
ROY C. VAN ORDEN
J. BRENT HOERNER

CHARLES F. RICHTER
RICHARD H. JAHNS
RONALD F. SCOTT
C. ERIC LINDVALL

March 15, 1977

Professor Ioan Ursu
Embassy of Romania
1607 23rd St. N.W.
Washington, D.C. 20008

Dear Professor Ursu:

Thank you for your letter of March 10, with its kind invitation to visit Romania.

I decline with great regret; but I feel that in my present circumstances I must leave this to younger and healthier men.

Some of our best seismologists and engineers are now in Romania, or on their way. I look forward to learning their conclusions.

I feel that there is not much anyone can teach the seismologists in Romania about their special problem. They have been working with it for many years, and are well aware of their unique situation. Nowhere else in the world is a center of population so exposed to earthquakes originating repeatedly from the same source. The only similar occurrences are the repeated earthquakes deep under the Hindu Kush region.

However, this repetition does not justify the sort of warning that has been appearing in the news media, to the effect that another large event is immediately expected. Such rumors always are put into circulation after every earthquake disaster; they cause excessive alarm to no good purpose. It is still worse when they originate in official statements, or misinterpretations of such statements.

As you undoubtedly know, in 1940 a damaging earthquake in Romania in October was followed by a larger and disastrous one in November. As yet, there is no way of forecasting such happenings in advance. It may be that observations made preceding the present disaster may lead to progress in that direction.

Very sincerely yours,

Charles F. Richter

c:Ambassador Nicolae

Fig. 2.5
Letter from Charles Richter.

Prediction efforts attempt to establish a stress increase prior to rock rupture by monitoring motions and possible effects of stress accumulation such as changes in magnetization or temperatures, gas releases, animal behaviour, etc. At best, they can assess increased probability of seismic activity, but not predict an actual event.

Effect of earthquakes

Earthquakes have been part of our life throughout history, which has recorded their effects from antiquity.

Even the Seven Wonders of the World have not been safe and some were lost because of earthquakes: The Colossus of Rhodes was destroyed by an earthquake in 224 BC, as was the Mausoleum of Halicarnasus in 1402. The Alexandria Lighthouse resisted a first earthquake in AD 500, and having survived deliberate Arab attempts to demolish it in the ninth century, and more earthquakes in 1182 and 1303, finally succumbed in 1375 to another earthquake. At the time it was buried by the volcano eruption, Pompeii was repairing damage caused by an earthquake.

Earthquakes cause devastating loss of life and destruction of man-made structures such as buildings, roads, and dams. They also trigger fires, landslides, and flooding. As loose soil, such as landfill, loses the ability to bear loads, the ground behaves like quicksand making buildings sink and disappear. At sea, they cause the giant tsunamis described above, which devastate shorelines.

Loss of life is linked to the density of population on the particular location more than the magnitude of the earthquake. Tables 2.3 and 2.4 illustrate the point.

Effect of earthquakes and seismic design principles

The high concentration of seismic events of the last decade has highlighted the vulnerability of certain buildings such as the reinforced concrete buildings of the 1930s or those designed in accordance with seismic regulations of the 1960s.

The physical effects of an earthquake on a building can be examined more fully nowadays because scientists are able to travel to the place

Table 2.3
The deadliest earthquakes on record.

Date	Location	Deaths	Magnitude
23.01.1556	Shansi, China	830000	Not known
27.07.1976	Tangshan, China	255000	8.0
9.08.1138	Aleppo, Syria	230000	Not known
22.05.1927	Nr Xining, China	200000	8.3
22.12.856	Damghan, Iran	200000 (estimated)	Not known
16.12.1920	Gansu, China	200000	8.6
23.03.893	Ardabil, Iran	150000(estimated)	Not known
1.09.1923	Kwanto, Japan	143000	8.3
5.10.1948	Ashgabat, Turkmenistan	110000	7.3
28.12.1908	Messina, Italy	70000–100000	7.5
Sept. 1290	Chihli, China	100000	Not known
Nov.1667	Shemakha, Caucasia	80000	Not known
18.11.1727	Tabriz, Iran	77000	Not known
1.11.1755	Lisbon, Portugal	70000	8.7
25.12.1932	Gansu, China	70000	7.6
31.05.1970	Peru	66000	7.8
1268	Silicia, Asia Minor	60000	Not known
11.01.1693	Sicily, Italy	60000	Not known
30.05.1935	Quetta, Pakistan	30000–60000	7.5
4.02.1783	Calabria, Italy	50000	Not known

Source: National Earthquake Information Center, US Geological Survey, C/O Infoplease.com © 2002, Learning Network (http: //www.infoplease.com/ipa/A0884804.html).

Table 2.4
The 10 most powerful earthquakes of the twentieth century.

Number	Location	Date	Magnitude
1	Chile	22.05.1960	9.5
2	Prince William Sound, Alaska	28.03.1964	9.2
3	Andreano Island, Aleutian Islands	09.03.1957	9.1
4	Kamchatka	04.11.1952	9.0
5	Off the coast of Equador	31.01.1906	8.8
6	Rat Islands, Aleutian Islands	04.02.1965	8.7
7	India–China border	15.08.1950	8.6
8	Kamchatka	03.02.1923	8.5
9	Banda Sea, Indonesia	01.02.1938	8.5
10	Kuril Islands	13.10.1963	8.5

Source: National Earthquake Information Center, US Geological Survey,
C/O: Infoplease.com © 2002, Learning Network
(http://www.infoplease.com/ipa/A0884804.html).

where a disaster took place as soon as it happens and immediate observation of damage details has facilitated the improvement of building techniques in very efficient ways.

Effective design relies on understanding the way in which earthquakes affect building structures. In general terms, the effect can be direct, from the motion induced stresses and indirect from the associated events associated with or triggered by earthquakes.

Direct effects

Ground failure, which causes structures to become unstable or collapse. Ground failure can take place in a number of ways:

- *Surface faulting or fault rupture*. Faults are fractures in the Earth's crust where most earthquakes occur. They are usually most active along the plate boundaries, but can also occur within a plate. As the tectonic plates move against each other, seismic energy builds up along the plates and remains 'locked' along the faults due to friction and rock interlock. Once the energy accumulated is large enough, it is released through the slippage of rocks along the fault ruptures. Earthquakes can trigger or inhibit the release depending on the fault geometry. Surface faults ruptures are fault ruptures which break to the surface (see Fig. 2.4). If a structure, such as a building or a road, straddles a fault, the ground displacement that occurs during an earthquake will seriously damage or rip apart that structure (see Figs 1.2 and 2.6). A surface rupture of about 60 km long was the main feature of the Chi-Chi Taiwan earthquake, which took place on 21 September 1999 (see Fig. 2.6). The rupture caused extensive devastation at the Shih-Kang dam, located about 50 km north of the epicentre as it passed directly beneath one end of the dam. The large vertical offsets (10 m vertical and 2 m horizontal) were curved which is typical of thrust faults due to the dip of the fault. In other areas, buildings not directly

Fig. 2.6
Dam rupture in Taiwan Earthquake.
© EERI / J.P. Bardet.

Fig. 2.7
Liquefaction example, Izmit, Turkey.
© EERI.

within the rupture zone showed no apparent damage compared to those located within the 15–20 m wide rupture zone, which suggests that the motions associated with permanent fault offset take place slower than dynamic shaking.

- *Soil vibration*. This can either literally shake a building off its foundations, modify its support or cause foundations to disintegrate.
- *Liquefaction*. In liquefaction conditions, buildings can start to lean, tip over, or sink into the ground. Liquefaction occurs when sediments below the water table lose strength temporarily and behave as viscous liquids rather than solids (Fig. 2.7). Liquefaction occurs predominantly in recently deposited sands and silts with high ground water levels. When saturated, soils such as loose sands, lose their bearing capacity during severe ground shaking, and become fluid due to a sudden reduction in shear resistance caused by the temporary increase of the pore fluid pressure (Fig. 2.8). High-density areas, built on loose

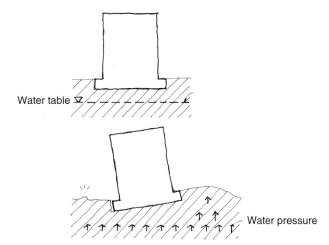

Fig. 2.8 Structural tilting due to liquefaction – diagram.

Water table

Water pressure

ground material, can suffer devastation even from relatively small earthquakes as a result. After the earthquake, the ground usually firms up and the ground water recovers its deeper level. However, as the soil consolidates after the earthquake, further damage to buildings can occur as a result of more settlement and 'sand boil' eruptions (water and sediment bursts from the pressure charged liquefied sand). Liquefaction can also cause an increased lateral pressure on retaining walls, which can be displaced, tilt, or collapse altogether. This effect can often be observed during earthquakes in waterfront walls retaining loose saturated sand.

- *Ground lurching*. Strong surface seismic waves make the ground heave and lurch and damage the buildings in their path.
- *Differential settlement*. Earthquakes shake the ground beneath buildings causing it to settle at a different level to its initial one. This can be particularly damaging when liquefaction occurs (see Fig. 2.8).
- *Lateral spreading*. As a result of liquefaction, large masses of soil can be displaced laterally with catastrophic consequences. At their worst, they take the form of *flow failures*, when large volumes of soil travel down steep slopes, sometimes for tens of kilometres. On slopes of less than 3°, lateral displacement caused by the liquefaction of subsurface layers can determine horizontal displacements of several metres. The displaced ground suffers cracks, rifting, and buckling. As a result, lateral spreads disrupt foundations of buildings built across the failure, cause engineering structures such as bridges to buckle and service pipelines to break. The damage from lateral spreading can be extensive. In the 1906 San Francisco earthquake, all major pipelines were broken by a ground failure displacements of less than 2 m. This relatively small event caused extensive devastation because it hindered fire fighting and 85% of the total damage to San Francisco was caused by fire.

- *Landslides and mudslides*. The shaking of the ground can cause landslides, mudslides, and avalanches, which can damage buildings and cause loss of life. Amongst the many landslides that took place during the 1999 Taiwan earthquake, some were enormous like the one at Tsaoling, located 30 km from the epicentre. Its debris travelled nearly 3 km carrying with it buildings, cars, and roads, destroying everything in its path and killing 34 people.

Vibrations transmitted from the ground to the structures: The shaking of the ground is transmitted to buildings in different ways, subject to the type of Earth's motion. The way the buildings will be affected will depend on their shape, construction, and characteristics.

Earth motion types

Seismic waves are of two main types: *deep* and *surface* waves. Deep waves travel from the Earth to the surface and can be *primary* or *P* wave, a back and forward motion felt like a sharp jolt; and *secondary* or *shear* or *S* wave, a rolling motion.

Surface waves travel along the Earth's surface, and can be *Love* wave, a horizontal type of surface wave, with no vertical motion; and *Rayleigh* wave, a retrograde surface wave, travelling along a free interface with an elliptical motion.

At any given point, a combination of these types of waves results in a complex random motion, often is predominantly horizontal, but with considerable vertical motion as well. Figure 2.9 showing the trace scratch made on the floor by a kitchen range during the 1933 Long Beach, California earthquake, illustrates the random nature of the ground movement. From a design point of view, structures must assume that earthquake waves may come from any direction.

Fundamental period

Tall buildings undergo several types of vibration, of which the *fundamental* or *first mode* is the most significant. Whilst a stiff object, such as a bulky piece of furniture, will only vibrate in the first mode, a flexible object such as a tall building, will vibrate in a number of modes, which change direction at node points (see Fig. 2.10).

Fig. 2.9
Scratch left on floor by kitchen range in the 1933 Long Beach, California earthquake © EERI.

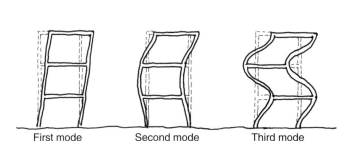

First mode   Second mode   Third mode

Fig. 2.10
Vibration modes diagram.

The initial ground motion is often amplified, depending on the nature of the soils and rocks of a given site. Soft soil can amplify the motion several times, as much as six times, and consequently earthquake damage tends to be more severe in areas of soft ground.

Every object has a fundamental period at which it vibrates if set in motion. The ground also has a fundamental period of its own. If an object is set in motion by an external force such as the ground shaking, which would be at the fundamental period of the object, the result will be dissonance and the motion of the object will tend to increase.

In building structures, the main determinant of the vibration period is height and proportions. A tall slender building will have a long vibration period and will swing back and forth quite slowly. A 40-storey building will sway every 7 s while a single storey for every 0.1 s, and a filing cabinet only every 0.05 s (see Fig. 2.11).

A child's swing will behave like a pendulum and continue to swing for a few minutes without assistance, but buildings and other objects will not do the same because their vibration is reduced or damped by their construction, thereby stopping their vibration after a few seconds. The extent of damping depends on the materials of construction, their connections, and architectural elements such as partitions, ceilings, cladding, etc. Ductility is an other important characteristic of building structures because ductile structures can absorb much more force than a rigid ones. Non-ductile structures such as non-reinforced masonry or inadequately reinforced concrete can be at risk because of the possibility of brittle failure.

Pancaking
When subjected to lateral forces, vertical members, such as columns or walls, fail by buckling when the building mass exerts its gravity force on

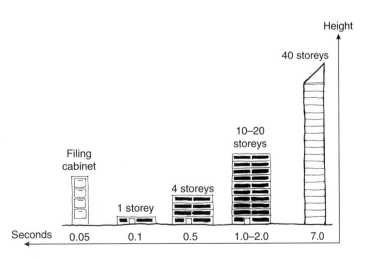

Fig. 2.11
Fundamental period diagram.

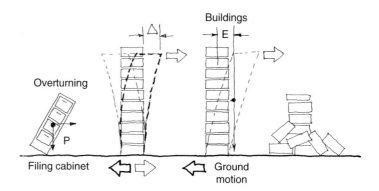

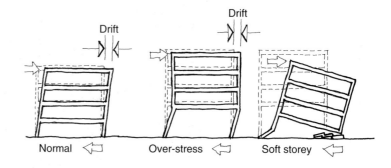

Fig. 2.12
Pancaking.

Fig. 2.13
Soft storey principle.

Fig. 2.14
Building collapse due to soft storey – earthquake in Greece. © EERI.

a member distorted or put out of plumb by lateral forces. This is known as the P–e or P delta effect, where P is the gravity load and e or delta are, respectively, the eccentricity or extent to which the forces are offset.

Buildings seldom overturn in this situation (as would a piece of equipment or a filing cabinet), they fall apart or 'pancake' (see Fig. 2.12). This is due to the fact that they are composed of many elements connected together and when the earthquake forces pull these components apart buildings collapse vertically rather than fall over. Overturned buildings, usually, are structures with strong shear walls which retain their integrity when upset by a soft storey action (see Figs 2.13 and 2.14) foundation failure, or a combination of these.

Stiffness

Lateral forces are distributed in proportion to the stiffness of resisting members. In turn, stiffness is related to shape and is measured by deflection. Horizontal storey to storey deflection is known as *drift* and it relates to storey height (see Fig. 2.15). A very important aspect of stiffness in lateral force design is that earthquake force distribution tends to be proportionate to the stiffness of the resisting elements. The forces are attracted to the stiff elements and this is an important consideration for relative column stiffness, which varies approximately as a cube of its length (see Fig. 2.16).

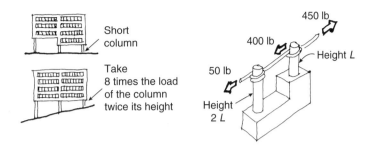

Fig. 2.15
Drift principle diagram.

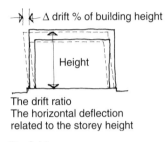

The drift ratio
The horizontal deflection
related to the storey height

Fig. 2.16
The 'short column' principle diagram.

Fig. 2.17
Earthquake provoked innundation in
Golcuk, Turkey. © EERI/Ascheim.

Indirect or consequential effects

- *Tsunamis.* These are series of ocean waves induced by earthquakes. They usually take place along the subduction zones and are very common in the Pacific Ocean. Earthquakes cause ripple motions in water, barely noticeable in the open ocean, despite their speed which can reach 750 km/h, but as they travel thousands of miles when they reach shallow water they can reach heights of 30 m causing severe damage to coastline cities.
- *Seiches.* Seiches are similar to small tsunamis and occur as a result of the sloshing of enclosed water in reservoirs, lakes, and harbours shaken by earthquake waves or intense storms. Only a few feet high, they can nevertheless flood or knock down houses, and topple trees.
- *Landslides.*
- *Floods.* Earthquakes can rupture dams, water pipes, or levees (raised river embankments). The water from reservoirs and rivers then flood the area damaging buildings, sometimes even sweeping them away with considerable loss of life (Fig. 2.17).
- *Fires.* Fires are one of the main hazards when an earthquake takes place. During the first moments after an earthquake, there is often darkness and dust. People try to get light striking a match and start

fires from broken gas mains and appliances. Other fires are started by the short-circuiting of broken power lines or by fractured heating and cooking devices. The fact that often the water mains are also severed makes fire-fighting difficult and means that fires spread easily. As mentioned earlier, most of the damage in the 1906 San Francisco earthquake was caused by the raging fire which burned for 3 days destroying most of the city. This was mostly due to the fact that ruptured water mains made fire-fighting virtually impossible.

Seismic design principles

Specialist studies show that the ability to construct buildings that have both *flexibility* and *cohesion*, is one of the most important considerations when designing earthquake-resistant structures. A main objective is to provide an effective linking of different parts of a building so as to enable them to work together and avoid the dislocation which causes collapse. As well as considering the form of a building and the materials employed, good design also entails choosing a judicious location. When examining the effects of earthquakes on buildings, three main areas can be identified as vulnerable and requiring specific design attention:

The ground and the ground–foundation–structure interaction

Buildings located close to valleys, near rivers, or on mountain slopes have been shown to be more at risk from earthquake, and in the construction of seismic-resistant building it is essential to an understand all aspects concerning the nature of the ground such as rigidity and energy dispersion.

Before making design decisions, it is important to understand the physical mechanisms of the ground. Seismic calculations determine the way in which, when shaken, a building will respond to the movement of the Earth and how this will affect its foundations. This involves considering following aspects:

(a) applied stress;
(b) restrictions;
(c) movements;
(d) deformations.

The reactions of a building are closely related to the nature of the ground and soil. Experience shows that the degree of intensity to which an earthquake is felt depends on the nature of the ground throughout which the seismic vibrations travel. Buildings situated on mobile ground suffer much greater damage than those located on rocky ground because they associate themselves to oscillators amplifying the shocks applied to the base. The adjustment ground/structure will depend on the specific location and characteristics such as the building height and its vibration sequence.

Fig. 2.18
Nikaia Hall, Nice, France. © W. Jalil.

Modern buildings in seismic conditions are often built of reinforced concrete material considered to satisfy the necessary ductility criteria. The association between concrete and reinforcement is complementary providing resistance in both compression and tension. The adherence between these two components is of prime importance in transmitting stress loads. A good transmission will be provided through the existence of sufficient friction between them, which can be achieved if the reinforcement bars are ridged. Considerably more reinforcement is necessary in seismic zones to cope with the increased stress (see Fig. 2.18).

To ensure the rigidity of a structure, it must be anchored and tied to form a 'cage' like unit. This is particularly important in smaller buildings, as it ensures a good redistribution of forces between the different bracing elements. The load-bearing walls and their connection to the foundations and slabs should be reinforced to counteract the shearing effect that stress the vertical elements. The foundations must have additional steel provision to allow the fixing of vertical anchor ties which should be provided at each angle and opening being tied to reinforced lintels. Each level should have horizontal ties linked to the vertical elements.

The geometry of the load-bearing structure
To absorb the wave vibrations transmitted by the Earth's movements; it is recommended that expansion joints and a homogenous distribution of the structural volumes complement the ductility of reinforced concrete. The role of the expansion joints is to separate the building in several independent blocks, able to move freely when an earthquake shakes the building. (In France, standards require joints of up to 60 mm in areas most at risk) (PS92) The joints should be continuous and linear both in plan and elevation and continued in basements if the soil is not of homogenous type.

In earthquake areas, buildings with discontinuous, stiff, or asymmetrical volumes are not suitable as each asymmetrical element introduces a

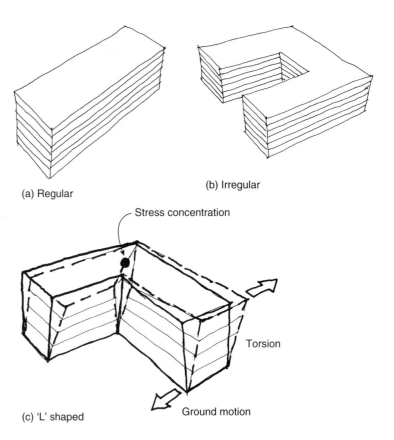

(a) Regular

(b) Irregular

Stress concentration

Torsion

Fig. 2.19
Effect of building shape in seismic
conditions.

(c) 'L' shaped

Ground motion

weakness encouraging a multilayered type of collapse. Regular configurations are essentially symmetrical in plan and elevation and have no setbacks or complicated layouts in plan (Fig. 2.19a). Irregular buildings have geometrical complexities of plan or elevation. In this example (Fig. 2.19b) the building is regular in elevation, but has re-entrant corners in plan and is symmetrical along one axis only. In an L-shaped building, the movement of the wings will result in a concentration of stress at the junction point whilst the asymmetry will result in torsion, which can cause the building to literally tear itself apart at the notch point (see Fig. 2.19c).

Torsion occurs when the centre of the mass and the centre of resistance do not coincide, or there is a difference of stiffness in materials or as a result of the way the resisting elements are arranged. Lightweight architectural components such as partitions or asymmetrical facade panels can create an unbalanced resistance and subject the building to torsion forces (see Fig. 2.20).

The resistance of the structure to earthquake forces
The structure design must provide adequate resistance to the earthquake forces to which a building is likely to be subjected. For lateral resistance, *braced frames* will provide the necessary resistance through triangulated

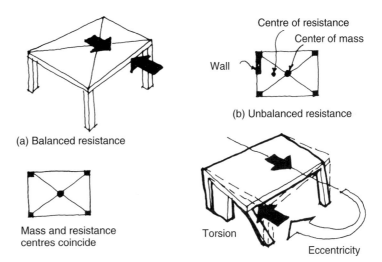

Centre of resistance
Center of mass
Wall

(b) Unbalanced resistance

(a) Balanced resistance

Mass and resistance centres coincide

Torsion

Eccentricity

Fig. 2.20
Torsion effect in seismic conditions.

geometry. Connections must be strong and elements must be able to resist buckling and tension. Most braced frames are concentric, but eccentric brace frames are increasingly used with link beams replacing the connection points, making it possible to reduce failure to localised points, leaving the structure intact.

Other solutions consist of the provision of *shear walls* (which provide resistance along the plane of their length) or *moment resisting frames* (which rely on the joints to provide lateral resistance). The latter are usually constructed of steel so as to make use of the material's inherent ductility, but they can also be of reinforced concrete.

Architects designing buildings in earthquake prone-areas must take into account the effects of stress concentration and avoid:

- volumes which are excessively projecting or set back;
- 'transparent' stories susceptible to shearing;
- clear, unbraced, or discontinuous ground floor elevations.

Potential earthquake damage often involves vertical irregularity; one storey, usually the first, has taller, fewer columns which makes it significantly weaker or more flexible than the storeys above (see Fig. 2.21). Whilst a regular building would distribute its drift equally to each floor, in soft-storey buildings, although the overall drift is the same, the second floor connections will be subject to almost all the drift and fail. Stress concentrations means that an undue proportion of the overall forces is concentrated at one or a few points of a building. Isolated elements such as a particular set of beams, a wall or several columns may be stressed beyond their design capacity and fail, and in doing so they may bring the whole building down in a chain reaction. Also, as forces tend to be attracted by

Stress concentrations

The most serious condition of vertical irregularity
is the soft or weak storey, in which one storey, usually
the first with taller, fewer columns, is significantly
weaker or more flexible than the storeies above.

Flexible first floor   Discontinuity   Heavy superstructure

Fig. 2.21
Examples of 'soft storey' design.

stiffer elements these too will tend to be stress concentration points. Just as demolition techniques seek to weaken a few key columns and connections, in earthquake conditions these 'weak' points will be the cause of final collapse while the upper floors, which have been subjected to little or no drift, remain almost undamaged.

Examples of serious danger of dislocation and collapse can be found in:

- heterogeneous masonry;
- buildings where the centre of gravity is too high;
- building with too heavy roofs;
- verandas;
- projecting features;
- chimneys.

Once a structure type is chosen, attention must concentrate to making the building as balanced as possible, if necessary by decomposing it into geometrically simple elements. For example, an L-shaped building can become two rectangular blocks.

Rehabilitation of old structures

When considering the rehabilitation of an old structure, it is important not to assume that it would be sufficient just to revise the structural dimensions. Each building must be considered on its individual merits, as many buildings were not designed with earthquakes in mind.

Apart from improving the structural size of main components, ties and anchoring are useful methods. External ties consisting of reinforced concrete ring beams (see Fig. 2.22) or metallic ties and crosses would counteract the horizontal thrust linking columns and beams.

For masonry buildings, a basic technique involves bonding a layer of reinforced grout shell to the outside of the walls. The shell is made to function integrally with the wall through a grid of studs hooked and welded to mesh reinforcement on the outside, tightened with nuts and bearing plates on the inside (see Fig. 2.23). Another method, known as

(a)　(b)

Fig. 2.22
Concrete ring beam strengthening to building in Chisinau, Moldova.

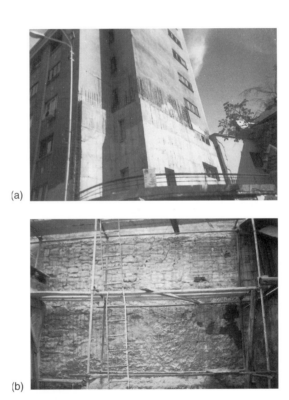

(a)

(b)

Fig. 2.23
Rehabilitation of old structures in Bucharest, Romania (a) Reinforced concrete 40s building being upgraded; (b) Consolidation of solid masonry exterior and (c) interior views.

(c)

the composite reinforced masonry, aims to achieve a ductilization of the brick masonry through the insertion of a reinforced grout web.

In the case of historic buildings, in addition to structural consolidation there is the added problem of maintaining the historic appearance and proportions. Chapter 9 looks at some of the methods used to achieve this. Subject to what materials existing structures are made of, consolidation aims at either adding rigidity to a flexible steel structure or reducing the brittle element of a concrete one by adding steel.

New ideas, research, and recent developments for seismic-resistant construction

Although we understand earthquakes better now, than say 50 years ago, predicting them remains mainly guesswork. Scientists try to determine where and when earthquakes occur by observing the movement of the tectonic plates and by looking at the history in a particular region and detecting the pressure and fault lines. However, predictions remain vague and only aftershocks can be said to be easier to anticipate. What can be done? Efforts are best directed into raising preparedness and designing buildings to specific standards. The *1973 Uniform Building Code* sets out an international standard for construction and structural strengthening.

General guidelines recommend:

- strengthening of support material;
- designing buildings so that they are flexible enough to absorb vibrations without falling or deteriorating.

A *Eurocode 8* is currently being prepared aiming at harmonizing European standards. For example, the British and French principles of design differ and adjustments will be required. In France, the protection of the building's occupier takes precedent over the preservation of the building in earthquake conditions, and this is reflected by a reduced use of reinforcement in high-rise blocks. This is not acceptable in countries which have statutory requirements seeking to limit the effects of the earthquake on buildings to an absolute minimum, and who tend to impose high reinforcement provisions of about $10–50 \, \text{kg/m}^3$.

Established systems seek to reduce the failure of structural steel or increase the ductility of concrete An example is the composite structural steel-reinforced concrete system which was developed in Japan in order to overcome the reduction in the ductility of structural steel by local buckling in framed structures requiring a significant energy dissipation capacity and the associated problems posed by the confined reinforced concrete. A light steel frame with castellated beams is built with solid continuous shapes at the joints providing the necessary anchorage which will then be covered with confined reinforced concrete to avoid buckling This type of composite structural is commonly used in Japan for mid- and high-rise building material.

New systems tend to seek to:

• modify the seismic forces transmitted from the ground to the building; or
• modify the response of the building.

Amongst systems developed in the past decade are:

Base isolation – This system works through lengthening the period of the building superstructure to about 2 s and it is particularly useful in the case of buildings where the disturbance of the interior and contents should be kept to a minimum, such as historic buildings, laboratories, museums, and hospitals. It involves the insertion of special bearings under the structure.

Passive energy dissipation – This system reduces building drift slowing down the building motion through the insertion of devices that dissipate the earthquake energy by friction or deformation of specially located materials. One such material is the magnetorheological (MR) fluid (fluid, fluid that changes to near solid when exposed to a magnetic force and back to liquid when the force is removed) used inside large dampers to stabilize buildings during earthquake. The fluid was developed in North Carolina's Lord Corporation Laboratory, used in dampers in buildings and bridges in research seeking to create 'smart structures' that are able to automatically react to seismic activity.

Scale model testing – Experimental research has been conducted in the Structural laboratories of the University of California at Berkley and as part of a comprehensive US – Japan research programme testing scale models with earthquake simulators at the Science City of Japan, Tsukuka. They aimed at finding ways to improve seismic-resistant design and construction of buildings, and have highlighted the importance of three-dimensional interacting behaviour of walls and surrounding frames. Results of tests have also indicated the need for considering the contribution of slab reinforcement to the negative moment capacity of the girders cast monolithically with the floor slabs.

New technologies and methodologies are being used to provide the necessary information for the prevention and mitigation of earthquake impact.

• *Global positioning system* (GPS) a space-based technology is being used to provide real-time measurements of the way the ground is being deformed in seismic risk areas.
• *Synthetic aperture radar remote sensing* is being developed to provide continuous images of crustal deformation.
• *High-performance seismometer stations*, recording broadband high dynamic range ground motion, are being systematically installed

worldwide to provide emergency response and record strong earthquake data for building design parameters.

• *Paleoseismic methods* enable the identification of prehistoric earthquakes aimed at improving the estimation of earthquake recurrence intervals.

• *Advanced modelling and simulation of the response of constructed facilities* such as the Tsukuka model (Fig. 2.23) discussed above.

• *High-performance composites for strengthening existing structures*: High-performance materials such as high-strength, highly ductile, and weldable steel and alloys or super strong and durable cement-based materials are becoming common in seismic zones infrastructure construction.

• *New generation of data collection methods*:

– Non-destructive evaluation methods such as ultrasonic, acoustic emissions, infrared thermography are employed to detect structural weaknesses that would make a building susceptible to earthquake damage.

– Fiberoptic sensors embedment are being successfully used in sensing the dynamic response of structures in seismic conditions.

– Neutral networks and fuzzy logic techniques can be effectively used in identifying the reaction and damage potential of complex structures.

Case study: Vrancea, Romania

Vrancea zone in Romania illustrates the complex interaction of factors that must be considered when assessing the effects of earthquakes: the tectonic processes, the soil composition, the magnitude and intensity of the event and the man made structures.

General
The tectonic plates

A moderate to high seismic area, Romania is located at the intersection of three tectonic plates (Peceneaga-Camena, Intra-moesian and Moesian). At the point where the three fault lines converge, an area called Vrancea, has been the scene of intense seismic activity for centuries as a result of the subduction movement of the Moesian plate, which has caused about 95% of this country's seismic events (see Figs 2.24 and 2.25).

Research in recent years has made progress in understanding better the geodynamic evolution of the Carpathian region where a subduction towards the Southwest, coupled with a notheastward retreat of the subduction zone, forced the intra-Carpathians to move into the same northeasterly direction. Whilst a collision between the northern block and the European foreland was followed by a break-off in the north, with the detached slab segments sinking into the mantle, the southeastern zone beneath the Carpathians bend (the Vrancea Region) appears to be a slab segment *still detaching*, and this is thought to be responsible for the seismicity of the region.

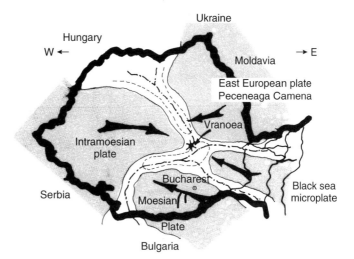

Fig. 2.24

Map of Romania showing location of
Vrancea focus. © Alexandru Cismigiu.

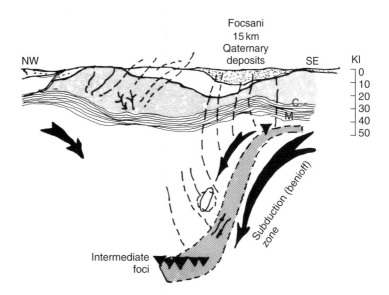

Fig. 2.25

Vrancea subduction focus.
© Alexandru Cismigiu.

The Vrancea zone is characterized by the occurrence of intermediate
depth earthquakes in a narrow epicentral and hypocentral region. The
epicentral area is within a zone of 30 km × 70 km and earthquakes occur
at between 70 and 200 km depth within an almost vertical column.

Shallow events (focal depth of maximum 60 km) and very deep (sub-
crustal depth of over 200 km) have also been recorded but with smaller
magnitudes. The Vrancea events tend to be *strong* (Richter scale magnitude $M = 7.8–8.0$), and *persistent* (systematic strong events occurring
three to four times per century, the average recurrence rates making
another strong event within the next two decades highly probable).

The focal depth of some Vrancea seismic events means that they are felt and cause considerable damage over large areas, unlike shallow earthquakes, which are only of local influence.

The soil structure

As was discussed earlier, the effect of an earthquake is strongly influenced by the soil structure, especially 50–60 m near the surface, as it affects the way in which the seismic waves are transmitted. The softer the soil, the slower the waves' travel and the greater the damage incurred.

Vrancea is largely made of soft material and Bucharest is located on soft sedimentary type sub-soil. The thickness of the unconsolidated layer is in the range of 100–200 m. The city centre sits on a bed of clay with shallow layers of sand and loess, while the northern and the eastern parts are on silt, clay, fine sand, and gravel. These different types of sub-soil, observed during the construction of the underground, account for the seismic risk zoning of Bucharest, the largest risk areas being associated with the softer soil profiles.

Measuring the impact

Table 2.5 gives an indication of the frequency of major earthquakes ($M > 6.8$) in the last 200 years and their measurement on the Richter and Mercalli scales.

While magnitude is expressed by measuring the amplitude of a seismic wave against an open-ended scale, intensity expresses the surface impact on a scale of I–XII, from imperceptible to major damage being caused and the destruction of 'life lines' such as roads, water and power liner, and total collapse of buildings taking place. In Romania, intensity charts used to assess risks, relate to return periods and place Vrancea and Bucharest in the high-intensity zone of VIII.

In recent times, the earthquake on 4 March 1997 has been the most devastating. Although it lasted only 60 s, it caused the death of 1580 people

Table 2.5
The magnitude, intensity, and focal depth of major earthquakes in the last 200 years in Romania.

Year	Focal depth H (km)	Magnitude M (Richter)	Intensity I_{max} (MKS)	Year	Focal depth H (km)	Magnitude M (Richter)	Intensity I_{max} (MSK)
				1908	125	6.8	VIII
1802	–	7.7	X	1940	135	7.4	IX
1829	–	7.0	VIII 1/2	1977	94	7.2	IX
1838	–	7.3	IX	1986	145	7.0	VIII 1/2
1894	–	6.8	VIII	1990	99	6.8	VIII

Source: 'The Seismic Pathology of Religion-related Buildings in Romania', A.I. Cismigiu and M.A Cismigiu.

injuring a further 11 000. Thirty-three thousand dwellings were destroyed and 20 high-rise blocks collapsed. Most of the devastation occurred in the capital city of Bucharest. The loss has been assessed to have been in the region of US$ 2 billion.

Charles Richter, the well-known seismologist, remarked about the effects of Vrancea earthquakes (see Fig. 2.5):

> Nowhere else in the world is a populated centre so exposed to earthquakes originating repeatedly from the same source. The only similar occurrences are the repeated earthquakes under the Hindu Kush region

The building types

During the 4 March 1977 earthquake, Bucharest suffered substantial damage, much more than during the 1940 earthquake. This was partly as a result of the different dynamics of the rupture causing a different damage pattern and partly due to the design and construction of some of the buildings. Countless nineteenth century buildings were destroyed and, more unexpectedly, many 'modern' multistoried buildings too, with devastating loss of life, and economic consequences.

The city's buildings can be divided in two general categories:

- Constructed before the Second World War – they range from solid masonry one-storey buildings, typical of the nineteenth century, to reinforced concrete frame buildings with brick partitions, most of which were not designed to withstand seismic stress, only to compensate vertical loading. Twenty-eight reinforced concrete frame buildings, 8–13 storeys high, collapsed partially or entirely. These buildings were part of a group of 100–150 blocks of flats built between the two World Wars, and which were constructed without particular concern to anti-seismic provisions, their lateral strength being strictly random. Furthermore, some were of poor quality, others had sustained damage in the 1940 earthquake, which was not repaired, and others had been modified for functional reasons with little regard to the structural implications. There are still some 400 such buildings in Bucharest and despite official efforts to highlight the risks and list the dangerous structures, very little change has occurred to date.
- Constructed during the communist era of monolithic reinforced concrete – 2–16 storeys, of uneven workmanship, many are in need of upgrading and a large number remain unconsolidated after the last three earthquakes. Lack of resources has meant that no repair and renovation were undertaken to counteract the effects of poor construction and lack of maintenance over many years.

The effect of 4 March 1977 earthquake on structures

The earthquake impact on the existing buildings took a number of forms.

Degradation/disintegration of the fabric due to alternating over-stress

The destruction of the fabric can be either brittle or ductile, depending on the type of material the structures were made of. Brittle materials such as concrete, masonry, or mortars have a tendency to revert to their original granular form, becoming friable, an irreversible change. Ductile materials such as construction steel or plastic, having a polycrystalline internal structure, tend to incur a rearrangement of the crystals resulting in pronounced deformation or plastic fatigue or deflection.

In structures constructed of mixed materials such as reinforced masonry or reinforced concrete, the brittle component tends to revert to its initial constituents (sand, gravel, and dust). A solid block, whose stability is ensured by dry friction between particles, changes into a granular mass, its usual shape being a rubble heap with the natural slope of the material.

In Bucharest, as a result of the predominant type of construction, the brittle destruction was the more devastating. Its manifestation ranged from 'micro-cracking' not easily distinguishable in large masses, to 'visible cracks' along preferential lines, culminating in 'explosive dis-locations', the result of massive dismantling of intermolecular connections and total collapse. This behaviour could be localized at the level of a structural component or, at the limit stage involve the structure as a whole. During the 1977 earthquake in Bucharest, several multistorey blocks of flats, such as Scala or Continental, collapsed in heaps of rubble with natural slope.

Failure of the vertical elements

Characteristic of seismic damage in structures not designed for seismic conditions, the weakest parts were shown to have been the columns, and more generally, the vertical components. Typical column failure occured due to:

(a) Weakness to shear and a lack of adequate transverse reinforcement were in evidence. When reinforcement is insufficient, it bends under the seimic shear stress and typical failure occurs at 45° such as can be seen in Figs 2.26 and 2.27. The inadequate and suitable reinforcement are apparent in Fig. 2.27 where the bent three vertical bars can be seen clearly distorted. If we compare the reinforcement diagram of this case (Fig. 2.28a) with a typical reinforcement for a seismic resistant column (Fig. 2.28b) the way in which the shear is counteracted becomes obvious.

(b) Excessive axial loading and insufficient transverse reinforcement This induces the crushing of concrete and the buckling of longitudinal reinforcement (Fig. 2.29). The principle is illustrated by the

Fig. 2.26
Columns, Bucharest earthquake of
4 March 1977, showing typical shear
failure due to insufficient transverse
reinforcement (stirrups). © Alexandru
Cismigiu.

~45°

Fig. 2.27
Typical shear failure of column detail.
© Alexandru Cismigiu.

Typical shear failure due to lack
of adequate reinforcement

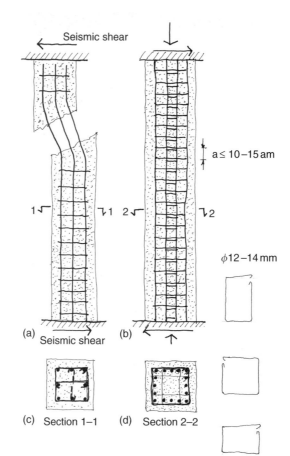

Fig. 2.28
Diagramatic representation of typical shear failure and corrective reinforcement.

Fig. 2.29
Column failure due to excessive axial loading and insufficient stirrups resulting in concrete crushing with buckling of longitudinal reinforcement.

diagram in Fig. 2.30, which shows the effect of a vertical force on a simple concrete cube in different friction conditions.

(c) Weak column – strong beams design. This caused a failure of the column below the frame joint (see Fig. 2.31) because of lack of transverse reinforcement.

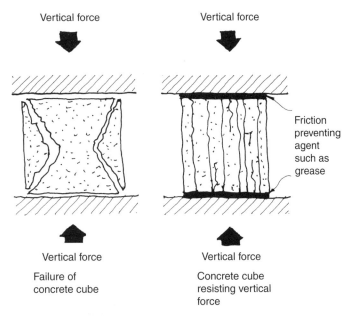

Vertical force

Vertical force

Friction preventing agent such as grease

Vertical force

Vertical force

Failure of concrete cube

Concrete cube resisting vertical force

Fig. 2.30
Diagram of brittle failure principle (a) failure of concrete cube without friction prevention; (b) Concrete cube resisting vertical force with friction prevention agent.

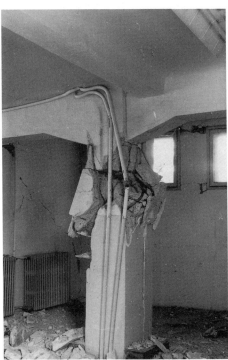

Fig. 2.31
Shear failure of column below frame joint due to lack of reinforcement and disregard to the 'weak beams – strong columns principle'.

The effect of 4 March 1977 earthquake on Romanian historic buildings

Romanian historic monuments such as churches, monasteries, or palaces were traditionally built with solid stone or brick masonry, which being brittle materials, did not resist well to dynamic action, especially at the points of discontinuity or openings, thus being susceptible to the brittle explosion damage described earlier. Traditionally built churches, examined after being subjected to seismic action, tended to present the following types of damage (see Fig. 2.32):

- A longitudinal dislocation, almost always extending from the altar to the porch, tending to cut the church nave in two halves. It is accompanied

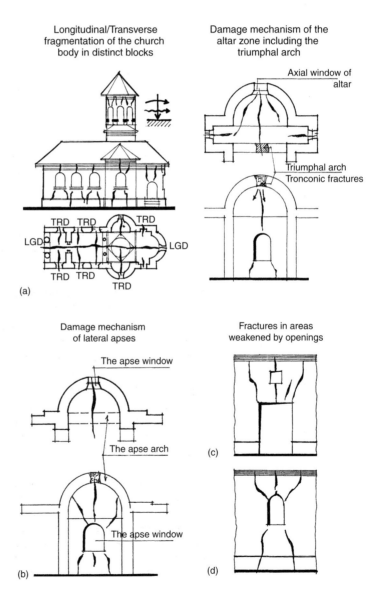

Fig. 2.32
Typical distribution of earthquake damage to church. © Alexandru Cismigiu.

by cracks and dislocation in the altar vault and fractures in all the arches, etc.
- Transverse dislocations and fractures along the axis lines of the Naos, Vortex, and Porch, systematically occurring at the weaker points of the nave walls such as the vertical narrow window openings.

The two types of associated dislocations/fractures tend to transform the main body of the building into an assembly of almost independent blocks, each acting separately. Projecting features such as bells, drums, bell towers, are always vulnerable during an earthquake. Built of brittle materials with low tensile and shear strengths, these elements are exposed to high overturning moments and shear forces at the base.

When consolidating existing buildings, Romanian engineers favour the insertion of a compatible and closely associated three-dimensional new structure into the existing structure. In the case of a traditional church building, this consists of two macro-structures: roof and foundations, linked by horizontal and vertical lamellar components (floors/beams, walls/columns) thus creating a new composite system (Fig. 2.33).

The link between the old and the new structures is achieved by bonding and mechanical enclenching. Bonding is obtained by using cementitious materials at specific ratio mixes of coarse and fine grout, and mechanical enclenching is achieved with the help of steel insertions buried in non-active cement. The enrobed mixed matter, or 'bulbs', achieves the ductility of composite materials: 'steel–grout masonry' and in time, the permanence in time of stone masonry. Fig. 2.34a–c illustrates such consolidation work stages at a traditional church building.

Romanian consolidation techniques, anti-seismic design, and legislation

In recent years, solutions have been sought to make possible the transition from gravitational capability to seismic strength. Encasing the brittle material (i.e. the concrete) or inserting a three-dimensional longitudinal and transverse reinforcement system are methods currently adopted (see Fig. 2.35a–c). The techniques employed are generally based on the mixed structure of composite materials (MSCM) concept, as illustrated by consolidation work in progress in Bucharest (Fig. 2.36). The consolidation of public buildings has been a priority; some examples are given below.

The Intercontinental Hotel Bucharest (Fig. 2.37a and b) (*Bucharest International Project; Structural Engineers: Gabriela Pop, Stefan Mihailescu, Lucian Dogariu; Consultant: Alexandru Cismigiu*). The existing central columns of the 22-storey high building required consolidation as they showed signs of stress after the 1977 earthquake. Constructed of reinforced concrete, $1\,m \times 1\,m$, they were designed for a high axial force ($N = 1444$ tonnes). The solution opted for consolidation was transversely

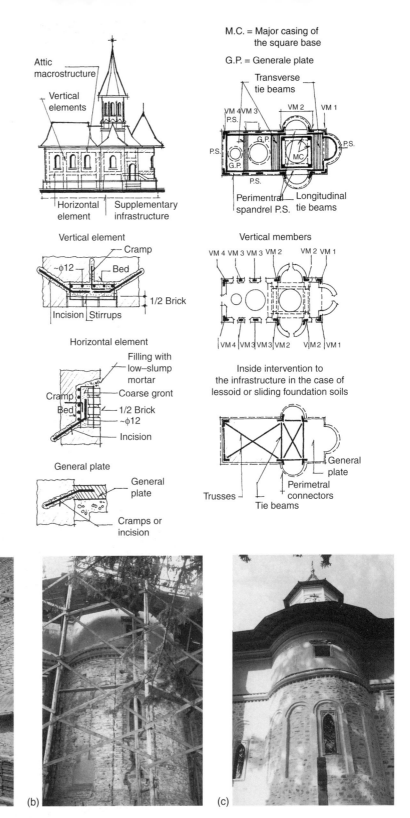

Fig. 2.33
Traditional church consolidation concept. © Alexandru Cismigiu.

M.C. = Major casing of the square base

G.P. = Generale plate

Attic macrostructure

Vertical elements

Horizontal element

Supplementary infrastructure

Transverse tie beams

VM 4 VM 3
P.S.

VM 2   VM 1

P.S.

G.P

P.S.

G.P.

MC

P.S.

Perimentral spandrel P.S.

Longitudinal tie beams

Vertical element

Cramp

~φ12

Bed

1/2 Brick

Incision   Stirrups

Vertical members

VM 4 VM 3 VM 3 VM 2   VM 2 VM 1

VM 4   VM3 VM3 VM2   V|M 2 VM 1

Horizontal element

Filling with low–slump mortar

Coarse gront

Cramp

Bed

1/2 Brick

~φ12

Incision

Inside intervention to the infrastructure in the case of lessoid or sliding foundation soils

General plate

General plate

Cramps or incision

General plate

Perimetral connectors

Trusses

Tie beams

Fig. 2.34
Mirauti Church, Romania, repairs in progress and completed. © Alexandru Cismigiu. (a) Reinforcement being inserted; (b) Masonry cover in progress; (c) Consolidation work completed.

(a)   (b)   (c)

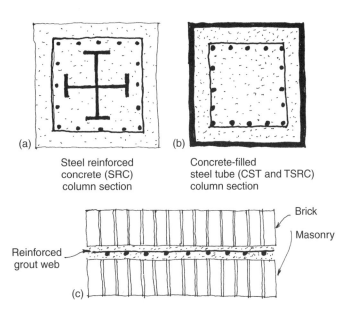

(a) Steel reinforced concrete (SRC) column section

(b) Concrete-filled steel tube (CST and TSRC) column section

(c) Reinforced grout web   Brick   Masonry

Fig. 2.35
Structural consolidation techniques diagrams (parts a, b, and c).

Fig. 2.36
Consolidation work in Bucharest.

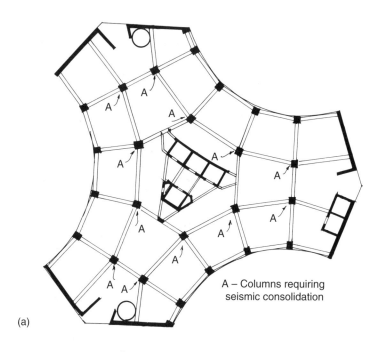

A – Columns requiring seismic consolidation

(a)

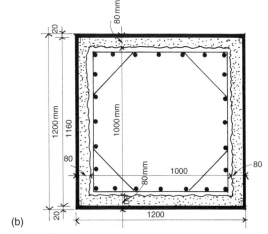

(b)

Fig. 2.37
Intercontinental Hotel, Bucharest:
(a) plan; (b) detail. © Alexandru
Cismigiu.

super reinforced concrete (TSRC) where a steel skin, 20 mm thick and 80 mm expanding grout were installed to encase the existing columns.

The Parliament House, Bucharest (Fig. 2.38) (*Coordinating engineers: Alexandru Cismigiu, Traian Popp, Mircea Mironescu; Architect: Anca Petrescu*). The largest structural complex ever built in the MSCM concept, using SRC as building material. It consists of shear walls, either alone or grouped in tubular zones, associated with frames and framed shear walls; torsional effects very well taken care of. The design brief was that the building should be viable for *a minimum of 500 years*! Architecturally, more than controversial, from an engineering point of view it constitutes a unique and outstanding example of the MSCM–SRC technique.

The Telephone Exchange building Bucharest (Fig. 2.39) (*Design Institute of the City of Bucharest; Structural engineers: Dragos Badea, Dan Popescu,*

Fig. 2.38
'Casa Poporului', Bucharest.

Fig. 2.39
Telephone exchange building
consolidation in Bucharest.
© Alexandru Cismigiu.

Ilie Canciovici; Consultant: Alexandru Cismigiu; Architect: Popescu Greaca). Built in 1936 as pure steel frame, the building suffered important plastic displacements in the 1977 earthquake. The MSCM concept was applied here with the construction of a full peripheral SRC skin 40–50 cm thick, connected to the existing steel skeleton, from the outside, as access into the building for construction work was not permitted in order not to iterrupt its functionality. Peripheral masonry panels were strengthened in the CRM system.

Legislation and building control

Following the devastation from the 1977 earthquake, Romania has adopted a building code, currently P100-92, which lays down regulations for the construction of earthquake-resistant buildings. The main consideration is to limit and prevent earthquake damage such as:

- loss of human life and material damage;
- disruption of the socioeconomic life;
- destruction of the cultural assets;
- damage from hazardous substances.

The code sets safety levels related to specific parameters such as:

- the seismic grading of the area (maximum ground acceleration);
- geological conditions;
- the importance of the building;
- time spent in the building;
- type of forces acting on the building.

The code also sets out guidelines and restrictions in respect of a building's configuration, materials used, existing buildings, structural alterations, etc. At the time of writing, work was in progress to align the code with European prescriptives.

Disaster mitigation

A number of new techniques are being pursued to aid populated centres such as Bucharest in the case of a new powerful Vrancea earthquakes:

1. The use of carbon fibre reinforced plastics (CFRP) sheets to facilitate a quick and cheap intervention after an event, as they can be attached to walls from the outside to secure unstable buildings.
2. Airborne laser scanning of urban areas: after a strong earthquake, this method enables the detection of changes in man-made structures through comparison with pre-event data and classification of damage detected.
3. Seismic instrumentation of Bucharest combined with geological micro-zoning for fast post-event maps locating the ground motion and consequential damage distribution.
4. Development of an early warning system designed on the basis of travel time between S and P waves from the Vrancea epicentre to Bucharest. The difference of travel time should give a 25 s warning.

3 Volcanoes

What are volcanoes and how they erupt

A volcano is a mountain or hill containing openings and channels, which connect to the earth's crust and through which lava, ashes, and gases are expelled continuously or at certain intervals.

The Earth consists of three main layers: the core, the mantle, and the outer crust. We live on the outer crust, which is about 5–10-km thick under oceans and 30–70-km thick under the earth. This, in relation to the rest of the planet, is quite thin, comparable to an orange skin. The mantle, which is the largest layer of the earth, is extremely hot and mostly solid because of the high pressure it is subjected to. In certain conditions it melts forming 'magma', fluid molten rock, which penetrates the outer crust (see Fig. 2.2).

The most common cause for magma production is the movement of the earth's crust, which as we have seen earlier is divided into seven large plates (see Fig. 2.1). The movement, known as plate tectonics, can determine different forms of volcanoes and volcanic activity:

- *Spreading centre volcanism* is a type of movement where the plates move away from each other forming a ridge. As the two plates separate, the pressure on the mantle rock reduces, allowing it to melt and magma is formed; as it flows out it cools, thus hardening and filling the space created by the diverging plates.
- *Subduction zone volcanism* occurs when the moving plates collide and one plate is pushed under the other, sinking into the mantle. This forms a trench, usually in the ocean floor. The pressure created by this type of movement increases the water content of the mantle, lowering its temperature, which causes it to melt into magma.
- *Hot spot* occurs less often and is the result of a unusually hot lower mantle pushing into the upper mantle and creating a plume-shaped mantle material forming magma just under the earth's crust. If the continental plates move over the hot spot (which is stationary), the magma will create a string of volcanoes, such as the Hawaii volcanoes.

As magma forms as a result of one the processes described above, being less dense than the surrounding solid rock it pushes upwards through the crust. If the downward pressure of the rock exceeds its upward pressure, magma collects in *magma chambers* below the surface of the earth, but if the pressure is high enough or the cracks open magma will flow forming a volcano. Flowing magma is called *lava*.

Volcano types

Magma eruption force is due to the pressure from dissolved gases suspended in the magma solution. When the confining pressure decreases or when the gas pressure increases because the magma cools the dissolved gas is allowed to expand forming bubbles (vesicles) in the magma. As the bubbles escape, they push the magma out with them (rather like a flowing champagne bottle when opened) and an eruption occurs. There are two categories of eruptions:

1. *Effusive* – happens when the pressure is low and the lava flows slowly onto the earth's surface, causing damage to wildlife and man-made structures.
2. *Column eruption* – when pressure is very high, a great deal of material, hot gas, ash, and pyroclastic rocks, explode high up into the air.

Within these categories there are several types of eruptions:

- *Plinian eruption* – a column eruption caused by a powerful upward thrust of expanding gases, rising up to 48 km into the air, producing a towering eruption plume that can last for days and causes 'tehphra' volcanic material to fall on the surrounding area and very fast moving lava destroying everything in its path. Pompeii and Herculanum were buried by a Plinian eruption of mount Vesuvius (see Fig. 3.1).
- *Hawaiian eruptions* – an effusive type of eruption, produce a sluggish flow of low-viscosity, low-gas-content lava. These eruptions are slow enough to enable people to escape to safety. Sometimes there are 'fire fountain' displays, an orange lava upward flow of a few minutes or 'lava lakes', ponds of lava created in craters or other hollow cavities in the land. This type is common to Hawaii volcanoes, from where its name is derived.
- *Strombolian eruptions* – impressive but not very dangerous, these eruptions thrust very short bursts of lava high into the air. They are regular, but quite small and do not produce lava flows. They take their name from the Stromboli volcano on the Italian coast.
- *Vulcanian eruptions* – similar to Strombolian eruptions, but have slightly larger columns and are mostly made of ashy pyroclastic material. They also launch football-sized 'pyroclastic bombs'.
- *Hydrovolcanic eruptions* – occur in wet conditions near oceans or saturated clouds. The hot magma heats the water causing it to expand, resulting in eruptive columns and fine ash.
- *Fissure eruptions* – some eruptions do not start with an explosion; magma simply flows through the cracks in the ground. Characteristic 'curtains of fire' occur: lava curtains burst at a small height above ground. Although there can be a large quantity of lava, it is slow moving.

Fig. 3.1
Vesuvius lava flow. © NASA.

Statistics (*Source:* Volcano World)

It is widely accepted that there are more than 500 'active' volcanoes in the world (volcanoes recorded to have erupted within historic times), about the same number of 'dormant' volcanoes (those that erupted before historic times but less than 10 000 years ago) and many 'extinct' volcanoes (those that erupted more than 10 000 years ago). Of the 500 active volcanoes, 10 erupt on any given day.

The largest eruption in the world this century took place in June 1912 at Novarupta Alaska. An estimated 9 miles^3 of magma erupted for 60 h, over twice the 1991 Pinatubo eruption and 30 times the 1980 St Helens eruption. The deadliest eruption of the century occurred at Mont Pelée Martinique in 1902 when 30 000 inhabitants were killed. In 1985, 23 000 people died when mudflows inundated the city of Armero following a small eruption of the Nevado del Ruiz volcano in Columbia, which melted the ice cover causing the mudflow.

Effects of volcanic eruptions

Volcanic eruptions have devastating effects through a number of manifestations that can take place all at the same time or in various combinations depending on the type of eruption and its location. The potential hazards include the following:

- *Ash fall* (*pyroclastic falls*) – fine material (millimetre sized) resulting from the eruption can get carried by currents in the eruption column and travel vast distances downwind. Ash falls can cause substantial damage, depending on the thickness of the layer deposited: For example,

  At less than 1 mm ash will act as irritant to lungs and eyes, force closure of airports due to potential damage to aircraft, and contaminate roof-fed water tank supplies.

  At 1–5 mm ash will cause minor damage to buildings, blocking air filters and soiling interiors. May also cause electricity cuts due to conductivity of wet ash, short-circuiting transformers, etc.

  At 5–100 mm ash will destroy crops and pasture, cause lightweight buildings to collapse under the ash weight over 100 mm, and affect rail transport through signal failure. Major ash removal operations will be required in urban areas.

  At 100–300 mm roofs of buildings risk collapse under the weight of wet ash if not cleared.

  Over 300 mm livestock and wildlife are killed or very distressed, major collapse of roofs, roads unusable, power and telephone lines broken.

  Ash clouds can also generate powerful electric fields causing frequent lightning, damaging electrical installations and starting fires in buildings and installations.

- *Ballistic falls* – lava and volcanic rocks exploding like bombs.
- *Pyroclastis flows* (*ash flow*) – the flow of hot volcanic debris from the collapsing eruption column, advancing as a wall of fire in a melting gas cloud. They are the most destructive manifestation of volcanic activity: people rarely survive if caught in its path and buildings are often destroyed.
- *Lava flows* are molten rocks travelling down the volcano slopes at varying speeds depending on their geological make up, how steep is the slope, obstructions, etc. Despite their spectacular appearance they do not threaten life because of their slow movement, but they do cause total destruction of buildings and infrastructure in their path.
- *Lahars* are mudflows of volcanic ash mixed with water. They can crush people to death, erode riverbanks, and destroy buildings.
- *Volcanic gases.*
- *Volcanic earthquakes.*

Most of these hazards will only affect the area close to the volcano, except for ash fall, which can be found as far as thousands of kilometres from the site of an eruption.

The damage can be considerable. In 79 AD, Mount Vesuvius erupted burying without trace all surrounding cities in over 30 m of ash. Only in the eighteenth century were some of these cities (Pompeii and Herculanaeum) re-discovered. When they were excavated in the twentieth century, cataclysmic devastation and loss of life was revealed. Vesuvius is still active today (see Fig. 3.2) and could erupt at any time again.

Mount Ruapehu's 1995 and 1996 eruptions lasted a total of 4 months and cost New Zealand some $130 million. Of this tourism accounted for the biggest loss, $100 million, electricity for $22 million as two power stations were severely damaged, aviation industry $2.4 million, whilst emergency services cost $6.5 million.

Fig. 3.2 Vesuvius detail.

4 Flooding

How does flooding occur

If the total amount of water on Earth has remained fairly constant for millions of years, this is not, the case for its distribution. Although a small amount of water is lost everyday high in the atmosphere, by the breaking of water molecules by ultraviolet rays, an equal amount of new water is emitted from the inner parts of the earth through volcanic activity.

Water takes a number of forms:

- liquid in seas, rivers, etc.;
- solid in glaciers of North and South Poles;
- gaseous as vapours in the air.

And it changes from one form to another as it is moved around the planet by winds.

When the sun heats certain zones more than others, a heat discrepancy is created and cycles of air movement are initiated by the hot air rising and cool air sinking. These cycles determine consequential water cycles: The heat causes water to evaporate, the heated air rises and when meeting colder layers condenses into droplets, which form clouds. As the clouds become saturated with droplets they begin to fall through the air forming precipitation: rain, snow, sleet, hail, etc. The water so created forms rivers and streams and some accumulates underground.

At certain times, these cycles are affected by an unusual interaction of certain factors, like the development of a hurricane, resulting in an uncharacteristically large amount of water being produced. When this sudden, greater than normal, volume of water appears it causes the normal waterways to overflow and water engulfs the surrounding land. Flood is an unusually large accumulation of water in an area of land.

Causes and effects of flooding

Causes of flooding
- The most common cause of flooding is the succession of storms bringing massive amounts of water through rain. This often tends to be

seasonal due to the different amounts of time the sea and land take to heat up or cool. In winter, the air above the sea is warmer than that above the land and the wind flows away from the sea, but in summer the process is reversed and more water is carried.
- Wind currents creating a monsoon effect.
- Melting snow.
- Unusual tidal activity, such as tsunamis (giant waves triggered by earthquakes).
- Dam breaks. This can happen either as a result of a dramatic ground shift due to earthquakes or land slides, or due to design parameters not anticipating the extent of the amounts of water occurring.

Flooding and its severity is subject to a number of factors:

- The amount of water which accumulates as explained above.
- The absorbency of the land: land, which is saturated with water and cannot absorb any more will cause the surplus to overflow as runoff. Farm areas will be less absorbent than rock and concrete, asphalt and man-made cover even less as they reduce the Earth's natural absorbency.
- Flood relief systems, which conduct rainwater through culverted flood relief channels into other areas.
- Levees – raised embankments along rivers built to keep them from overflowing and which whilst protecting the local area from being flooded, may cause worse problems further down the line. They can also break in which case, like dams, can cause even more dangerous flooding.
- Excessive water along coastlines.

Effects of floods
Of all natural hazards, floods account for the highest death toll and most significant damage (see Disaster impact statistics page)

- Damage caused by the force of the flowing water. The worst damage is caused by the enormous force of the flowing water, at 6 in. (15 cm) being able to knock a person down. Pressure exerted by flash floods, which occur as a result of sudden intense accumulation of water is the worst especially if this happens on mountains. The water flowing down gathers tremendous speeds devastating anything in its way.
- Damage from dampness and the mud brought with the water. When the flood is over and water level drops, things are back to normal but mud and debris picked by the water stick as a general slime.
- Spread of disease. Flood water seeps in everywhere causing sewers to overflow into the drinking water system, washing away chemicals and all sorts of waste products. Rats and other wildlife may take shelter in human settlements.
- Indirectly, through damming and artificial draining to avoid damage to humans, floods can be responsible for dramatic changes in the natural

ecosystems such as in the case of the Grand Canyon, where an artificial flood had to be created to re-establish the natural balance.

Flood damage

Damage to property is only part of the 'human cost' of a flood. The upset caused by loss of personal belongings, some, of sentimental value and irreplaceable, the stress of living in temporary accommodation, the trauma of cleaning up, the smell, the loss of employment as business fails, the loss of pets, reduction in property value, the fear it may happen again, all these have a traumatic effect. Damage to property is related to the level reached by the floodwater. Table 4.1 indicates typical damage to a residential property. Flood can damage property outside the buildings such as outhouses, cars, fences, and gardening equipment.

The length of time the floodwater remains in contact with buildings is a key factor in the level of damage caused. It can be anything from a few hours to several weeks or even months. In March 2001, over a hundred homes were damaged in the village of Gowdall, United Kingdom. The water stayed for 2 weeks in most areas and some for 2 months.

Table 4.1
Damage to residential property.

Depth of flood water	Damage to building	Damage to services and fittings	Damage to personal possesions
Below ground floor level	Minimal damage to the main building Floodwater may enter basements, cellars and under floor voids Possible erosion beneath foundations	Damage to electrical sockets and other services in basements and cellars Carpets in basement and cellars may need replacing	Possessions and furniture in cellars and basements damaged
Up to 0.5 m above ground floor level	Damage to internal finishes such as wall coverings and plaster linings Wall coverings and plaster linings may need to be stripped to allow walls to dry Floors and walls will become saturated and will require cleaning and drying out Damp problems such as mould may result Chipboard type flooring likely to require replacement Damage to internal and external doors and skirting boards	Damage to downstairs electricity meter and consumer unit (fuse box) Damage to gas meters and low-level boilers and telephone services Carpets and floor coverings may need to be replaced Chipboard kitchen units are likely to require replacement Washing machines, free-standing cookers, fridges, and freezers may need to be replaced	Damage to sofas, other furniture and electrical goods Damage to small personal possessions such as books, audiocassettes, video and photos Food in lower kitchen cupboards may be contaminated
More than 0.5 m above ground floor level	Increased damage to walls Possible structural damage	Damage to higher units, electrical services and appliances	Damage to possessions on higher shelves

Source: DTLR (Department for Transport Local government and the Regions).

Inhabitants were told in February that it will be a year before they could return to their homes and people lived in caravans while repairs took place.

Preparing for floods

1. Assessing the risks
   - Obtain information on the likelihood of flooding occurring by establishing whether the property is near the sea, a river, stream, ditch; in a location where water could collect such as a hollow or at the foot of a hill; it is protected by river or coastal flood defences.
   - Obtain information about the history of flooding in the area (local library, The Environmental Agency, local records). The Local Authority's Building Control and Highway Departments may have information on more localized floods and water and sewerage companies may also provide information about sewers.
2. Deciding what level of flood to defend against
   - Information obtained from consulting records would establish the maximum levels reached in the past and how often it occurs.
   - Assess the likely cost of damage and choose the appropriate option for the specific property. After identifying the likely points where flood water could enter the property, look into ways of reducing the risks. For example: if air-bricks are present, an alternative way of ventilating the void can be found.
   - If records show flood duration can be significant, look at effects such as water seeping through external and party walls, or the ground and consider measures to increase resistance.
3. Measures to reduce effects of flooding:
   - Dry proofing measures – prevent water ingress with flood barriers at doorways, covers for air bricks and other vents (always ensuring alternative means for ventilation).
   - Wet proofing measures – by raising electrical sockets above flood level, improving the resistance of internal walls, floors and fittings to withstand the effects of flooding. The cost will provide long-term financial savings reducing costs of repairs, temporary accommodation, reduced business, etc.
   - Flood barriers erected away from the buildings with proprietary temporary and demountable defences.

Elements of design

Individual properties

When a property is located in a flood risk area, there are a number of simple steps, which can be taken to prevent or reduce flood damage:

(a) Identifying the likely points where flood water could be entering the property:
   - around closed doorways;
   - through air-bricks, air vents in walls, and the ground floor;

- backflowing through surcharged drains and discharging inside through toilets and sinks located below the flood line;
- seepage through cracks and joints in walls and gaps around service cables and pipes.

(b) Improving the flood resistance of the property.

There are two main categories of measures: dry-proofing – aimed at keeping water out of the property; and wet proofing – improving the building's ability to withstand the effects once the water has entered the building.

Dry-proofing measures can be:

- Provision of movable flood barriers for doorways and low sill windows. These may not entirely prevent the ingress of water; they could provide valuable time to move personal possessions out or to a higher level. Barriers have to be strong enough to withstand the pressure of water and should be put in place as soon as there is a flood warning. Barriers for external doors windows or garages usually are plastic or aluminium flood boards which can slide into a frame attached to the doorframe in a manner creating a watertight seal.
- Installing air-brick and vent covers – they take the form of a plastic cover, available in do-it-yourself stores, which can be clipped on to a frame fixed around the brick or vent opening. It is important that all covers are removed after the danger passes.
- Installation of non-return valves on sewers to prevent back flow.
- Sandbags can be effective as a barrier.
- Flexible skirting systems – they can enclose the lower parts of buildings to a height of 600–900 mm and although costly, can be justified in cases of regular flooding.

Wet-proofing measures can include:

- Improving the resistance of internal walls, floors, and fittings to enable them to withstand internal flooding. When undertaking repairs after flood damage, the opportunity should be used to replace damaged elements and finishes such as plaster, flooring, or kitchen units with materials that are more flood resistant.
- Raise electrical sockets above the established flood level.

General approach

Case study – Thames barrier

The water level at London Bridge has been rising by about 2.5 ft each century. Probably the main cause for London flooding are the surge tides, originating in the North Atlantic. Normally, they just pass by the British Isles, but when Northern winds force them into the North Sea, millions of additional tons of water are sent up the Thames, putting 1 250 000 people at risk.

A barrier across the Thames was considered the best way to protect London from a flooding disaster after a serious flood occurred in 1953, but the considerable volume of active shipping was causing design limitations, as it needed wide passageways. Only when, with the development of container shipping, the old London Docks became redundant it was possible to limit openings to only 200 ft. From a number of solutions put forward, it was decided to build a barrier with movable gates across the river at Woolwich, where the river bed is solid chalk and narrow enough to be spanned easily. The barrier covers 1716 ft width of the river and it consists of nine reinforced concrete piers forming six openings for ships and four other openings. Ten steel gates are positioned end to end across the river. Four main gates, 200 ft wide, are open at normal times and in flood control position when there is a danger of flooding. Each gate is set on pivots supported by the piers, which house the operating machinery and control equipment. If a surge tide threatens, the rising sector gates swing up through 90° forming a continuous steel wall, sealing off the upper Thames from the sea (see Figs 4.1 and 4.2). When open, the gates rest out of site in curved recesses set in concrete sills built in the riverbed, allowing traffic to circulate freely. The barrier is controlled by computers, which operate hydraulic machinery in the piers. Each gate has two sets of identical machinery and controls, three mains supplies and three back up generators.

The construction work started in 1974 and the barrier was officially open in 1984. Apart from the barrier, additional protection is provided to the east as new walls to a level of 23 ft have protected 11.5 miles of riverbank. The design of the gates is simple but efficient: they rotate from an

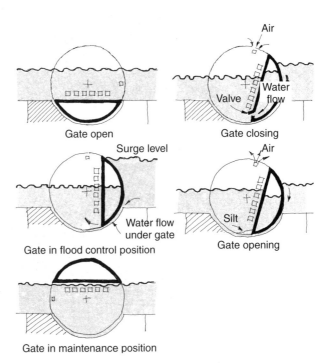

Fig. 4.1
Thames barrier: operation diagrams.
Source: Environment Agency, Thames Barrier Centre.

(a)

(b)

(c)

Fig. 4.2
Thames barrier – gates and shore
details.

open position to flood control position or to an underspill position to allow flow near the river bed and to eliminate the possibility of a reflective wave being brought by the initial closure. To allow for maintenance, there is a further position where the gates can be raised horizontally, completely clear of the high water level, which gives access to both faces.

The Thames barrier represents one type of solution, best suited for protecting a densely populated centre of a primarily industrial country which has traditionally used the river for trade and transport. In the case of a predominantly agricultural country like France, the approach is different as the flooding of a river has been traditionally regarded as beneficial by those living off the land.

Case study – The Loire river, France

The Loire (Fig. 4.3) is the longest river in France. It flows for 634 miles starting in the Cevennes and ending in the Bay of Biscay in the Atlantic Ocean. Along its course, it descends cutting gorges which account for some of the most beautiful scenery in France. Although usually tranquil and majestic, it has had furious moments with terrible effects. One of the worst periods of flooding in the Loire's history stretches from 1846 to 1866. June 1846 stands out as the most violent and devastating: the water level rose by an incredible 7.70 m and only areas placed on high ground were spared. A debit of 7000 m³/s was suddenly produced, frightening when compared with the more usual 11 m³/s!

The flooding was caused by the compounded effect of rain from the Cevennes, in turn caused by violent storms in Puy-en-Velay and precipitation from the Atlantic in the mid-Loire region. Other rivers in the area were affected: The Cher, The Indre, the Vienne and The Maine and though they did not flood on the same scale, the floods lasted longer.

Fig. 4.3
Loire River view.

Despite the horrific effects of the mid-nineteenth century floods, not many safety measures were taken and an estimated 300 000 people are currently at risk. Research shows that due to the lowering of river beds as a result of gravel extraction and the construction of the dam near Roanne, a possible surge at the Bec d'Allier, of some 8000 m^3/s could submerge embankments in the Sully valley, Orleans, and Langeais, with the Tours area being most threatened to incurring considerable damage.

Throughout the history of the Loire valley, there have been attempts to protect man from flooding. Embankments and earth walls have been built since the twelfth century, some major ones are 200 years old, but their protection is now considered to be to a certain extent illusory, as they can, if they burst, cause even more devastation than if they did not exist, gushing large amounts of water which they were suppose to contain.

The 1980s were another period of sustained flooding and during this period dams were considered the best solution. However, when the French government decided to commence constructing a number of dams along the Loire, there was strong opposition from environment bodies who won the day with a case for employing 'natural' methods, with a system of 'levées', strategically located earth banks, which would allow the river to flood but in a controlled way. Proposals also aim to take into account the natural effects of strategic planting and a reduction of water levels with the aid of locks, which would be opened allowing water to flow in order to reduce its level by 20–30 cm.

The levées

There is a certain amount of scepticism as to the effectiveness of these methods and whilst detailed studies and research is still in progress, and are not expected to be finalized before 2006, efforts are directed towards prevention and reduction of the flooding risks by:

- identifying areas at risk;
- improving the alert system, for example, installing a meteo-radar systems on the higher basin;
- re-opening secondary branches of the river;
- reinforcing the base and fabric of strategically located embankments;
- adjusting overflows such as the one between La Bouillle and Blois.

Infrastructure control is being reinforced with state-initiated Plans for the Prevention of Natural Risks (PPRs), and a number of initiatives by river villages organizations attempting to limit the building in flood-prone areas and experimental projects.

To a certain extent, the success of these attempts depends on finding the necessary financial backing and each community acts proportionately with the funds it can raise as neither the state nor insurance companies are prepared to foot the bill.

Case study – Reignac sur Indre

Reignac sur Indre is a typical picturesque French village (Fig. 4.6). It has been a settlement on the river Indre, a tributary of the Loire since Roman times. It has a centuries old church, a château associated with the Marquis de La Fayette, a water mill, and a Town Hall. Because of its position above the confluence of the river Indre and its tributary the Indrois, and the geological features, it has, throughout its history, been prone to severe flooding. The worst on records has been in 1770 when the waters carried people away, but there have also been floods in 1850, 1910, and 1982. In December 1982, the water mounted to its highest level with extreme speed overnight. The water was reported to have been gushing through the floor tiles and stripping the tarmac off the roads. The following images show the extent of the flood (Fig. 4.5) compared

Fig. 4.4
Reignac sur Indre village square, usual view.

Fig. 4.5
Reignac sur Indre flooded village square.

with the same view of village in normal time (Fig. 4.4). Figure 4.7 shows the level it reached inside the houses.

The stress and devastation caused by the flood decided the community to take steps in preventing it happening again. As the plan in Fig. 4.8 shows, a series of earth embankments (levées) have been created to contain future floodwater. The earth mounds have been successfully landscaped to blend into the existing surroundings (Fig. 4.9).

Fig. 4.6
Reignac sur Indre aerial view.

Fig. 4.7
Reignac sur Indre – interior view of flooded house.

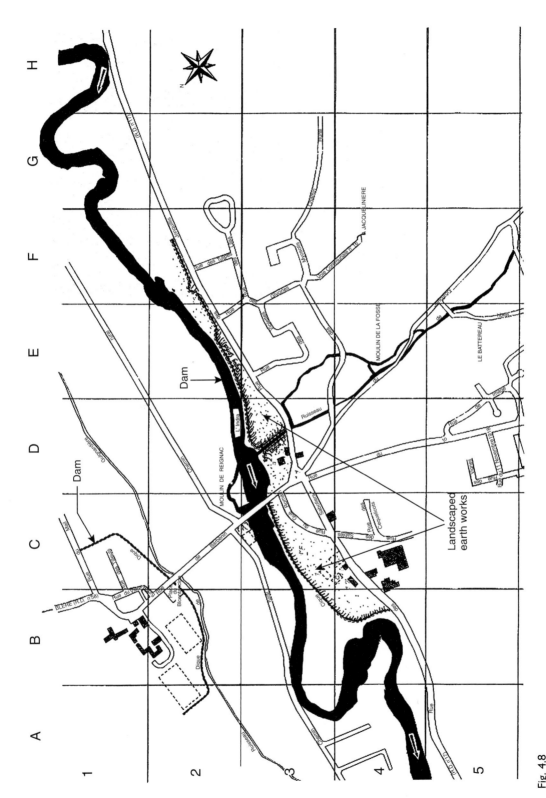

Fig. 4.8
Reignac sur Indre – plan of flood defence earthworks. © Bertrand Penneron.

Fig. 4.9
Reignac sur Indre – view of
landscaped earthworks.

5   Weather conditions

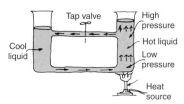

Fig. 5.1
Hot water circulation principle.

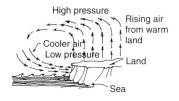

Fig. 5.2
Sea breeze principle.

Storm

What is a storm and how it occurs
Wind

The atmosphere is never at a standstill and air moves constantly between high- and low-pressure areas. This movement of air is *wind*.

The principle of air circulation can be illustrated with a simple experiment using two connected water-filled containers, of which is one heated. The expansion of the hot water increases the pressure near the top at which point, if the controlling tap is opened at the upper level, the heated water will flow into the cool one, thus decreasing the pressure at its lower part. This, in turn, will cause the cold water to flow into the warm vessel (see Fig. 5.1).

Air behaves in the same way: when heated by the Earth's surface, pressure decreases at the lower levels and increases at the higher ones. Nearer the Earth's surface, air flows *in* from high pressure and at the upper regions *away* from high to low.

The sea breeze follows the same principle in conditions created by the unequal capacity of land and water surfaces for absorbing radiating heat. On a hot day, land heats up quickly whilst the sea becomes warm slowly. At the same time, once warm, the sea will keep the heat longer than the land. Whilst both land and sea lose heat by evaporation and conduction, land does so very rapidly. The effect of the land being heated during the day is to induce a breeze near the coast, and to a lesser extent, cooling at night induces a land breeze (see Fig. 5.2). The sea breeze effect is persistent and presents a fair resistance to land wind, which is forced to mount over it, creating a lift effect often used by gliders.

The alternation between night and day, summer and winter cause variations in the intensity and spread of sea breezes. Air movement increases in strength from gentle sea breeze to continental wind systems, culminating in monsoons.

On a larger scale, three constant low-pressure belts (one over the Equator and one over each Pole) condition the atmosphere's circulation.

Air rising over these regions creates a low pressure over the Earth and a high-pressure layer at the upper levels of the atmosphere, with winds flowing into lower layers and overflowing at the higher ones. The actual weather effect is considerably more complex and other factors such as the distribution of land and water on the earth's surface or the earth's rotation, which deflects winds, influence it.

In continental wind systems, airflow is also influenced by the configuration of the land. For example, when blowing over a mountain range flow is not only deflected from its horizontal course but also directed upwards into cooler layers causing cloud formation and release of latent heat. This raises the temperature of the atmosphere and changes the pressure.

Wind scale

High-level winds attain great speeds as observed in the movement of clouds from 225 miles/h to 660 m/h, whilst meteor trails indicate the presence of high winds at even greater heights.

Admiral Sir Francis Beaufort compiled in 1803 a wind scale for the guidance of sailors, which gives a simple explanation of wind speeds at ground level and is still valid today, although speed values would differ as modern equipment enables more accurate measurement (see Table 5.1).

In simple terms, a *storm* is a violent disturbance of the atmosphere with strong wind, heavy rain, snow, or hail.

In certain conditions, there is also thunder and lightning, the occurrence of which is explained in Section C.

Table 5.1 Wind scale for the guidance of sailors.

Number	Wind	Speed (mph)	Effects
1	Calm	0	Calm, smoke rises vertically
2	Light air	2	Wind direction shown by smoke drift but not by weather-vanes
3	Light breeze	5	Wind felt on face, leaves rustle, vane moves
4	Gentle breeze	10	Leaves and small twigs in constant motion, wind extends light flag
5	Moderate breeze	15	Raises dust and loose paper, small branches moved
6	Fresh breeze	21	Small trees in leaf begin to sway, crested waverlets on inland water
7	Strong breeze	27	Large branches in motion, whistling heard in telegraph wires, umbrellas used with difficulty
8	Moderate gale	35	Whole trees in motion, inconvenience felt when walking against the wind
9	Fresh gale	42	Breaks twigs off trees, generally impedes progress
10	Strong gale	50	Slight structural damage occurs (chimney pots and slates removed)
11	Whole gale	59	Seldom inland, trees uprooted, considerable structural damage occurs
12	Storm	68	Very rarely experienced, accompanied by widespread damage
13	Hurricane	Above 75	—

Wind effects on buildings

All structures move under *wind pressure*. Their resistance depends on their shape and type of construction, namely:

- the ratio between their height and width;
- the rigidity of construction, ranging from a heavy solid structure with stiff cladding to a framed structure with light curtain walling.

A structural frame under wind pressure will act as a

- cantilever – where the floors remain plane; or as a
- portal frame – where the floors bend.

A tall slender structure will act predominately as a cantilever whilst a short stubby building will act mostly as a portal frame.

In the case of very tall buildings, lateral movement will result in a pronounced deflection and bending moment, just as a cantilever under load, with consequences such as cracks in finishes at the upper levels and difficulty of use.

Top deflection limits are set and used for structural design calculations. In the United States these limits vary with the type of building: from $0.001 \times$ the height – for buildings with curtain walling and low rigidity to $0.002 \times$ the height – for building in the case of heavy structures with stiff cladding.

The twin towers of the World Trade Centre were designed to withstand a wind pressure of 13 000 tonnes! Resistance to winds of up to 100 m/h was a major design consideration as the effect of the wind would not only cause the building to lean back, but also induce side to side movement, which, if unrestricted, would literally 'shake' the building to pieces. Experts assess that the effect of New York's notorious strong wind push is 4–5 times stronger than that of the Los Angeles or Tokyo earthquake.

Wind loading is defined by a *dynamic pressure*, which is calculated by taking into account:

- the appropriate wind speed for a given location of a building (taken from the area's isopleths map);
- topographical factors;
- building particulars such as height above ground and size.

By applying the corresponding coded coefficients to the *dynamic pressure*, the actual pressure or suction applied to a specific surface of the building can be established and used in the structural design.

The distribution of wind pressure is not uniform and so the effects vary: near the eaves it is stronger and suction at the ends of walls is greater,

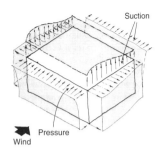

Fig. 5.3
Wind effect on buildings.

resulting in a curvilinear representation (see Fig. 5.3). The effect of the wind on buildings includes

1. pressure on roofs and walls;
2. suction effect on roofs (which varies with the pitch) and on walls;
3. lateral pressure on solid walls;
4. lateral pressure on framed structures;
5. uplift forces at foundation level from pressure on soil due to suction on the roof or lateral wind pressure, which in tall light structures tends to cause overturning.

Resistance to the effects of wind can be provided in a number of ways:

1. Judicious choice of design: shape and rigidity of construction.
2. Adequate lateral resistance in the form of rigid frames, bracing, and shear walls.
3. In some cases, foundations are designed with a view to holding the building down against the uplift of the wind and the nature and type of soil are considered before positioning a building. The building's form and height are also considered. Soil mechanics will differ on the same type of site with different types of buildings and identical buildings will perform differently on variable sub-soil.
4. Design of fixings for claddings should be designed with particular regard to wind loads, which increase with the height above ground and exposure.
5. Provision of adequate fastenings to prevent the wind stripping off the roof, with particular attention to the eaves and gable ends where the maximum suction occurs and the ridge when pitched. Industrial flat roofs are often a problem.
6. Selection of roof shape should be made with due consideration to the wind effect (see Figs 5.4 and 5.5 – showing flat, pitched, or doubly

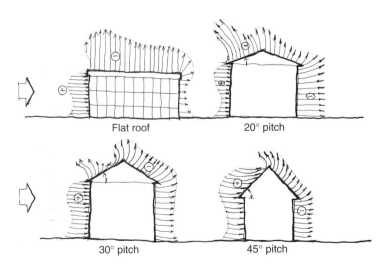

Flat roof   20° pitch

Fig. 5.4
Wind effect relative to roof shape.

30° pitch   45° pitch

Fig. 5.5
Repairing storm wind roof damage.

Fig. 5.6
Tree felled by storm.

curved roofs, the latter requiring tying down the unsupported corners, especially if not enclosed).

Case study – The Storms of 1987 and 2000 in the UK (as reported by the UK Met Office)
Storms of 1987

In southern England, 15 million trees were lost, among them many valuable specimens. Trees blocked roads and railways, and brought down electricity and telephone lines. Hundreds of thousands of homes in England remained without power for over 24 h.

Falling trees and masonry damaged or destroyed buildings and cars (see Fig. 5.6). Numerous small boats were wrecked or blown away. A ship capsized at Dover and a Channel ferry was driven ashore near Folkestone. The storm killed 18 people in England and at least four more in France. The death toll might have been far greater had the storm struck in the daytime.

Four or five days before the storm struck, forecasters predicted severe weather on the following Thursday or Friday. By mid-week, however, guidance from weather prediction models was somewhat equivocal. Instead of stormy weather over a considerable part of the United Kingdom, the models suggested that severe weather would reach no farther north than the English Channel and coastal parts of southern England.

During the afternoon of 15 October, winds were very light over most parts of the United Kingdom. The pressure gradient was slack. A depression was drifting slowly northwards over the North Sea off eastern Scotland. A cool weather prevailed over England, Wales, and Ireland. Over the Bay of Biscay, a depression was developing.

The first gale warnings for sea areas in the English Channel were issued at 0630 UTC on 15 October and were followed, 4 h later, by warnings of severe gales. At 1200 UTC on 15 October, the depression that originated in the Bay of Biscay was centred near 46°N, 9°W and its depth was 970 Mb. By 1800 UTC, it had moved northeast to about 47°N, 6°W, and deepened to 964 Mb. At 2235 UTC, winds of Force 10 were forecast. By midnight, the depression was over the western English Channel, and its central pressure was 953 Mb. At 0135 on 16 October, warnings of Force 11 were issued. The depression now moved rapidly northeast, filling a little as it did, reaching the Humber estuary at about 0530 UTC, by which time its central pressure was 959 Mb. Dramatic increases in temperature were associated with the passage of the storm's warm front.

It is clear that for sea areas warnings of severe weather were both timely and adequate. Forecasts for land areas, however, left much to be desired. During the evening of 15 October, radio and TV forecasts mentioned strong winds but indicated that heavy rain would be the main feature, rather than strong wind. By the time most people went to bed, exceptionally strong winds had not been mentioned in national radio and TV weather broadcasts.

Warnings of severe weather had been issued, however, to various agencies and emergency authorities, including the London Fire Brigade. Perhaps the Met Office issued the most important warning to the Ministry of Defence at 0135 UTC, 16 October. It warned that the anticipated consequences of the storm were such that civil authorities might need to call on assistance from the military.

In southeast England, where the greatest damage occurred, gusts of 70 knots or more were recorded continually for 3 or 4 consecutive hours. During this time, the wind veered from southerly to southwesterly. To the northwest of this region, there were two maxims in gust speeds, separated by a period of lower wind speeds. During the first period, the wind direction was southerly. During the second, it was southwesterly. Damage patterns in southeast England suggested that whirlwinds accompanied the storm. Local variations in the nature and extent of destruction were considerable.

Comparisons of the October 1987 storm with previous severe storms were inevitable. Even the oldest residents of the worst affected areas could not recall winds so strong, or destruction on such a massive scale:

- the highest wind speed reported was an estimated 119 knots (61 m/s) in a gust soon after midnight at Quimper coastguard station on the coast of Brittany (48°02′ N, 4°44′ W);
- the highest measured wind speed was a gust of 117 knots (60 m/s) at 0030 UTC at Pointe du Roc (48°51′ N, 1°37′ W) near Granville, Normandy;
- the strongest gust over the UK was 106 knots at 0424 UTC at Gorleston, Norfolk;
- a gust of almost 100 knots occurred at Shoreham on the Sussex coast at 0310 UTC, and gusts of more than 90 knots were recorded at several other coastal locations;
- even well inland, gusts exceeded 80 knots: 82 knots was recorded at London Weather Centre at 0250 UTC and 86 knots at Gatwick Airport at 0430 UTC (the authorities closed the airport).

TV weather presenter Michael Fish will long be remembered for telling viewers, the evening before the storm struck, that there would be no hurricane. But he was unfortunate. Fish was referring to a tropical cyclone over the western part of the North Atlantic Ocean that day. This storm, he said, would not reach the British Isles – and it did not.

It is worthwhile to consider whether or not the storm was, in any sense, a hurricane – the description applied to it by so many people.

In the Beaufort scale of wind force, Hurricane Force (Force 12) is defined as a wind of 64 knots or more, sustained over a period of at least 10 min. Gusts that are comparatively short-lived (but cause much of the destruction) are not taken into account. By this definition, Hurricane Force winds occurred locally but were not widespread.

A 10-min mean wind speed of 70 knots (an average over 10 min) was recorded at Lee on Solent in Hampshire and an hourly mean speed of 68 knots at Gorleston. The highest hourly mean speed recorded in the UK was 75 knots, at the Royal Sovereign Lighthouse. Winds reached Force 11 (56–63 knots) in many coastal regions of southeast England. Inland, however, their strength was considerably less. At the London Weather Centre, for example, the mean wind speed did not exceed 44 knots (Force 9). At Gatwick Airport, it never exceeded 34 knots (Force 8).

The Great Storm of 1987 did not originate in the Tropics and was not, by any definition, a hurricane – but it was certainly exceptional.

Southeast of a line extending from Southampton through north London to Great Yarmouth, gust speeds and mean wind speeds were as great as those that can be expected to recur, on average, no more frequently than once in 200 years. So, comparison with the great storm of 1703 was justified. The storm of 1987 was remarkable for its ferocity, and affected much the same area of the United Kingdom as the 1703 storm.

Temperature and pressure
The 1987 storm was also remarkable for the temperature changes that accompanied it. In a 5-h period, increases of more than 6°C per hour were recorded at many places south of a line from Dorset to Norfolk. Especially rapid and large was the increase at South Farnborough in Hampshire, where the temperature rose from 8.5 to 17.6°C in 20 min. The return frequency for a temperature increase this rapid is, like the return frequency for the wind strengths that occurred in the storm, about once in 200 years. Across southern England, rapid increases in temperature were followed by sharp decreases.

Ahead of the storm, barometric pressure had fallen rapidly, but neither the magnitude of the fall nor the rate of decrease was remarkable. The subsequent rise in pressure was, however, exceptional. Over much of southern England, increases of more than 8 Mb per hour were recorded, with the most rapid at Hurn in Hampshire, where pressure rose 12.2 Mb in 1 h. The greatest rise over 3 h occurred at the Portland Royal Naval Air Station in Dorset, where, between 0300 and 0600 UTC, the rise was 25.5 Mb. This was, by some margin, the greatest change in pressure – either upwards or downwards – ever recorded in 3 h anywhere in the British Isles. At many places in southern England, the pressure rose more than 20 Mb in 3 h. The return period for such an occurrence is, again, roughly once in 200 years.

The storms of 2000

Introduction

The autumn of 2000 was the wettest since records began in 1766. In all, 503 mm of rain fell during this exceptionally wet and unsettled period. In October, 188 mm of rain was recorded in England and Wales, followed by 182 mm in November. In all, the total for 2000 was 251 mm above the average for this season. Not surprisingly, many parts of the United Kingdom experienced flooding, and there was major disruption to travel and sporting events as frontal system after frontal system swept across the country. The problems began during the period between 9 and 12 October, when a complex low-pressure cell built up over Northern Ireland and Scotland, bringing heavy rain and wind. Then, between 11 and 12 October, a slow-moving area of heavy rain affected the southern parts of the country. In Kent and Sussex, torrential downpours occurred, with between 4 and 6 in. (100–150 mm) of rain falling overnight.

Further frontal systems passed over the United Kingdom during the next fortnight or so, as a low-pressure cell gradually established itself to the Northwest of the country. This drove belts of rain and heavy showers across the country and, in some parts of the country, quite significant amounts of rain fell on every day of the month. By the final week of October, many rivers in the country were either swollen with floodwater or had burst their banks.

News bulletins were full of flood warnings and stories of areas being evacuated as the Environment Agency issued flood alerts. It was then that meteorological events took a further turn for the worse.

The storms of 28–30 October

A major *cyclogenesis* (i.e. formation of a depression) took place on 26 October in the northwestern part of the Atlantic Ocean – the result was a deep low pressure, anchored between Greenland and Iceland, and, over the next 2 days, an extensive cold front built up, stretching its way well towards the southwest. This became the 'birthplace' for the first in a series of highly potent wave depressions that tracked across the United Kingdom between 28 and 30 October.

The 'parent' low and its trailing cold front are clearly seen on the Atlantic infrared satellite image for 0600 UTC on 27 October. Over the following few days, three 'daughter' depressions swept across the United Kingdom, bringing heavy rain, strong winds, and further flooding in addition to extreme weather events such as tornadoes.

The first storm – 28 October: The first of the daughter depressions deepened quickly as it crossed the country during 28 October. It brought a milder 'tropical maritime' air mass, so, for a while, the passage of the warm front was accompanied by a period of heavy rain in many places, with up to 8 mm being reported in an hour across parts of the Home Counties. This rainfall can be seen on the radar image for 0700 UTC.

During the afternoon, the cold front swept eastwards across Wales and England, accompanied by gale force winds as the depression continued to deepen. A tornado was reported in Bognor Regis shortly before 1700, resulting in local severe damage.

Later in the day, the centre of the depression turned towards northern Scotland and brought a spell of gale force winds to much of the north during the following 12–24 h. The cold front had, by now, swept into the North Sea, so, clearer, chilly conditions prevailed across most of the United Kingdom overnight and into the early part of 29 October.

The second storm – 29 October: Many people in Britain woke up on 29 October to find sunshine and blue skies. A few showers spread inland during the morning and it was cold enough for a little snow to be mixed in over parts of northern Britain. However, out to the southwest, a duo of wave depressions hurtled in from the Atlantic.

The visible satellite image for 1200 UTC shows most of the country still in reasonably fair weather, although the dappled pattern of clouds indicates showers over some northern areas. Towards the southwest, a large bank of cloud can be seen, with the second depression forming over Eire and the third depression forming near 52°N, 30°W.

The veil of upper cloud ahead of the second storm spread very quickly northeast across Wales and all but the far north of England by mid-afternoon on 29 October. Rain set in soon afterwards, becoming steadily heavier and more persistent as dusk approached. By 1700, heavy rain had spread across much of the southern part of the country, accompanied by strong winds. Some of the strongest gusts were experienced across Wales and southwest England, for example, 76 knots (87 mph) at North Hessary or on Dartmoor.

The centre of the depression crossed Wales and the Midlands before heading into the southern part of the North Sea, still deepening quickly. But worse was to follow, as, after a temporary lull during the evening, the next wave depression became centred off southwest Ireland, and all the signs suggested that this would be the most damaging of the three depressions.

The third storm – 30 October: Rain continued to fall across southern areas during the early hours of 30 October and, during the second half of the night, the new and rapidly deepening depression crossed Ireland, the Irish Sea, Wales, and then on into the southern parts of northern England. The steep pressure gradient resulted in strong winds and widespread gusts of between 70 and 90 mph.

As is most often the case, the strongest winds were experienced to the south of the centre of the depression, while, to the north, most of

Scotland, Northern Ireland, and parts of northern England escaped with much calmer conditions. Wind speeds reached a peak in the early hours along the South Wales coast, touching 84 knots (96 mph) at Mumbles.

During the following few hours, the strongest winds transferred east, with the Isle of Portland in Dorset reporting a gust to 81 knots (93 mph) at 0600. The strongest winds accompanied the passage of the cold front that passed through London between 0600 and 0700, and cleared into the North Sea by around 0800. Langdon Bay near Dover registered a gust of 76 knots (87 mph) between 0600 and 0700, and, by 1000, this weather station had been reporting gusts to 60 knots (69 mph) or more for 16 h! At inland locations, typical gust strengths were 50–70 knots (57–80 mph). Some structural damage accompanied these gusts, with trees being brought down and roads and railway lines blocked.

Rain had fallen all night, so, by 0900, 24-h totals of between 25 and 50 mm were commonplace, with locally 75 mm and more. Local flooding occurred and caused major disruption to commuters during the morning rush hour of 30 October. In a number of areas, the cumulative effect of these heavy storms brought the situation close to breaking point, and the heavy rain on 30 October resulted in much more serious flooding problems, in areas as far apart as Kent, Wales, and Yorkshire.

Another area of severe weather developed as the depression crossed northern England and the pressure at its centre continued to fall. The warm and cold fronts formed a sharp apex, in between which was located a narrow band of warmer air from further south. Temperatures at some locations rose some 5–7°C within the hour. But as the cold front crossed, the temperature fell dramatically.

The depression had by now developed a wrap-around of thick cloud, and heavy precipitation occurred to the west and northwest of the centre, as seen on the 0900 UTC radar image. However, the precipitation, falling into the already chilly air, turned first to sleet and then to snow, and swept eastwards just to the west of the retreating depression. Locally, the temperature was observed to fall as much as 10°C within 1 h, and a short spell of quite heavy sleet and snow set in. Several roads were badly affected, notably those across the Pennines. During the morning, the depression moved out into the North Sea, deepening even further, and, during the afternoon, storm-force winds were recorded over the North Sea, with some in excess of hurricane force. Later in the day, the storm finally began to lessen in intensity as it neared the south of Norway.

Hurricane and tornado

What is a hurricane and how it occurs
Every year during the 'hurricane season' (from June to November), eastern and gulf coasts of the United States, Mexico, Central America, and

the Caribbean are threatened by huge storms, hurricanes, also known in other parts of the globe as *typhoons* or *cyclones*.

'Hurricane' (from indigenous term Hura Kan – winds of the gods) is a name for a *tropical cyclone* occurring in the Atlantic Ocean.

Tropical cyclone is the generic name for low-pressure systems, which develop in the tropics. When tropical cyclones have a maximum sustained surface winds of 39 mph they are called *tropical depressions*, up to 73 mph they become *tropical storms*, and at wind speeds greater than 74 mph they are called *hurricanes*. The weakest Hurricane (category 1) has wind speeds between 74 and 95 mph.

Hurricanes occur as a result of very low pressure zones occurring over warm oceans, usually in late summer and autumn when seawater is at its warmest. Hurricane winds often generate *tornadoes*, which are smaller, more intense cyclonic storms where a spinning vortex reaches down from the base of a thundercloud. A hurricane, when formed, includes

- *the eye*: the low-pressure centre of circulation;
- *the eye wall*: area around the eye with the strongest winds;
- *rain bands*: thunderstorms moving outward from the eye, part of the evaporation/condensation cycle that feeds the storm (see Fig. 5.7).

How a hurricane works
The whole process of hurricane formation is not fully understood, but it has been established that a number of conditions are present when it

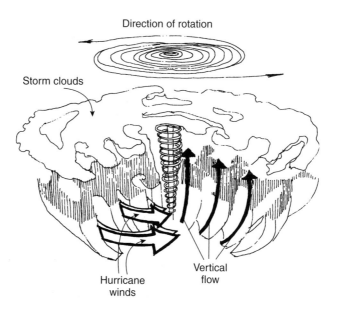

Fig. 5.7
Hurricane development diagram.

develops from a thunderstorm:

- *A cycle of warm humid ocean air evaporation – condensation*. As explained in Section 5.1, the rising warm air from the sea surface condenses in contact with colder layer, releasing latent heat of condensation, which heats cooler air causing it to rise and in turn be replaced by warm air from the ocean below. This continuing cycle creates a pattern of wind, which circulates around a centre, similar to the pattern of water going down a plughole.
- *Converging surface winds pattern and high-speed-altitude winds*. As the cycle develops into a storm, several winds are moving in different directions colliding and pushing warm air upwards and increasing the speed of surface winds rising already. High-altitude winds maintain the storm if at uniform speeds at all levels, failing which *winds shears* form causing the storm to weaken.
- *Difference of air pressure between the surface and high altitude*. The high pressure in the upper atmosphere helps driving the air cycle. As high-pressure air is sucked into the low-pressure centre (the eye), the storm increases wind speeds.

Hurricane size

The destructive power of a hurricane is determined by two factors:

1. the wind speed and
2. storm surge (a wall of water pushed by the hurricane as the sea level rises due to wind and atmospheric pressure changes associated with storms).

Hurricanes are rated in five strength categories by the Saffir–Simpson scale system (see Table 5.2).

Table 5.2
The Saffir–Simpson hurricane scale.

Category	Wind speed	Effects
1	74–95 mph (119–153 kph)	Storm surge 4–5 ft (1.2–1.5 m) above normal Some flooding Little or no structural damage
2	96–110 mph (155–177 kph)	Storm surge 6–8 ft (1.8–2.4 m) above normal Trees down Roof damage (shingles ripped off)
3	111–154 mph (178.6–209 kph)	Storm surge 9–12 ft (2.7–3.7 m) above normal Structural damage to houses Mobile homes destroyed Severe flooding
4	131–154 mph (210–247.8 kph)	Storm surge 13–18 ft (4–5.5 m) above normal Severe flooding inland Some roofs ripped off Major structural damage
5	>155 mph (>249.4 kph)	Storm surge at least 18 ft (5.5 m) above normal Severe flooding further inland Serious damage to most wooden structures

Hurricane damage

– *Rain* – hurricanes bring vast amounts of rain, as much as dozens of inches in a day.
– *Flooding* – as a result of the sudden infliction of such huge quantities of rain and the combined effect of storm surge and high tide.
– *High sustained winds*, which cause structural damage, blow over trees and cars, beach erosion.
– Satellite smaller storms such as *tornadoes*.

The extent of the damage depends on

– hurricane strength;
– angle at which storm hits the land (head on or just grazing the coastline);
– which side of the hurricane strikes (on the right-hand side the hurricane is stronger as its motion and wind speed are complementary, on the left-hand side its motion reduces the wind speed).

Case study – Hurricane Andrew

Hurricane Andrew (see Fig. 5.8) has caused an estimated $26 billion damage and is being considered the most expensive natural disaster in the history of the United States.

It was also the third strongest after 1935 Florida Keys Labour Day storm and Hurricane Camille in 1969. Classified as a category 4 storm, Andrew had a central pressure of 922 mbar, its storm surge was a record for Florida, 16.9 ft (5 m), wind speed reached 145 mph, with gusts up to 175 mph, and destroyed an area of 1100 miles^2.

As with many Atlantic hurricanes, Andrew was formed as a result of a tropical wave, which moved off the West Coast of Africa and passed south of the Cape Verde Islands. It became a tropical storm on 17 August

Fig. 5.8
Hurricane Andrew. © NASA.

1992 and moved uneventfully west northwestward across the Atlantic. Significant changes occurred in the large-scale environment of Andrew on 21 August as a deep high-pressure centre developed over the southeast US and extended eastward to north of the tropical storm. In response to the much more favourable environment, Tropical Storm Andrew strengthened rapidly and turned westward. Andrew became a hurricane on 22 August and strengthened to a strong category 4 hurricane the next day. Eye temperatures, as measured by reconnaissance aircraft, suggest that convection in the eye-wall and the associated vertical circulation became more powerful as the storm moved ashore.

Damage

The storm devastated Dade County where it caused an estimated $25 billion in damage. After striking Florida, Andrew moved northwest across the Gulf of Mexico to make a second landfall in a sparsely populated area of south central Louisiana as a Category 3 storm on 26 August. In total, Andrew directly caused 23 deaths in the United States and indirectly caused 38 more (see Fig. 5.9).

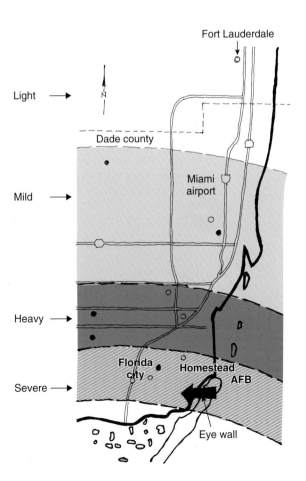

Fig. 5.9

Plan of Dade area affected by Hurricane Andrew. (Source: EQE Internation Inc.)

Businesses were damaged, an airforce base levelled, acres of tropical fruit trees were uprooted, and tourist industry was given a long-term blow, not only because of the actual damage to hotels, etc., but also by association with being a dangerous place to go to.

Impact on buildings

The worst hit were the residential buildings: 25 524 homes were destroyed and a further 101 241 were damaged, accounting for about 70% of the losses. The type of homes destroyed were:

- 63% single family homes;
- 29% apartments in condominiums;
- 8% mobile homes. (*Source*: project CHART – the Co-ordinated Hurricane Andrew Recovery Team, 1994.)

The actual damage was due to:

- water damage – apart from the rain the destruction of the roofs and windows enabled water to flow in freely;
- roof failure through inadequate fixings of sheathing, especially in gable-roof houses;
- flying debris breaking windows and damaging roofs.

It was found that the statutory design parameters such as wind speed were greatly exceeded. Also, a combination of poor materials, inadequate roof systems, unprotected openings facilitated the high degree of roof and water damage. The widespread destruction resulted in housing shortage and housing assistance was made available by public and private sources. Insurance covered three-fourths of the losses, FEMA provided 3600 mobile homes and travel trailers; rental vouchers were provided for disaster victims by HUD, who also assisted in repair and provided low-cost units in the region affected.

Project CHART has estimated that 75% of the housing lost was restored to 90% of its value within 2 years.

What is a tornado

Tornadoes are violent spiralling storms, which occur when a mass of cold air clashes with an opposing mass of warm, moist air. With a characteristic rotating motion, they are accompanied by funnel-shaped cloud and are seasonal.

In West Africa, they are in evidence at the beginning and the end of the rainy season and in the United States, which is one of the most tornado-prone countries in the world, from April to July, with variations for the north and the south. Tornadoes also tend to be afternoon or evening events.

Rated from 0 to 5, they can reach 260–318 mph, and are capable of lifting frame houses off their foundations or stripping the bark off trees. The damage is increased due to the debris they pick up: from hoardings and small objects to cars, trees, and even trucks.

Tornadoes only happen over lands and tend to appear at the trailing end of storms, born of a mix of three main ingredients: wind, temperature, and moisture. The warm air drawn by the storm raises and with the colder higher temperatures condenses into rain, which, in turn, sets off an opposing cool downdraft. Wind shear rolls together the cold and warm air into giant horizontal spinning tubes, which, when tilted with one end touching the ground, become tornadoes.

About 500 yards wide and lasting around 15 min, tornadoes leave a trail of destruction on average 2 miles long and 1000 ft wide, but sometimes their trail is significant enough to be visible from satellite as over Oklahoma (see Fig. 1.1).

It is not clear why some major storms, such as hurricanes, spawn tornadoes, while others, just as powerful, do not. United States, which is constantly hit by tornadoes (about 800 a year on average) has been making sustained efforts to improve the understanding of the causes of hazardous weather and provide better warning systems, currently averaging between 6 and 12 min.

A number of US government agencies (The National Severe Storms Laboratory and The Storm Prediction Centre) have been set up to undertake long-term research. Doppler radar can detect strong rotation within a storm and NEXRAD, a computerized Doppler system, has been effective at locating and analysing tornado producing storms.

Tornadoes are rated as shown in Table 5.3.

Table 5.3
Tornado ratings.

Scale number	Maximum wind
F0	72 mph
F1	112 mph
F2	157 mph
F3	206 mph
F4	260 mph
F5	318 mph
F6	379 mph

Lightning

What is lightning and how it occurs

When a cold front meets warm air it pushes it upwards and, as explained in Section A, a storm occurs in the process and thunderstorm clouds develop, becoming charged like giant electricity storing devices. Lightning is a very powerful spark between clouds with different potential or a charged cloud and the earth.

How lightning occurs

Ions and electrons in the atmosphere convert to water droplets of different charges (positive, negative, or neutral). It is not fully understood how these become separated into different clouds or, more often, in different parts of the same cloud with the upper part becoming positively charged and the lower part negatively charged, with the two separated by an insulating layer of air.

As the clouds grow, their charges increase until the voltage difference between the positive and negative parts is so great that it breaks down the resistance of the insulating layer and an electrical discharge occurs. The discharge starts with a negatively charged downward feeler (step *feeler*) seeking an easy path to a positively charged part that is sending upward seeking positive *streamers*. When these meet, the potential difference is equalized, causing a bright flash or a *return stroke*.

The charged cloud, or part of a cloud, will discharge towards another charged body as soon as the potential difference is high enough to overcome the resistance between them. Discharge between different portions of the same cloud happens more often than between two clouds or a cloud and the earth because of the way the air inside the cloud becomes ionized by the drawn out water droplets that create a path for the 'step leaders', also known as 'potential gradients'.

The lightning flash is the visible effect of the passage of the discharge, usually several miles long. When a discharge happens, ionization takes place and, almost simultaneously, ions and electrons recombine.

Light is emitted in the process accompanied by sudden expansion and a violent reaction of the heated air, causing the vibration that constitutes thunder. Thunder is the explosion that occurs at the same time with the flash, but due to the relatively slow speed of sound travel arrives much later.

A charged cloud will transmit a charge to the earth below by attracting opposite particles. This concentrates on any upstanding point such as a tree, chimneystack, or church steeple. These protruding objects begin to respond to the strong electric field by producing 'positive streamers' and a discharge takes place as soon as the surrounding air becomes sufficiently ionized.

When the potential gradient is extremely steep the objects need not be very high above the ground: a tent pole, tree, or human being, for example, will be sufficient to act as a conductor. A lightning conductor does not 'attract' lightning. A lightning conductor protects by providing the current with the easiest route to conduct it safely to earth, thus reducing the potential for discharge (potential gradient). The reduction of the potential gradient is why thunderstorms are correctly said to be less dangerous when accompanied by rain. Each raindrop carries a small amount of electric charge to the ground, thus reducing the difference between charges.

The average quantity of electricity carried by a lightning strike is about 20 C and the value of the current of the order of 20 000 A, at peak releasing 100 MW/m.

The power of current carried by discharges has been recorded to be as high as 250 000 A.

Types of lightning
- *Normal* lightning as described above.
- *Sheet lightning*: normal lightning reflected in the clouds.
- *Heat lightning*: normal lightning near the horizon, reflected by high clouds.
- *Ball lightning*: lightning forms a slow moving ball that can burn objects in its path before exploding or burning out.
- *Red sprite*: a red burst reported to occur above storm clouds reaching a few miles in length towards the stratosphere.

Effects of lightning on buildings
As lightning strikes it heats air to about 30 000°C, which expands explosively damaging the part of the building where it strikes. The extent of the damage will depend on the power released as well as the discharge's direction and 'striking distance' (length of the last step of the downward feeler of the discharge). British Standard 6651-1992 represents this distance as a sphere of 60 m diameter and when superimposed on the plan and elevations helps establish the protection required. The projecting parts of a building that are nearest to the downward feelers, such as chimney stacks, pinnacles, crosses, steeples, will be the most vulnerable.

The main causes for damage to the fabric of a building are:

- the consequences of the explosive air expansion;
- the effect of the mechanical force of the strike;
- the effects of the high temperatures involved;
- flying debris;
- weakening and/or dismantling of parts of the structure;
- dislocation along masonry joints;
- fire from igniting dust;
- the effects of the magnetic field created by the discharge causing damage to electrical circuits and electronic equipment.

Surge protectors deal only with surges in supply. To protect electronic items like TV, VCR, etc., a 'lightning arrester' is needed. It uses a gas filled gap that acts as an open circuit to low potentials, but becomes ionized and conducts at very high potentials.

Protecting buildings from lightning
- As a rule of thumb, lightning has been considered to affect an area contained within a 45° line drawn from the highest point of a building; thus, protection has been provided accordingly with a conductor placed at the highest point to cover this required zone of protection. Detailed advice and specification for protection and installation can be found in *British Standard 6651: 1992 – Protection of Structures against Lightning*.
- Lightning has also been observed to strike at the sides of buildings, seeping in through joints, dislocating whole blocks away, and splitting

masonry. The phenomenon is still being researched, but buildings need to be protected from this *side flash* type of hit too. Current recommendations suggest that protection can be achieved with a series of down conductors protecting the entire building; towers and spires requiring two down conductors diametrically opposite to each other and horizontal conductors (coronas) at 20 m centres. A 20 m × 10 m grid would protect the rest of the building projecting features requiring additional air terminals. Positioning of conductors is important for safety reasons, but, in the case of historic buildings, for also being able to provide the necessary protection without altering the character and appearance of the monument.

- To ensure adequate earthing and protection the installation must be regularly inspected and maintained. A qualified contractor should carry out checks once a year and after each lightning strike checks the electrodes. Maintenance of the system is of paramount importance, as the provision of a lightning conductor will not prevent lightning from striking, just direct into the earth safely. If through lack of maintenance this is not possible the building and its occupants will lose protection.

Case study – Reconstruction of church spire
St Quentin-sur-Indrois, France (contributor: Bertrand Penneron, Architect, Tours, France)
Historical background

The St Quentin sur Indrois church was built in the eleventh century, probably as a replacement of an earlier timber church, on being granted to the Abbey of Marmoutier. The Bell Tower was erected at the beginning of the twelfth century with a vaulted stone first floor. The Chancel has been subject to substantial alterations from the end of the fifteenth century to the beginning of the sixteenth century. To enable their vaulting over, the walls were raised, additional supports built, and buttresses added. The Nave roof structure was comprehensively restored.

In 1614, a manorial chapel was built against the chancel and bell tower, which is now the Vestry. The two asymmetrical altars on the east side of the nave were also erected during this period. Another major transformation took place during the eighteenth century. The nave walls were reduced by about 1 m; the roof structure was restored re-using salvaged elements. The gallery, which at that time still existed on the south elevation of the nave, was part demolished, part incorporated above the portal. Finally, it was the nineteenth-century refurbishment that gave the church its present appearance: the bay openings, the panelling of the underside of the nave's roof timbers, the erection of the dais, and the removal of the Southern gallery.

During this time, the church was almost entirely restored: the walls and vaults, the Bell Tower base, and spire were renewed in ashlar and rubble stone and re-rendered. The roof structure was refurbished, the Vestry and Chancel roof coverings repaired, and that of the nave completely renewed. The Chancel's render was renewed to give the appearance of stonework, and was painted in distemper. The vault supporting the Bell Tower was restored; the Belfry refurbished with an oak copy. The inside of the spire was cement rendered. The spire base was strengthened with a metal device, but it is difficult to be specific about this as several projects are mentioned in the archives.

The works executed are described as follows in a November 1880 account:

> An external strapping with iron circles tied internally by tie-rods of the same metal and supported by vertical uprights. (…) Dressing of the Spire and the bell Tower, rendering with hydraulic lime. This render covering the irons will preserve them from the direct action of the air and oxidation. The iron used come from the Berry forge will be soft, treated with a minimum of two oil-based coats before use. All assemblies will be executed with the greatest care, the bolt and nut fillets will be regular and thick, the nuts will always be used in pairs, one over the other, and the bolts level on the last nut

The church was listed on the Historic Monuments Supplementary List on 28 October 1926.

On 21 June 1957, the Bell Tower was hit by lightning and suffered substantial damage. The repairs consisted of the re-building of the Belfry, repair of a crack on the north side of the Tower, rebuilding of the finial of one the pinnacles, repairs to the lower part and replacement of the upper part of the Bell Tower, the readjustment of the cross, and the renewal of the weather vane cock. Lightning struck the Bell Tower again on 16 May 1988, causing minor damage. It is likely that the strengthening of the tower with concrete was undertaken at this time: a concrete floor supporting the belfry, concrete perimeter tie-beams replacing or complementing the metal devices. It is amazing that despite repeated damage from lightning a lightning conductor was not installed!

On 12 April 1998, the Bell Tower was hit by lightning once again. This time the stone rubble Spire was almost entirely destroyed, its fall causing substantial damage to the roof timbers and coverings of the entire church, the chancel vaults, the furnishings, and the flooring (see Figs 5.10 and 5.11).

Emergency measures were then undertaken: the remains of the chancel vault was enclosed in shuttering, a tie-rod was inserted between the north and south nave walls, which were no longer linked by the roof timbers, and a temporary roof cover was installed over the damaged roofs.

An architect experienced in historic building restoration and familiar with traditional buildings techniques (Bertrand Penneron) was appointed to oversee the repair works (see Contributors notes). The rebuilding work was financed mostly by insurance funds and by some grants from

Fig. 5.10
St Quentin sur Indrois – church spire damaged by lightning.

Fig. 5.11
St Quentin sur Indrois – damage to church roof detail.

regional and departmental funds, as well as by The French Ministry of Culture. However, as a result of administrative and insurance procedure requirements, it was only at the end of January 2001 that funds were secured and remedial work initiated.

Building survey following the disaster
The nave
The roof timber structure was constructed with truss forming rafters, and panel lined with nailed but jointed boards. There are five apparent main trusses with tie beams and octagonal king post and secondary trusses at approximately 65 cm centres.

The eastern half of the nave was entirely destroyed. The furnishings were partly destroyed. The nave had two Altars, constructed in timber with plaster reredoses, all decorated in 'faux marble' style. One has been destroyed and the two reredoses damaged when the roof fell in. A great number of pews were destroyed. The five plaster statues placed on brackets along the walls were damaged.

The chancel
A large part of the roof timber structure was destroyed by the fall of the stone spire and the parts, which remained in situ, were disturbed (breakage of assembly). The floor was partly smashed by the fallen stone vault. The plywood Altar used for Mass was destroyed by the falling structural timbers.

The bell tower
The spire was almost entirely destroyed as a result of the explosion caused by the expanding heated air and debris flying hit the stone facades across the road leaving marks resembling bullet holes. The base, which remained in situ, was completely disturbed (see Fig. 5.12).

Fig. 5.12
St Quentin sur Indrois – church spire damage. © Bertrand Penneron.

One part of the bay level was also destroyed. One of the little towers, also in rubble stone, had shifted away from the group. The rest of the tower remained in relatively good condition.

The vestry
Falling masonry and roof timbers disturbed the vault

The re-building work

The principle adopted was to reinstate what was lost exactly in the same way as it was before the damage occurred, and to restore all the elements damaged by the disaster (see Figs 5.13 and 5.14).

Contractors were selected amongst professionals experienced in historic building restoration, with specific qualifications such as those issued by QUALIBAT or other similar references.

The nave
The part of the structural roof that was destroyed was entirely re-built, copying the components of the surviving portion using the same type of timber, the same section, and type of decoration. The timber structure of the roof and the timber boarding were re-built using traditional methods and re-using as much as possible the old timbers. The surviving part was inspected (in particular the assembly joints that had been shaken by the strike). The roof was entirely recovered with slate, matching the rest of the church. In order to retain the unity of the volume, it was decided to renew the entire floor, not just the part that was destroyed in the nave, and part of the Chancel. A combination of clay tiles and chalk stone slabs was used and advantage was taken of the restoration work to install an under-floor heating system, replacing the existing heating system that did not comply with building safety standards. The Altars and the pulpit were

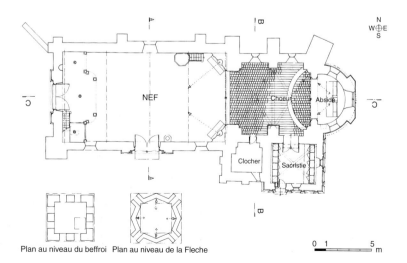

Fig. 5.13
St Quentin sur Indrois – church plan.
© Bertrand Penneron.

Plan au niveau du beffroi   Plan au niveau de la Fleche

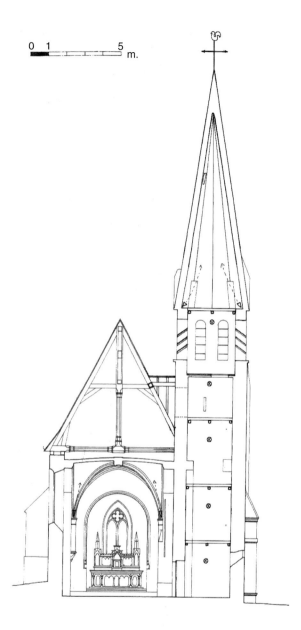

0 1   5
                         m.

Fig. 5.14
St Quentin sur Indrois – church
repairs section. © Bertrand
Penneron.

reproduced exactly as the originals, in accordance with surviving features
and the record photographs from the archives kept in the Town Hall.

The chancel

The vault was rebuilt as an exact replica of the surviving bay, and has
been decorated in 'faux' stone as the existing one, which has been
restored. The roof coverings and timber structure has been renewed as for
the nave. Taking advantage of the works, it was decided to reinstate a
junction between the chancel and the bell tower. This existed in the past
as witnessed by the remains of the flashing mark on the bell tower; it had

the advantage, amongst others, of improving the disposal of rainwater and of allowing access into the roof space of the Chancel from the bell tower, through an opening that existed in the rubble stone wall. The Altar, of a very modest construction (plywood covered by a piece of cloth), was entirely destroyed and the opportunity arose to design a more noble piece of furniture. With the agreement of the clerics, a solid wood altar is being constructed.

The apse
The roofing was renewed as for the rest of the church. The existing roof was executed on cut slopes, probably for economic reasons; advantage was taken of the works to renew it in a conical shape, more suitable for a circular apse.

The bell tower
When the lightning hit the masonry, the extreme heat caused it to explode. Here, almost the whole of the spire had fallen. The base, which remained in place, was entirely disturbed and had to be dismantled and rebuilt. The perimeter ties at the base of the spire has allowed the upper part of the belfry to remain in place. Nevertheless, the lightning has probably passed along the chamfer of the southern bay of the east face, and the entire corresponding angle had to be refurbished. An opening existed in the slopes of the spire, visible in the photographs; this was reinstated. As witnessed by the numerous estimates in the Town hall archives, at the end of nineteenth century the bell tower was showing serious structural problems. Apart from the age of the masonry, it was due to the excessive thrust exerted by the vault supporting the belfry, which was removed and replaced by a wood and metal floor, and then by a concrete one, thus removing one of the causes of the problem. The bell tower was otherwise strengthened.

The reinforced concrete strengthening was maintained, checked, and restored. As the concrete floor supporting the belfry was very thin (10 cm) it was strengthened. The checking and restoration of the belfry, bells, and mufflers were also undertaken. At long last a lightening conductor, protecting the entire building, was installed!

The vestry
The timber roof structure and coverings over the nave were renewed. Here too it was decided to take advantage of the works to reinstate a valley forming roof slope (of which there still remained traces under the form of a flashing) in order to improve the disposal of rainwater. Certain sections of the cornice and stained glass were also renewed. The church's lighting scheme was entirely re-designed, the existing installation no longer complying with the safety standards; the lighting was designed to allow, on the one hand, the conduct of the religious service and, on the other, to enhance the remarkable features of the monument (Altars, vaults, panelling). Figure 5.15 shows the church building after restoration work was completed.

Fig. 5.15
St Quentin sur Indrois church
after repairs.

Extreme temperatures

Temperature records – extreme cold
General
In central Europe, records go back to the sixteenth century; in central England, to the seventeenth century.

The Climatic Research Unit (CRU) at the University of east Anglia, Norwich (UEA), widely recognized as one of the world's leading institutions concerned with the study of climatic change, used 17 sets of data to build up a record of average summer temperatures for both hemispheres from the year 1000 to 1991, with 10 applying to the Northern Hemisphere. Five are from tree rings from northern Sweden, Siberian, Alberta, and Idaho. Ice core data are two from Greenland and one from Spitzbergen.

The result has been that the temperatures currently being experienced are higher than at any time over the last 1000 years, with 1998 being the hottest single year on record.

The CRU team is examining patterns past and present that have had a forcing effect on climate, including events like volcanic activity and solar cycles. The aim is to compare patterns of the past with those of today to prove conclusively if current temperature changes are significantly different from patterns of natural variability in the past. Climate models suggest that anthropogenic global warming will show a distinctive pattern, for example, that it will be greatest in northern latitudes of the great continental landmasses. Already recent summer temperatures in Siberia are higher than for a 1000 years.

Summary of changes occurred over the last 100 years, attributable to human-induced global warming (Source: CRU)

- Sea level has risen up to 250 mm since 1860 and could rise by 1 m by 2100.
- There has been a marked increase in the incidence and severity of storms.
- El Nino has produced effects of unprecedented severity effects due to the warming in the Pacific.
- Receding polar ice is resulting in the rapid expansion of flora; Antarctic summers have lengthened by up to 50% since the 1970s and new species of plants have appeared as glaciers have retreated.
- In Switzerland, glaciers have retreated by up to 50%.
- Global mean surface air temperature has increased between 0.3 and 0.6°C since the later part of the nineteenth century. The hottest year on record was 1998.
- Seasonal shifts and changes in rainfall patterns are becoming increasingly pronounced.
- Spring in the northern hemisphere is arriving at least 1 week earlier than 20 years ago.
- Deserts are expanding.
- Pests and pathogens are migrating to temperate latitudes, most notably vector-borne malaria.

Extreme cold

November 1998 was the coldest in Moscow and other parts of European Russia since complete records were first kept in 1879. In Petropavlosk, the city's mayor told residents to take to their cellars and cover the radiators in their apartments with blankets to save the heating system from total collapse. In Vladivostok, Russia's main Pacific Ocean port, the cold spell that has already brought daytime temperatures to −25°C (−13°F) was forecast to be the longest in any December since 1941. Coal reserves at a power station that provided the city's central heating stood at 80 000 tonnes, compared to 250 000 tonnes the previous year. A spokesman for the local electricity company said that if the next delivery of fuel were held up at all, the heat would have to be shut off.

Subsequently, 17 frozen apartment blocks had to be abandoned in the town of Alapayevsk near Yekaterinburg in the Ural Mountains because fuel was late in arriving at the town. In the remote Arctic outpost of Cape Schmidt opposite Alaska, vanishing fuel supplies forced 190 families to abandon their frozen apartments and relocate to military barracks or move in with relatives.

January 2001 was the coldest in 50 years in Siberia. (Northern Hemisphere's low-temperature records were not surpassed however.

They remain: −90°F in Verkhoyansk on 5 and 7 February 1892, and in Oimekon on 6 February 1933, both in Siberia.) There were two episodes of unusually cold weather in Siberia in 2001: 1–13 January and 27 January to 6 February. The lowest temperatures in the western political subdivisions (oblasts) of Siberia (Tomsk, Novosibirsk, Omsk, and Altay Kray) occurred during the first episode, with minimum temperatures ranging from −42 to −61°F.

The normal daily average temperature for stations in these oblasts ranges from 6 to −9°F during early January. The observed average temperature at these stations on the coldest days ranged from −31 to −51°F. The lowest temperatures at stations farther east in the east Siberian region (most notably in the Irkutsk oblast) occurred during the second episode, mostly on 31 January and 1 February, with minimum temperatures ranging from −48 to −72°F. Daily average temperatures ranged from 28 to 46°F *below normal*.

The coldest weather actually occurred in what is known as the Russian Far Eastern Region, in Oimekon (−78°F) and Verkhoyansk (−73°F) on 29 and 27 January, respectively.

In Table 5.4, some of the coldest days observed at Russian stations in January and February 2001 are shown. (The 'WMO number' identifies a particular surface station in the World Meteorological Organization.)

Although the weather in January 2001 was unusually cold in Siberia and the Far East, it was not the coldest in the last 50 years. The average monthly temperatures in 1969, 1977, and 1972 (for some stations) were probably lower (see Table 5.5).

Vostok, Antarctica, is the home of the coldest temperature on Earth at a cool −89°C (183 K). At the Russian research station the temperature is regularly in the −30 to the −60°C mark. This chilly weather is due to

Table 5.4 Coldest five days observed at Russian weather stations in January and February 2001.

Date	WMO number	City	Minimum (°F)	Maximum (°F)
29 January 2001	24 688	Oimekon	−78	−65
27 January 2001	24 266	Verkhoyansk	−73	−67
15 January 2001	24 678	Zapadanya	−70	Unknown
28 January 2001	24 382	Ust-Moma	−69	−62
31 January 2001	24 817	Yerbogachen	−69	−54
1 February 2001	24 688	Oimekon	−72	−59
1 February 2001	24 817	Yerbogachen	−72	−68
2 February 2001	24 918	Zhdanovo	−71	−65
2 February 2001	30 127	Yuktukon	−71	Unknown
1 February 2001	24 713	Nakanna	−69	−68

Table 5.5 Coldest temperatures on earth.

Bibliographic entry	Result (with explanation)	Standardized result
Earth Science Revised, 3rd edition. New York: Prentice Hall, 1987: 217	'... the temperature in Vostok, Antarctica, dropped to nearly −89.2°C, the lowest temperature ever recorded on Earth'	−89.2°C
World Book Encyclopedia. New York: World Book, 2000: A530	'Scientists recorded the world's lowest temperature, −128.6°F (−89.2°C), at Vostok Station...'	−89.2°C
Weather at the Coldest Place on Earth: Vostok Antarctica. Central Atlantic Storm Investigators (CASI), 1999	'Vostok, Antarctica holds the world's record for coldest temperature: −129°F (7/21/83)'	−89.4°C
McFarlan, Donald. *Guinness Book of Records*. New York: Guinness Publishing, 1992: 42	'−126.9°F. Vostok, Ant. Aug. 25, 1960'	−88.3°C
Antarctica Weather. The Antarctic Connection, 2000	'Antarctica has the coldest average annual temperatures, and the lowest temperature ever recorded on earth (−129°F) was at Vostok on July 21, 1983.'	−89.4°C
Pomeroy, Marc. *Antarctic Facts*. 1999	'Vostok station (Russian) NEW RECORD SET IN 1997!!! This is an unconfirmed report from Vostok Station during the winter of 1997. −91°C (−132°F). This is colder than Dry Ice! The "official" record is also from Vostok station on July 21, 1983 −89.2°C (−128.6°F)'	−91°C (unconfirmed), −89.2°C (confirmed)

the exceptionally high speed of the arctic winds. The katabatic or down-ward type winds that bring the brisk temperature travel with speeds up to 200 mph (about 90 m/s) from the inland towards the coast of the continent. As one moves toward the higher region inland – that is, towards the true pole – the temperature drops from its normal −40 to −80°C. The coldest temperatures usually occur during the winter months of around 22 March, when Antarctica has completed days of darkness. Warmer temperatures, usually still well below freezing, occur during the all-day summer months around 22 September. Antarctica also holds the previous record of the lowest temperature on earth at −88°C. Although still unofficial, Vostok Station may have broken its own record for the coldest temperature on earth. It has been reported that Vostok reached the temperature of −91°C during the winter of 1997. (*Source*: Yong Li Liang, 2000.)

Temperature records – extreme heat
Our life depends on the Sun heating and lighting the Earth.

The Sun's surface temperature is 5500°C, and whilst the Earth is much cooler, temperatures can still reach levels man find difficult to tolerate. At 41°C, proteins begin to denature and cells begin to be irreversibly damaged. A body temperature of 45°C is lethal for humans and at temperatures exceeding 50°C almost all cells are destroyed if exposed for a few minutes.

The hottest air temperature ever recorded was 58°C, measured in the shade in Lybia (El Azizia, September 1992); temperatures of over 45°C are recorded routinely in Central Australia, The Gulf States, and Sudan. High temperatures can be registered in normally cold environments such as mountain tops – Everest snowfields have recorded 30°C, but the highest temperatures on earth are found in deserts. *Deserts* are defined as areas that receive less than 10 in. of rain a year. The extreme heat can be further increased by hot dry winds and the lack of clouds allows the intense sun radiation to build up rapidly during the day and cool equally quickly at night.

With protective clothing humans can tolerate temperatures above boiling point but only for short intervals as the body temperature inevitably rises and brain cells, extremely sensitive to heat, cannot withstand more than 42°C, after which the brain function is severely impaired. Consequently, our ability to survive in extreme heat depends on being able to keep body temperature below 42°C. An example of the devastation that hot weather can cause was witnessed in July 2000 in South East Europe, when record-breaking temperatures caused deaths due to heat stoke, high blood pressure, and heart attacks in Greece, Romania, Turkey, Bulgaria, and Italy.

In Romania, hospitals were overcrowded with sufferers, pavements melted in the heat and nearly 200 fires occurred within 24 h due to the hot and dry conditions. Government employees were told to stay at home because of lack of air conditioning and power failures. Similar reports came from Bulgaria, Macedonia, Belgrade, and Turkey. The region's average top summer temperature, usually between 30 and 35°C, was reaching 42°C in the shade and was set to rise due to a thermal air heat mass flowing in from the Sahara desert.

In Italy, wildfires spread across the from Rome to Sicily and in Greece authorities provided air-conditioned public auditoriums and halls for the public, activating a civil defence fire and medical emergency alert.

Long-term planning to ensure communities at risk are better prepared when they involve reviewing shelter and housing construction.

Traditionally, survival in hot climates has meant that man has sheltered from heat in cooler underground locations and constructed buildings so as to reduce heat absorption and maximize cooling effects.

The Matmata houses of the Sahara are sited 10 m below the ground and some people in the Australian desert town of Coober Pedy still live in homes below the ground. In lesser heat, built-in features help to reduce heat; for example, the wind catchers in Pakistan or the sliding walls in traditional Japanese houses, which allow cooling through winds. In more temperate conditions, but still subject to periods of hot climate, such as Italy or the south of France, stone walls, several feet thick, are employed for their insulating qualities to provide refuge from intense heat.

Design elements for buildings in hot climates are discussed in detail in the following chapter.

General design features

'Climate sensitive design' has become a high priority in recent years. Sometimes referred to as 'solar architecture', 'climatic or bioclimatic architecture', it represents the acknowledgement of the significant role climatic factors have in determining the basic internal environmental conditions and, ultimately, the quality of buildings.

It has been possible to overcome some of the negative effects of poor design that has disregarded the effect of climate conditions by the use of heating, ventilation, and air conditioning, but the consensus is that an extravagant use of such systems is becoming unacceptable, not least because of its effect on energy consumption.

Climate-sensitive design is now adopting a number of factors in building construction, in recognition of their considerable impact within the context of varying environmental conditions:

1. design of an appropriate building form avoiding unnecessary over-shadowing of one building by another;
2. use of suitable construction techniques such as the relative positions and thickness of insulation materials to maximize beneficial heat gains or to exclude excess heat;
3. adapting the internal layout to climate and building orientation so that rooms or spaces with specific functions are located adjacent to the most appropriate facades;
4. division of buildings into thermal zones with buffer areas, such as balconies, verandas, atria, courtyards, and arcades; avoiding the creation of barriers to cross-flow ventilation where this is required;
5. judicious choice and positioning of appropriate building materials within the internal and external fabric, particularly where thermal mass effects can be used to dampen temperature fluctuations;
6. location, size, and type of openings in the building envelope (including glazing type) chosen so as to exploit an advantageous solar gain (glazing facing south in northern latitudes is easier to shade);
7. careful co-ordination between the building and the site so that site disadvantages are not exacerbated.

Many of these features can be incorporated within the usual building process, often at minimal additional cost. A recent example of a climate-sensitive-design building, The City Hall London (Fig. 5.16) is not only a remarkable landmark, but also ensures that it will run on a quarter of the energy of a conventional office building.

Materials, thermal mass, and energy storage

One of the constituent elements of good climate-sensitive design involves the choice of appropriate materials for energy absorption. In many climates, ambient temperature varies in a daily pattern with maxima during the middle of the afternoon and minima overnight in the

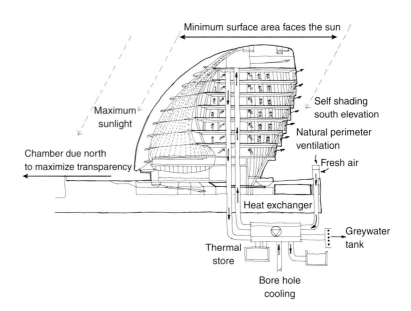

Fig. 5.16
City Hall London.
(Source: World Architecture
July/August 2002) Architect: Foster
and Partners; Structural, Services and
Acoustic engineers: ARUP. The
building uses glass extensively as a
design statement to express
accessibility and transparency. At the
same time, it is environmentally
efficient combining energy saving
measures such as judicious
orientation and shape to reduce
energy consumption.

Labels in figure: Minimum surface area faces the sun; Maximum sunlight; Self shading south elevation; Natural perimeter ventilation; Chamber due north to maximize transparency; Fresh air; Heat exchanger; Greywater tank; Thermal store; Bore hole cooling

early morning. Maximum solar input also occurs during the middle
of the day. By choosing suitable building materials with appropriate
'thermal mass' (the accepted term for the overall effect of the amount of
material combined with its thermal capacity), heat can be stored and
temperature fluctuations reduced, with the result of more acceptable
thermal conditions.

Recent innovations include the promotion of *cold storage* in which building materials are pre-cooled overnight so as to be able to absorb and counteract some of the next day's overheating. A Scandinavian system, known
as Termodeck, involves using an interconnected network of tubes running
through floor slabs. Cool air can be circulated at night to pre-cool the floor
slabs. Water, which has a high thermal capacity, may also be used to
absorb heat. Another interesting possibility involves the use of phase-
change materials. When water changes from a solid (ice) to its liquid form,
it absorbs a large amount of heat without changing its temperature.

When adopting climate-sensitive design modern designers follow the
same principles used in the historic vernacular architecture of many
areas of the world. A number of scientific studies have confirmed that
traditional design was often extremely well suited to the specifics of its
local climate and the general trend is to revert to the traditional concepts,
which in the past were abandoned in favour of fast and cheap 'modern'
building. (See Fig. 5.17a and b.)

Bioclimatic design
An analysis technique that considers thermal comfort zones in terms of
air temperature and moisture content (humidity), from which alternative

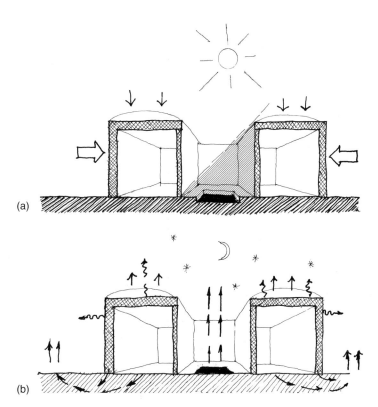

Fig. 5.17
Traditional hot dry house.
(a) day-time heat absorbtion;
(b) night-time cooling effect.

(a)

(b)

solutions can be devised, includes:

1. use of increased thermal insulation levels in the building fabric;
2. increase of effective thermal mass arising from choice and location of construction elements and materials;
3. increased natural ventilation and associated heat transfer encouraged by building openings;
4. increased night-time ventilation (when external temperatures are likely to be at their lowest) to promote cooling;
5. use of evaporative cooling on building surfaces or at openings;
6. use of radiative cooling from building surfaces.

Solar design
Whether the priority is to encourage or exclude solar radiation from affecting a building, design should consider a number of parameters in relation to the site; for example:

1. the sun's position relative to the building (solar altitude and azimuth);
2. site orientation and slope;
3. existing obstructions on the site;

4. potential for overshadowing from obstructions outside the site boundary;
5. grouping and orientation of buildings;
6. road layout and services distribution;
7. proposed glazing types and areas, and facade design;
8. nature of internal spaces into which solar radiation penetrates.

Effect of extreme temperatures on buildings
Cold

Extreme cold does not affect buildings in isolation, but only in conjunction with moisture through the process of freezing. The resulting expansion of ice when the temperature drops and the subsequent thaw when it rises subject buildings to movements that sometimes are sudden and excessive, thus causing structural or morphological failure. The common effects of low temperatures are

- *Frost heave* – an expansion causing the sub-soil to move and affect foundations that are not deep enough. This is often the case when buildings are constructed on fine sand, silt, or clay soil where the water table is close to the ground level. When the ground below the floor slabs lifts and expands sideways it causes tilting and horizontal cracks in walls.
- *Damage to porous building materials* such as brick or stone, especially when saturated with water. Ice forms in the pores and when these are not able to expand, either due to rigidity or hydrophilic characteristics, they 'cleave', crumble, and disintegrate (see Fig. 5.18).
- *Snow* – whilst providing good insulation it can also cause *structural failure* through its weight if inadequate loads have been allowed in this respect.
- *Melting snow* on an inappropriate roof slope can degenerate into avalanche-like descents damaging structures below or cause flooding through blockages and overflows. Some of these aspects are further examined in Section D.d. Simple precautions such as snow boards, duckboards, and regular maintenance are cost-effective prevention measures.

Heat

A building undergoes a constant heat exchange process with the outdoor environment. This can take place in a number of ways:

- inwards or outwards by *conduction*;
- *heat gain* from solar radiation, or the internal output of appliances, human bodies, lamps, etc.;
- movement of hot and cold air, that is, *ventilation*;
- *mechanical control of temperature* (heating or cooling);
- *evaporation* of water, either externally such as pooling rainwater on the roof, or internally from human sweat, baths, drying laundry, etc., which can have a cooling effect.

Fig. 5.18
Stone masonry affected by frost.

The effect of alternating extreme heat from direct solar radiation by day and the cooling convection at night subjects buildings to a cycle of expansion and contraction, known as *thermal movement*.

The way in which building materials heat up is subject to a number of factors such as their colour (light colours absorb less heat), absorbency, surface treatment, thermal expansion coefficient, etc.

Building materials respond differently to thermal movement, depending on their capacity for dimensional change, rigidity, plasticity, structural restraint, and variations in moisture contents. For example, the increase in length of a 30-m element will be 20 mm for aluminium, 58 mm for wood across the grain, but only 3.36 mm for limestone or 6.7 mm for brickwork. Thermal movement can affect:

1. *An existing building element such as a roof or a wall.* Unrestricted it will expand freely, but if restricted or longer than 30 m the element will be stressed by the constraint. Walls will develop longitudinal and diagonal cracks (see Fig. 5.19a–c). It is, therefore, important in

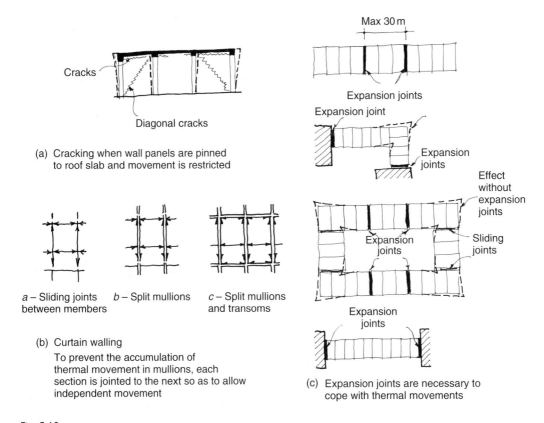

Cracks

Diagonal cracks

(a) Cracking when wall panels are pinned to roof slab and movement is restricted

a – Sliding joints between members   b – Split mullions   c – Split mullions and transoms

(b) Curtain walling

To prevent the accumulation of thermal movement in mullions, each section is jointed to the next so as to allow independent movement

Max 30 m

Expansion joints

Expansion joint

Expansion joints

Effect without expansion joints

Expansion joints

Sliding joints

Expansion joints

Expansion joints

(c) Expansion joints are necessary to cope with thermal movements

Fig. 5.19
Thermal movement: (a) building structure; (b) curtain walling; (c) expansion joints.

conditions of substantial seasonal variation (which even in Britain can be as high as 50°C) to incorporate suitable provisions, such as expansion joints to facilitate unimpeded movement of the structural elements.

2. *An entire structure* is also subject to movement and the length and shape of the building play a major role in ensuring that adequate provisions are available to permit the necessary expansion. The spacing and width of the joints depend on the materials and temperatures involved, and their location is determined by the size and shape of the building.

General design considerations with respect of the effects of extreme temperature variations have been mentioned in Section D.c. As an extensive specialist subject, the design of buildings in hot climates could not be considered in depth here, but looking at the general principles of a typical *house design for a hot and dry climate* will give an idea of the main aspects involved:

1. *Objective*: to provide reasonable comfort and protection from the intense heat radiation coming from the sun, ground, and surrounding buildings during the day. This can be achieved by maintaining inner surface temperatures lower than the skin.

2. *Form and planning*: because of the hostile outdoors an essentially inward looking building is the most suitable. Surfaces directly exposed to the sun should be reduced to a minimum, and if possible the building should have a north/south orientation. West is to be avoided. Siting buildings close together will decrease heat gain thanks to mutual shading, which is why traditional settlements tend to have closely grouped buildings, narrow streets, colonnades, and small enclosed courtyards.
3. *Internal courtyards* can be used as thermal regulators and are the best external places, as they provide shade during the day and cooler surface earth that draws the heat during the night (see Fig. 5.17a and b).
4. *Adjustable openings* – small during the day and large during the night with heavy shutters or other type of screening, to regulate intake of hot and cool air.
5. *Use of the thermal capacity of structural elements*, especially roofs to enable the storage of day heat and its dissipation during the night.
6. *Suitable surface treatments* can help reduce the heat load. The absorbency and emittance of heat values of materials differ when receiving heat from solar radiation and this is a major consideration when selecting roof-surfacing materials. Traditional shelter in desert regions tends to use earth, brick, or stone painted white.
7. *Ventilation and airflow* must be designed to minimize the entry of hot air during the day and maximize the intake of cool night air. Whilst ventilation will not reduce the radiant heat transfer, it will help reduce radiant heat emission by lowering the temperature of the inner face of the outer envelope. Adequate ventilation of the roof space also helps and careful location and orientation of the openings is vital.

Case study – Anchorage Performing Arts Center roof repair (Contributor: Jon Kumin)
Introduction
Anchorage Alaska is located at latitude 60°N, a sub-arctic zone. (see Fig. 5.20). Although the weather is moderated by the nearby Gulf of Alaska, winters are long and by some standards quite cold. Extreme lows experienced in Anchorage approach −40°C, although this is unusual. Warmer periods with extensive snowfall are often followed by extended spells of clear, dry weather that can average −20°C for weeks at a time. Snow usually falls in significant quantities by mid-October and 5 months or more of snow cover is common. Although Anchorage does not experience the extreme arctic temperatures that embrittle common steels or congeal motor oil, this is a challenging climate for roofs.

Experience has shown that design approaches that work in regions at lower latitudes often do not work in Anchorage. This is true even for assemblies that have been proven in climates that for brief periods experience low temperatures that are similar to Anchorage. The extended duration of the winter severely tests a roof.

Selection of a roofing assembly is a complex balancing of issues. Typically, all roofs should have sufficient capacity to support the full

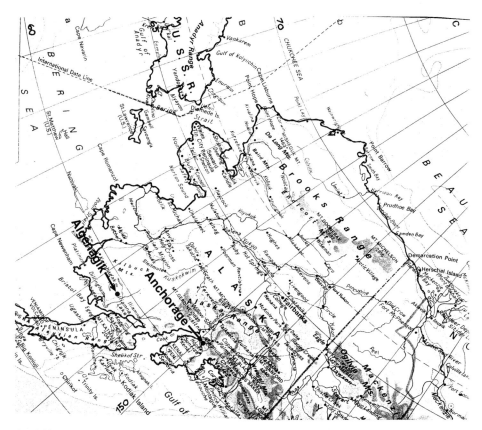

Fig. 5.20   Map of Alaska.

weight of the maximum expected snow load, which is $195\,kg/m^2$ in Anchorage. This is moderate – other communities in Alaska experience snow loads up to $600\,kg/m^2$. The snow can wind drift and slide to form extraordinary concentrations, and that is a key part of the difficulties faced by the roof considered in this example. Roofs should also be weather-tight, and if visible present an attractive appearance.

This discussion is offered as a cautionary tale of what can go wrong, and as an instructive one describing a successful repair.

Background

The Anchorage Performing Arts Centre (PAC) is a major public building, with construction completed in 1988. It encompasses about $16\,600\,m^2$ and has three theatres, the largest seating over 2000 people. The handsome steel and concrete framed structure has pitched roofs over major areas. The roof experienced difficulties virtually from the outset. There were several major issues – snow sliding, moisture build-up, and leaks.

Initial construction

The facility is covered with a mixture of steeply pitched and low slope – almost flat – roofs. This article focuses on the pitched roof areas. The structure is typically steel framed, with a corrugated metal deck. Over the theatres concrete fill was used on the steel deck for acoustic isolation. About 75 mm (minimum thickness) of concrete was placed on the 75-mm deep corrugated metal deck. Cold-formed light gauge galvanized steel purlins about 100-mm deep were fastened to the concrete, spaced about 1220 mm apart. Rigid phenolic foam insulation was placed between the purlins. This was covered by 19-mm thick plywood, treated with fire-retardant chemicals. The plywood was covered with stamped stainless steel shingles. The shingles formed a surface with little vertical relief, so that the seams between each shingle were close to the plane of the roof where runoff water flowed.

Over less acoustically sensitive areas, the concrete was not used. The corrugated metal deck has an initial layer of 13-mm gypsum board to create a level substrate. This was covered with Kraft paper. In these areas, 200-mm deep purlins were used, with the bottom 100 mm filled with fibreglass insulation and the top 100 mm again filled with phenolic foam. As with the other areas, a layer of 19-mm-thick fire-retardant plywood was screwed to the purlins, topped with the stamped stainless steel shingles. Slopes vary, typically running from 26.5 to 33.8°. The shingles were thin in profile with minimal overlap and had no underlying building paper or roofing felt.

Issues to resolve
There were three major problems areas – snow sliding, water intrusion (leaking) into the building, and moisture build-up within the roof assembly. They are interrelated as discussed below. A number of ancillary issues were also addressed, such as leaks at the low slope roof areas and intermediate gutters. This narrative focuses on the major issues.

As the pitched roof eaves are high above a busy downtown sidewalk, snow sliding was a concern from the inception. The original design used a series of large snow fences to block the sliding action. This was successful in keeping avalanches from injuring pedestrians; however, large quantities of snow would stack up against these fences, stressing the flashings.

A common cause of leaks in a snow country is water backed up by the formation of ice dams. These can be created by many factors. They are most common at the edge of poorly insulated roofs, where melt water encounters the cooler exposed edge and freezes. The piles of snow at the snow fences grew ice dams. The low-profile shingles had minimal resistance to water backing under them, causing leaks.

Moisture attacked this roof from both directions, not just from above. The building is humidified to about 45% relative humidity. As cold air holds little moisture, this creates a strong vapour pressure drive from the interior to the exterior. Water vapour pressure flow follows Pascal's 'law of partial pressure'. The cold exterior air holds little moisture, with consequently a much lower vapour pressure. The vapour is forced toward the exterior, cooling as it moves from the interior warmth towards the exterior. Once it cools to the dew point, it condenses into liquid water. This water can damage a roof assembly in a number of ways, such as fostering wood rot or corrosion of metals.

The standard response to this issue is a vapour-retarding membrane of some type, placed on the warmer side of the insulation. In this case, the vapour barrier selected was an emulsion of asphalt brushed on the concrete, and Kraft paper in the areas without concrete. These proved inadequate barriers, allowing water vapour to penetrate into the insulation. As it moved towards the outside, it cooled and condensed into liquid water.

This water combined with the water leaking from the outside to create a problem ultimately much worse than a simple leak. Phenolic foam insulation when wet produces a corrosive acid. The acid ate away the steel purlins, to the point where they crumbled at touch. This left the entire assembly vulnerable to blow-off in a strong wind.

Resolution

Although repair funds were limited, it was determined that partial measures would not do. A complete repair was instituted for the portion of the roof that could be afforded. This initial effort was completed in 1999; the remaining portion of the roof will be repaired as funds become available. Every component of the roof was replaced from the deck up. Typically, different materials were chosen to resolve specific issues. A key change was elimination of the snow fences, replacing them with a grid of square stainless steel tubes, placed perpendicular to the ribs of the new standing seam roof.

The original roof assembly was removed down to the concrete. A 0.25-mm-thick polyethylene vapour barrier was placed directly on the concrete. This has far more resistance to the passage of water vapour than the original asphalt emulsion. New galvanized steel purlins, 200-mm deep, were placed next, and secured at 610 mm intervals. Rigid expanded polystyrene foam, 200-mm thick was placed between the purlins. This material does not support development of a corrosive product, even when wet. This was covered with 19-mm-thick plywood, modified bitumen waterproofing membrane, and a new concealed fastener stainless steel standing seam roof. The waterproofing membrane acts as an additional layer of protection under the exposed metal roof. The standing seam material has 50-mm high ribs, and is therefore much less susceptible to water intrusion than the shingles. The panels are continuous from ridge to eave, and the lateral seams are raised 50 mm out of the plane of the water runoff surface. A transverse section below portrays the new assembly (see Fig. 5.21).

The 19-mm square tubes were placed on the ribs at 610 mm centres, over the entire roof. These act as snow guards, anchoring the snow to the roof. The attachment is by a clamp mechanism at the top of the ribs, so that there are no penetrations of the exterior surface.

19 mm² Stainless steel tubes
at 610 mm spacing
50 mm high ribs
Rubberized bituminous membrane
19 mm Plywood
Four layers of 50-mm thick foam insulation
200 mm Steel purlins
New vapour barrier membrane
Existing concrete deck

Section through new roof assembly

Fig. 5.21
Anchorage Art Centre, section through roof. © John Kumin.

Fig. 5.22
Anchorage Art Centre, view of roof under snow. © John Kumin.

Lessons learned

After three winter seasons, the repaired roof is performing well. No slides have been observed. It is instructive to compare the appearance of the repaired versus the original roof immediately after a snowfall. The photograph (see Fig. 5.22) was taken 24 h after a major snowfall (725 mm fell in a 24-h period). The portion on the left shows the new roof; the portion on the right is the original assembly. Note how the snow has slid down to the snow fences on the portion of the sloped roof not yet replaced. The areas with the new system show a uniform coverage, with the snow load distributed over the entire surface. Snow fences to avoid danger to pedestrians are unnecessary. There have been no signs of leaks or moisture build-up. Based on this performance, the intent is to complete the repairs as presently designed.

The lessons for future construction are evident. Moisture transport mechanisms must be understood. A competent vapour barrier on the warmer side of the insulation must be in place. Roofing materials in a snow country should be detailed to keep vulnerable seams out of the water drainage plane. Snow sliding on steeply pitched roofs must be considered. It is most useful to contemplate roof assemblies as systems, not isolated components. Each key element – underlying structural support, vapour barrier, insulation, and exposed roof – covering must be considered as part of an integrated whole.

Fig. 5.23
Algenak, Alaska – gymnasium roof
collapsed under snow weight.
© John Kumin.

The effects of snow weight can be dramatic as the unfortunate experience of an Alaskan school gymnasium whose roof collapsed under the snow load can illustrate (see Fig. 5.23).

New materials
The advance of science and technology has brought a new generation of materials that allow man to adapt to living in extreme temperature conditions and that can provide inspiration for building designers with their high performing insulation and flexibility characteristics.

Some examples from the NASA (National Aeronautics and Space Administration) innovation web site (http://nctn.hq.nasa.gov/innovation/Innovation51/insulatn.htm) are given below:

Layered composite insulation
NASA has developed layered composite insulation (LCI) technology for use in commercial applications. Designed by the Cryogenics Test Laboratory at the John F. Kennedy Space Centre (KSC) in Florida, this system can benefit multiple industries that depend on regulation of low temperatures in equipment and products.

The synergistic effect of improvements in materials, design, and manufacture of this new insulation technology exceeds current multi-layered insulation (MLI) or foam insulation products such as companies that transfer fluids (liquefied natural gas, refrigerants, chilled water, crude oil, low-pressure steam) or transport companies that move refrigerated containers by land and sea and need to protect food, medicine, and other perishable commodities. Similarly, it can have an application in the construction industry for buildings in areas of extreme temperatures.

The technology
The technology combines a unique layered cryogenic insulation system with specific manufacturing, packaging, wrapping, and rolling methods. One of the unique features of the LCI is its superior thermal performance: approximate R-values per inch for cryogenic conditions are R-1600 for

high vacuum, R-90 for soft vacuum (about 1 torr), and R-10 for no vacuum. This new LCI system surpasses the current limitations of current MLI systems and the insulation can currently be continuously rolled or manufactured in blanket, sheet, or sleeve form. This technology is part of the NASA Technology Transfer Program, which seeks to stimulate development of commercial applications from NASA-developed technology.

Milk bottle blankets 'better than wool'

Rescue blankets made of recycled plastic milk bottles are a new spin-off from NASA's research into the development of lightweight metal insulation for spacecraft. Using the same 'honeycomb' concept that will be used to make future spacecraft metal heat barriers, researchers working with scientists at NASA Ames Research Centre have created a lightweight plastic insulation for blankets and clothing that is 'better than wool'. Like wool, the new material can also keep a person warm, even when it is wet.

Eventually, about 70 000 emergency blankets are expected to be distributed annually by Thermalon Industries, Ltd., El Segundo, California. Currently, 250 blankets are being evaluated for use in emergencies by the Disaster Assistance and Rescue Team at Ames Research Centre. The blankets are reported to be better than wool or fleece because they are non-allergenic, and they dry five times faster. The new material is also four times warmer than wool in cold and damp conditions, and more efficient than fibres for insulation. The honeycomb is made from metals for high-temperature usage, and the plastic insulation can be made even from recycled milk bottles.

Space program insulation down to Earth

Space age insulation derived from NASA materials is finding a myriad of new applications right here on Earth.

Energy Q Radiant Barrier is the commercial name for the material, manufactured and marketed by Tech 2000 LLC of Roswell. NASA has used highly effective radiation barriers made of aluminized polymer film since the days of the Apollo missions. The insulation ensured constant, comfortable temperatures inside the command modules and permitted the astronauts to work in their shirtsleeves. The material has been used to protect the inner workings of satellites and a number of unmanned spacecraft, and it protects the Space Shuttles' computers. The double-sided material, made of 99% pure aluminium with a fire-resistant polypropylene insert, reflects 97% of the heat that strikes it.

Energy Q uses reflective technology to reduce energy consumption and is key for homes, offices, industrial plants and farm buildings. Energy Q is being used in protective clothing, sleeping bags, and emergency care thermal blankets. Researchers are investigating the use of Energy Q to line bridges and golf courses and to wrap water pipes for sprinklers and irrigation systems. Food storage systems from picnic coolers to pizza delivery bags to refrigerated vans and railroad cars are lined with the material.

Insulation technology

NASA Langley Research Centre has been promoting the commercial-ization of its line of innovative insulation technologies, which were developed with a number of manufacturing companies. The low-density foam can be processed into neat or syntactic foams, foam-filled honey-comb or other shapes, and microspheres.

The process for this foam begins with a monomeric solution with salt-like properties, which yields a homogeneous polyamide precursor solid residuum. It is this resulting precursor that can be processed into the foams and shapes that produce useful articles through normal foaming tech-niques. NASA/Unitika's process can produce foam and microsphere materials by reacting a derivative of a dianhydride (e.g. ODPA, BTDA, PMDA) with a diamine (e.g. ODA, PDA, DDS). An admixture of two or more polyamides can be combined or used separately to make a variety of polyamide foams with varying properties. These products can be used in a variety of ways: flame retardant and fire protection, thermal insulation, acoustic insulation, weight reduction, gaskets and seals, vibration damp-ing pads, spacers in adhesives and sealant, extenders, etc.

The NASA polyamide foam technologies resist fire, are non-toxic and non-fuming, and have low smoke emissions. They also offer several thermal performance benefits: low thermal conductivity from cryogenic to elevated temperatures, low coefficient of thermal expansion, and high glass transition temperature. Mechanically, they are highly resilient (i.e. low friability) and offer high compressive strength. Finally, these tech-nologies resist chemicals, solvents, and hot water, and they have a low dielectric constant. These products offer excellent thermal and acoustic insulation but their long-term effectiveness can only be proven in time.

Mass movement

What is mass movement and how it occurs

Mass movement can be defined as the large-scale down slope movement of rock, earth, debris, etc. (the mass) accompanied by a moving agent such as water from rivers, floods, glaciers, wind, etc.

This *movement* process is influenced by factors such as:

- *gravity* – acting proportionately to the weight of the moving material and the gradient of the site;
- *slope angle*;
- *pressure from the moving agent*, which can saturate or force apart particles increasing their weight and movement.

The movement eventually causes the *failure of the slope*.

This takes place through alterations of the *shear stress*, which can

- *Increase*, resulting in strong forces pulling the mass down the slope. This can be due to many factors, such as
  - a lack of friction, proportionate with the steepness of the slope;
  - lack of cohesive strength resulting in reduced binding and liquefaction;

- vegetation trapping moisture;
- large volume of water.
- *Decrease*, resulting in slope failure. Causes can be
  - weathering and water contents and table variations;
  - alterations to the slope (steepening, undercutting, etc.);
  - dumping of waste such as mine waste;
  - vibration shock such as an earthquake.

Types of mass movement and slope failure

Mass movement and slope failure can be classified according to the following considerations:

- the speed of the mass movement;
- the water content of the mass;
- the type of the movement.

These manifest themselves in different ways with different effects.

Speed of movement

Slow

Soil creep: a very slow continuous movement that is a result of repeated alternation of contraction and expansion (wet and dry or freeze and thaw). Its manifestations include large cracks in sloping roads, tilting of trees, telegraph poles, or tombstones and bulging walls due to soil pressure.

Solifluction: slightly faster activity, usually in periglacial conditions where surface water from melting cannot drain.

Fast

Landslide: a rapid movement occurring when an entire volume ruptures and slides along a straight, flat plane, retaining its shape and structure until it reaches the bottom of the slope. Weather events, earthquakes or volcanic eruptions often trigger landslides.

The world's two largest landslides of the twentieth century occurred at Mount St Helens, Washington, in 1980 where rock and mud broke free releasing pressure and a major eruption followed and at Usoy Tajikistan in 1911, which was triggered by an earthquake. The landslide moved a huge amount of material creating a dam some 1880 ft high on the Murgob River. Fortunately, casualties were low due to evacuation action at St Helen's and the relatively unpopulated area at Usoy.

The deadliest landslide, causing some 50 000 deaths, happened in 1990 in western Iran and was caused by an earthquake.

Weather-related landslides have become increasingly deadly in recent years. In Venezuela, some 30 000 deaths have been attributed to a landslide; whilst in 1998, Hurricane Mitch caused the side of Casito Volcano to collapse, creating a landslide that wiped out two towns in Nicaragua killing over 2000 people.

In 1983, El Nino caused a landslide that led to the flooding of Thistle, a Utaha town, creating the costliest landslide known in US history, with losses estimated at $400 million at that time.

Far removed from this large-scale tragedy, but no less relevant, are smaller landslides that can be just as destructive if not observed in time. One such example is described below.

Case study – The Dalles Middle School (Contributors: Anne Deutsch, Josh Glavin, and Assoc Prof Christine Theodoropoulos, University of Oregon)

Summary. The Dalles Middle School, a public school for students aged 11–13, in the northwest of the United States, illustrates the importance of siting buildings to avoid unstable soil conditions. The original school buildings were constructed on a portion of the site subject to landslides. Damage to the school buildings occurred over a period of several years. A proposed project to rebuild in 1999 was delayed in favour of mitigating the problem by stabilizing the landslide area. The school was finally demolished in 2001, and a new school building, now under construction, has been relocated to a more stable area of the same property.

Site conditions. The Dalles is a small Oregon town located approximately 30 miles Northeast of Mount Hood, in the northern portion of the Dalles Basin, in the Columbia River Gorge. It is part of the Colombian River Plateau Physiographic Province in which the bedrock units have been folded by primarily southwest to northwest trending synclines and anticlines and north and northwest intersect the structural folds to southeast trending faults.

The site is located at 280-ft elevation, about 200 ft above the Columbia River and slopes from the south to the north, with a drop in elevation of 80 ft. Originally, the site contained four existing buildings and four temporary classroom structures, with asphalt paved parking and play area in the northern portion of the site. The remaining space consisted of grass playing fields, sidewalks, landscaped areas, and a baseball field at the southernmost point.

The school property is mapped as landslide topography and is located on the toe of an active landslide. The landslide area is described as a combination of a deep bedrock translational slide and a rotational slump. A hazard study for the city of The Dalles indicated that the site is located in hazard zone B, a low to mid-risk to development based on landslide hazards and soil stability. Based on borings and test pit excavations, a near surface groundwater zone was observed at the project site between 5 and 10 ft below the ground surface. Groundwater was encountered at depths from 2.5 to 12 ft and flow varied from slight to moderate, with severe caving occurring where flow was moderate. Initially, the school district drilled down to the location of the water in an attempt to release the pressure that was causing the ground movement, and installed pumps to

Fig. 5.24
Dalle School – wall ceiling junction. © Anne Deutsch, Josh Glavin, and Christine Theodopoulos.

Fig. 5.25
Dalles school – infill panel/column detail. © Anne Deutsch, Josh Glavin, and Christine Theodopoulos.

discharge the water out to the Columbia River. Unfortunately, the ground continued to move and the buildings began to slide with it, down the slope.

Damage to buildings. The most recent land movement in 1991 caused extensive damage to the existing buildings on the site, forcing the school district to make the decision to vacate the premises and begin plans for a either a new building after stabilizing the soil or to find another site on which to build. Some of the damage to the buildings included exterior walls separating from the structural elements, and the sliding of the foundation causing the base of the exterior walls to move away from the floor slab, both of which required temporary bracing of the structure (see Figs 5.24–5.27).

School replacement considerations. Recent damage to three of the existing buildings resulted from ground movement associated with the Kelly Avenue Landslide. Immediate action was taken to analyse the site's stability, and propose a solution to reuse the site for a new middle school building. AMEC Earth and Environmental, Inc., were asked to conduct a geo-technical evaluation of the site and BOORA Architects were appointed to design a new school building. The solution provided by the geo-technical engineers, included cutting a key trench through the alluvium, ash and silt stone to the top of the weathered basalt to the north of the landslide location. The trench was then filled with basalt and covered with gravel fill and topsoil. The new school is restricted to the northern portion of the site to increase the safety factor against the building being affected by further possible land movement.

Slump: a rapid, rotational movement along a curved slide plane, usually occurring where weaker material such as clay overlies stronger layers such as limestone. This type of mass movement often happens along coastlines weakened by erosion and is facilitated by water action, which reduces friction thus helping flow. Such a situation was created along the North Yorkshire coast, south of Scarborough in the case of the Holbeck Hall Hotel.

Case study – Holbeck Hotel

On 5 June 1993, the north-east wing of the four-star Holbeck Hall Hotel, containing the lobby and several bedrooms, collapsed into Scarborough's South Bay, leaving the other half behind (see Fig. 5.28).

The area had a history of cliff movements: local records mention the spa being carried away by a landslide in 1770 and the Holbeck cliffs suffering a major slip in 1912. The East Yorkshire coast's steep clay cliffs has always been considered by geologists as vulnerable and the 40 miles of Holderness cliffs are probably the fastest eroding European coastline. The average rate of erosion was reported to be between 6 and 65 ft (Holderness Council).

Opinions have been divided as to the extent to which the sea erosion was the main factor causing the slump, considering the existence of a protective sea wall at the base of the cliff. Many have considered that the main

Fig. 5.26
Dalles school – partition wall detail.
© Anne Deutsch, Josh Glavin, and Christine Theodopoulos.

Fig. 5.27
Dalles school – slippage of exterior wall marked on external tap. © Anne Deutsch, Josh Glavin, and Christine Theodopoulos.

Fig. 5.28
Holbeck Hotel. © Yorkshire Press.

problem had been caused by the heavy rain that spring, which happened after several dry summers and which penetrated layers of sand and gravel in the cliffs.

This lubricated the clay, which had cracked in the dry weather; the saturated clay becoming unstable slumped along a curved plane. The only course of action left was to allow the slip to stabilize itself. Geologists estimated that this would happen when it reached 25°.

The engineers are considering a number of solutions to be undertaken once the movement has stopped: improving the drainage of the boulder clay, weighting the front end, and examining cliff stabilization schemes.

Water content

Wet (of fluid) movements
Flows: more continuous than slumps, they tend to redistribute the mass into a new form. Water-saturated particles lose cohesion and consequently flow.

They can take the form of *mudflows*, which occur on relatively bare, steep slopes, during heavy rain fall, or *earthflows*, which are more solid and slower and as such tend to be less catastrophic.

A well known tragic example of the deadly destruction mudflows can cause was the case of the village of Aberfan, South Wales, UK, where in October 1966 an estimated $100\,000\,m^3$ of spoil and water engulfed a primary school and 20 houses, killing 147 people, 116 of whom were primary school children. The problem was created by the existence of large amounts of spoil from the Merthyr Vale Colliery, stored 200 m above the village, on 25° slopes, and unwittingly located in a line of springs. When heavy rain combined with the water from the springs increased the weight of the spoil the catastrophe followed.

Dry movements or rock falls

These occur on slopes steeper than 40°. The process is started by the loosening of rocks due to weather variations such as frost, erosion, weak lines, wild fires, etc. When rocks start falling, gravity adds speed and momentum and they free fall or bounce at the bottom forming a 'scree'.

Type of movement

Expansive move

Heave: an expansion of the soil, which can occur as a result of:

– plastic failure of the soil under excessive load (see Fig. 5.29);
– frost action;
– swelling of clay saturated with moisture.

Receding move

Subsidence: the downward movement of soil, which can occur due to:

– ground movement;
– excessive loading;
– differential loading;
– soil recovery under variations of moisture.

Common causes

The common causes of subsidence are

1. *Variation in the moisture content of the sub-soil.* The nature and properties of soil determine the degree of settlement for the structure that it supports. Fine-grained cohesive soils such as clay will change considerably in volume with moisture content variations, which can occur due to weather conditions or the effects of tree roots.

   Shrinkable clays, like those in the southeast of England are most susceptible to these changes. They *shrink* when they dry and swell, or *heave* when wet. Both actions can cause considerable damage to the buildings supported by the soil in question. Normal seasonal variations affect depths of up to 1 m, but during times of long droughts, such as the one in 1976, the effect goes considerably deeper, and

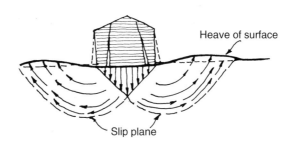

Fig. 5.29
Heave effect.

foundation design must ensure that these go to a sufficient depth to overcome this type of problem.

Tree roots extend in a circle with a radius equal to its height, sometimes more, and they extract water from the soil to considerable depths, drying out clay soil below any nearby building. Conversely, when the tree dies or is cut, the ground will re-absorb moisture and swell.

2. *Settlement of old mine works.* These may be quite a distance away from where the damage occurs. As often it is difficult to find records of their exact layout, specialist professional advice is required to ensure safety of buildings existing or knew.

3. *Long term consolidation of fill.*

4. *Modification in the nature of lower soil layers.* When watertable levels change, previously stable layers become biodegradable or dry out, and in both cases shrink. This causes the buildings supported by the soil to settle and crack. Sub-soils can also be damaged or 'softened' by water flowing through them from springs, leaking pipes, or drains.

5. *Instability of uneven ground.* This can often be the case with sloping ground such as coastal cliffs, which become unstable and begin to slip, or even collapse. Man-made excavations creating great differences in ground levels can also have the same effect (see Figs 5.30 and 5.31).

Type of damage

The most common is structural damage: cracks and distortions in the general fabric of the building (see Figs 5.32 and 5.33). These require assessment by a specialist professional to establish whether the main load bearing elements have been affected and provide recovery and consolidation solutions.

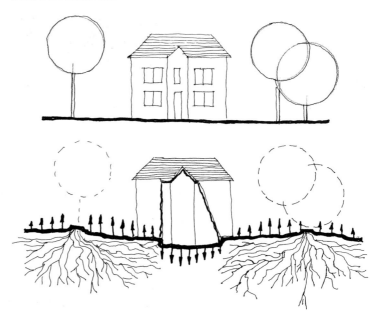

Fig. 5.30
Effect of trees on ground near buildings.

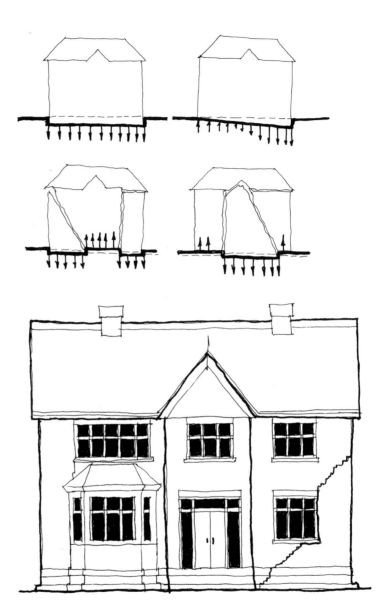

Fig. 5.31
Instability of uneven ground effect on buildings.

Fig. 5.32
Typical structural damage due to ground effects.

Subsidence is unlikely to cause instability suddenly. Cracks should be monitored and sub-soil analysed to establish its nature.

Initial signs that a building may be subjected to ground movement can be:

– doors or windows begin to stick even after being planed off and adjusted;
– wall paper begins to crease and ripple in places where it was smooth before;
– new cracks appear inside and outside, generally in one part of the building: corner, bay window, recent annex;

Fig. 5.33
Example of settlement crack.

– old cracks become wider;
– external brickwork may show fresh cracks;
– drains leak or do not work properly, gullies take longer to drain.

Preventing further damage

This can be achieved by dealing with the individual causes for the excessive movement:

– Repair leaking pipes.
– *Tree control.* It is advisable to manage vegetation in a way that will not allow significant fluctuations of moisture.
– Consolidation of foundations by underpinning, piling, or raft foundation.
– Design parameters selected to ensure that foundations extend deep enough to avoid the layer that could be affected by seasonal moisture.
– *Soil moisture management* – specialist process ensuring that the moisture content of a given soil is kept at an acceptable level regardless of external variations by re-hydration and tree control.

Part II
Man-made Disasters

6 Conflict

The Oxford Dictionary defines conflict as: *a fight, struggle (both literally and figuratively), a clashing of opposed principles.* Each individual has a unique viewpoint, understanding and experience of life. This human nature creates diversity, which can lead to disagreements and conflict within the context of social relationships.

Types of conflict

There are many types of conflict, each with complex implications and ways of expression. In broad terms, conflicts can be defined by the nature of their issues and by the methods employed to resolve the difference of opinion.

Conflict issues types
For example:

- *Religious* – initiated by opposing principles about values central to human existence. Religious beliefs sometimes become identified with tradition, or blurred by superstition. Theological issues have often been used as means of social control.
- *Sociopolitical* – initiated by different social expressions of economic and power struggles.
- *Ethnic* – stemming from racial prejudice and often relates to previously unresolved conflicts and is fuelled by economic factors.
- *Economic* – brought on by the increasing number of poor people and poverty-related crises.

When extremes are emphasized in each type of disagreement, the effect is of further polarizing the dispute, which can degenerate into aggression.

Methods of resolving conflict issues
These can be:

- *Peaceful coercion.*
- *Authoritarian socioeconomic control* – those dissenting are kept under strict control, like in the Eastern Block, 'police states', or by way of trade restrictions.

- *Segregation* – on the basis of race, religion, or ethnic origin creating ghettoes.
- *Use of force* – as in the case of social unrest, military coup, revolutions, etc.
- *Armed conflict* – the use of armed military force between governments, or organized armed groups, resulting in battle-related deaths.
- *Terrorism* – the worst use of force aimed specifically at killing innocent people.

In most instances, buildings are involved in the evolution of each conflict. From places of worship, to temporary shelters, they reflect the situation or can be caught between conflicting sides becoming targets for destruction. Governments and interstate organizations are attempting to find solutions and create infrastructures to cope with the effects. An example of the extent and complexity of the task can be seen from the intricate organisational infrastructure set up to manage and aid reconstruction outlined below.

The European Agency for Reconstruction is responsible for the management of the main European Union (EU) assistance programmes in the Federal Republic of Yugoslavia (the Republic of Serbia, Kossovo, and the Republic of Montenegro) and the former Yugoslav Republic of Macedonia (fYROM). It was established in February 2000 and has its headquarters in Thessaloniki, and operational centres in Belgrade, Pristina, Podgorica, and Skopje.

It is an independent agency of the EU, accountable to the European Council and the European Parliament, and overseen by a Governing Board composed of the European Commission and representatives from EU Member States. Its 2001 assistance programme amounted to some €525 million, while the 2002 figure will be some €510 million. It now oversees a total portfolio of some €1.6 billion across its four operational centres.

The agency's three main objectives are:

(i) to carry out immediate physical and economic reconstruction (rehabilitation and repair of key infrastructure and public utilities, such as energy, housing, water, transport);
(ii) to lay the foundation for the development of a market-oriented economy and to foster private enterprise (support to enterprise development, agriculture, health);
(iii) to support the establishment of democracy, human rights and the rule of law (strengthening of local administration, NGOs, the media and the judiciary).

The agency plays its part within a wider EU commitment to the Federal Republic of Yugoslavia and the former Yugoslav Republic of Macedonia. This, in turn, is part of the EU's process of Stabilization and

Association which is underway with five countries in southeastern Europe, also including Croatia, Bosnia and Herzegovina, and Albania.

Other EU assistance includes macro-financial, humanitarian, democratization; customs and fiscal planning aid, as well as support for educational exchange programmes. It also includes the bilateral contributions made by EU Member States. The extent of the task can be illustrated by the comparison of the before and after images of a simple house in Kosovo (see Figs 6.1 and 6.2).

Fig. 6.1
Kossovo, war damage.
© European Agency for
Reconstruction.

Fig. 6.2
Kossovo, new house. © European
Agency for Reconstruction.

Effect of conflict and terrorist attack on buildings

Whether in the context of social unrest, war, or terrorist attack, it is a sad reality of modern life that destruction of buildings will occur. It is important to understand the nature of the damage in order to be able to protect the occupants. Building professionals will be called to:

1. Assess the damage and making recommendations for reinstatement.
2. Incorporate damage limitation or prevention features in building design and specification.

Types of damage

The following types of damage may occur in these situations:

1. damage caused by explosive devices (bombs) or sabotage;
2. fires;
3. damage to glazing caused by ballistic or missile attacks.

Explosions

By far the most common occurrence, explosions occur when a quantity of gas or inflammable liquid undergoes a chemical reaction resulting in high pressure gases, which with intense heat expand rapidly into the surrounding space that becomes pressurized and creates an 'air shock wave'.

The effect of the air shock wave is to produce an immediate high pressure (the positive phase) followed by a rapid fall in pressure below atmospheric (the negative phase) (see Fig. 6.3). The magnitude of the various stages depends on the characteristics of the surrounding environment and the effects are greatly influenced by the ratio between the positive phase and the natural vibration period of the structures involved. The duration of impact being almost instantaneous, materials do not have the time to react before the negative phase begins.

The damage created by explosions occurs as a result of the air pressure and movement caused by the accumulation of gases which creates a dynamic pressure known as 'blast wind'. The dynamic pressure's effect is greater at the point of explosion and on nearby objects as under normal circumstances it diminishes rapidly as it travels away from the source.

The pressure also compresses the ground resulting in a 'ground shock wave', which has the effect of:

(a) radiant compression waves;
(b) shear wave at the point;
(c) surface (Raleigh) wave.

The ground wave diminishes in strength as it travels away from the source, depending on the position of the structural elements relative to the line of wave propagation.

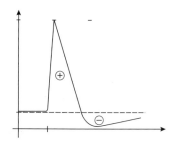

Fig. 6.3
Effect of explosion air shock wave: positive /negative.

Effect of explosion on structural components and materials

The shock wave from an explosion will cause structures to deflect or to be blown away depending on the extent of their rigidity, weight, degree of fixing, and the characteristics of the pressure applied. Ductile materials such as steel or plastic can withstand a great deal of pressure deflection, brittle ones like plaster, light masonry, or lightly fixed items such as slates, tiles, or suspended ceilings tend to disintegrate more easily, whilst timber would split. Heavy elements will be less affected.

In addition a building's type of structure, its condition, if defective, will compound the effects of an explosion. Reinforced concrete and steel-framed structures have been found able to withstand explosion effects without collapse if connections are suitably designed. Similarly, masonry buildings tend to suffer only localized damage.

Structural steel – if the design has allowed sufficient margin of size and shape and if adequate continuity has been provided, only localized distortions or misalignment would occur. Residual deflection may affect the load-bearing capacity in which case localized repairs and strengthening would be necessary.

Reinforced concrete – a certain amount of shrinkage and cracking happens under normal circumstances so it should not automatically be assumed, if these are in evidence that they are due to the explosion. Careful survey should reveal whether there is a case for replacement or *in situ* repairs. Design of connections between beams and columns can include preventive provisions (see Fig. 6.4a and b).

Brickwork and masonry – cracks and evidence of settlement should be carefully examined to establish whether they are not due to different response of materials or insignificant movement. Masonry is fairly tolerant of vibrations as can be seen in many industrial buildings and unnecessary removal of walls may disturb the building's new geometry

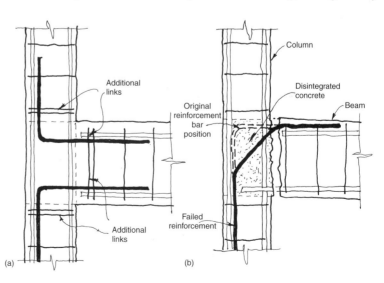

Fig. 6.4
Column beam connection design detail. (a) Improved R.C. beam Column Connection; (b) Common detail showing failure mode.

unnecessarily. Expert structural engineering trials and opening up should be undertaken before deciding on consolidation or replacement.

Foundations and underground services – other than fractured drains, gas or water supplies, it is not usual for serious damage to the sub-structure and soil to occur from short-term vibration, unless the explosion produces a localized damage.

Glass, cladding, and roof coverings – damage to windows and glazing is the type of damage that affects a wide area around an explosion. The blast can project deadly shards of glass in the immediate vicinity of the explosion. Further away glass can just fall out of the frames, or when it is strong enough, it is the frames that incur the damage, which they can also transmit to the surrounding elements. Cladding, if heavy could be fractured or if light, distorted or failing at fixing points, joint seals may be damaged and require replacement to restore weather-proofing. Similar damage can incur from loosely fixed panels and tiles. Internal finishes can suffer considerable damage either directly or due to vibrations, which can shake loose plasterboard fixings, for example.

Design considerations

Although it is not really possible to design a 'bomb proof' building that will survive completely unscathed, it is possible to design features that can help reducing injury and minimize damage to the fabric:

Planning stage

If there is a potential threat, consideration should be given to a number of relevant aspects at the planning stage:

- Increasing the distance between a likely bomb and the building. Strategically placed trees, bollards, and street furniture can ensure that in crowded, busy locations, as much stand-off distance as possible is provided (see Fig. 6.5; Royal Law Court bollards).

Fig. 6.5
Old Law Courts, Belfast.
© Andrew Beatty Grant (ABG).

Fig. 6.6
New Law Courts, Belfast. © ABG.

- Simplifying the shape of the building to avoid multiple reflections of the blast (see Fig. 6.6; Belfast New Law Court).
- Underpasses or car parking within the building are best avoided.
- Access, entrance areas, and public spaces should be easily monitored and free of obstructions, which would facilitate planting a bomb inside the building.
- Internal partitions in sensitive areas should be substantial enough to contain blast damage as much as possible.

Structural design

The following should be taken into account to improve blast resistance:

- Track record shows that reinforced concrete and steel frame structures with cast *in situ* floors have a better blast resistance; they should be preferred if possible.
- Framed buildings are usually designed to withstand gravity and wind loads and are not able to tolerate load reversal, which can take place by elastic rebound or blast load opposing wind or gravity load. Improved connections and additional cleats should be provided.
- There is also a high incidence of column/beam/ slabs failure and effective connections must be provided.
- Connection between components should be upgraded. For example, lateral restraint to the bottom flange of beams, additional ties between beams, and perimeter columns and moment resisting connections between beams and columns, continuous top steel in reinforced concrete slabs.

Windows and cladding

- The design of the windows is a priority when designing a blast-resistant building. Frame rebates should be 30mm thick and glazing beads should be capable of resisting movement in both directions. Openings should have strong hinges, multipoint locking for secure closing and fixings capable to withstand blast loading. When laminated glass fractures it becomes flexible, will fold up, and consequently can be pushed out of its frame. To overcome this problem, deep rebates should be provided for the frames, as they will prevent the interlayer to pull out at the corners, especially if associated adhesive and clamping are also in place.

- The choice of glazing is crucial, laminated glass being the most effective kind as it resists longer after cracking due to the interlayer membrane. Whilst plain glass would fail straight away, laminated glass will only incur total failure when coming away from the frames, with the added advantage of remaining in one piece with no flying shards. Glass can be chosen to remain integral or remain in place when broken. Given the necessary parameters, it is possible to design glass that will not break in an explosion, such as laminated toughened glass. A minimum thickness of 7.5 mm is recommended for laminated glass to be used in blast-prone situations, consisting of two 3 mm layers with a PVB interlayer of 1.5 mm, which is the key element in ensuring that the glass remains in place. If double-glazed, the inner panes should be of laminated glass, the outer pane preferably of toughened glass.
- In cost-prohibitive situations, a minimum provision can be made by using blast-resistant film on the outer glazing of ordinary windows and 'blast curtains' designed to enfold and capture flying debris. The disadvantage of this method is the limited life of the film and the fact that the curtains are only efficient if used in conjunction with the film failing, which would be ripped by shards of ordinary glass.

Security glazing

In conflict-prone areas, special provisions are required to protect buildings from aggression starting with casual vandalism, to deliberate manual and missile attack (stone, bricks, hammers) culminating with armed attacks (see Fig. 6.7).

BS 55 defines *anti-bandit glazing* as glazing that resists impact from a 1 kg object dropped five times from a height of 3 m and then once from a height of 9 m. A 6.4 mm laminated glass is not considered security glass but would deter a housebreaker. In the case of a blunt dead weight protection can be achieved by 7.5 mm laminated glass with a Poly Vinyl Butyral (PVB) interlayer of 1.5 mm. Objects that are sharp, have cutting edges or are dropped from a greater height, etc. can still cause substantial damage, so glass with higher performance is needed such as greater thicknesses of laminated glass 11.3 mm or more, with several interlayers.

Toughened glass does not offer adequate entry prevention as it is susceptible to impact from sharp objects, which is why is used in fire fighting routes as speedy access can be gained with axe blows.

The quality of framing should not be overlooked the method of fixing being as important as the glazing resistance. The highly resistant glass

Fig. 6.7
Smashed glazing phone booth.

would be useless if it can just betaken out by levering off beading, so suitably heavy duty hinges catches and fixings should be provided.

Bullet resistant glazing is defined by BS 5051 as glazing for interior use withstanding either three bullets spaced apart at 100 mm in a triangle, or in the case of a shotgun resisting at close range impact: two solid slugs in the same position. Specialist manufacturers like Pilkington Glass supply laminated glass of different qualities, conceived to provide resistance to standard bullets from a variety of weapons such as 9 mm Parabellum, up to shotguns and 7.62 mm rifles. Bulletproof glass is used for protective screening, and BS 1995 – Code of practice for installation of security glazing – gives guidance for installation principles.

Case studies

Northern Ireland

Whilst this section does not attempt to deal with the conflict itself, some awareness of the historic background is necessary to understand how deep rooted it is and to what extent *long term* is an inherent, relevant feature and constitutes an important aspect when analysing effect on buildings.

The following dates in the history of Northern Ireland give an outline:

- 1170: Settlers from Britain arrive in Ireland.
- 1608: Plantation of Ulster began.

- 1641: The Catholic–Gaelic rising in response to the Plantation and the confiscation of land by Protestant settlers from England and Scotland.
- 1690: The Battle of the Boyne and the victory of Protestant William III over Catholic James II – this victory is still celebrated in many parades in Northern Ireland.
- 1801: Act of Union which abolished the Irish Parliament and bound Ireland and Britain together as parts of the United Kingdom.
- 1912: Ulster Solemn League and Covenant signed by over 400000 Protestants who wanted to remain in the Union.
- 1916: The Easter Rising in Dublin against British rule.
- 1921: A treaty leading to the establishment of an Irish Free State of 26 counties, with the six counties of Northern Ireland remaining British.
- 1968: The starting point of the present 'troubles' arising, in part, out of the campaign by Catholics in Northern Ireland for civil rights.
- 1998: The Belfast Agreement, sometimes called the Good Friday Agreement.
- 1999: The setting up of a power sharing Assembly in Northern Ireland.

Northern Ireland has had more than its fair share of conflicts with many lives and buildings lost in the process.

'Peace lines', or peace walls, are physical barriers between the Protestant/Loyalist community and the Catholic/Nationalist community in certain areas in Northern Ireland. The walls are usually constructed of concrete, stone, and/or steel, and can be over 6m tall. There were approximately 35 peace lines in existence by 2001. Of these, 26 were in Belfast, mainly in the west and north of the city. Outside of Belfast there were six peace lines in Derry, two in Portadown, and one in Lisburn.

The 'official' peace lines grew out of barricades that the local communities erected themselves during periods of intense conflict in 1969 (and in later years). When the British Army was deployed in August 1969, it replaced the existing barricades with barbed-wire barriers of its own. It had been hoped that these would only be needed temporarily. However, the barbed-wire barriers were replaced with more permanent structures and over the years new peace walls have been erected and older ones extended in length and height. The peace lines represent the most visible form of the 'sectarian interfaces' between the two main communities in Northern Ireland. Currently there is no widespread support for the removal of peace walls, indeed there are demands from certain communities for additional walls (see Fig. 6.8).

Fig. 6.8
Peace line graffiti, Nortem Ireland.

In recent years, consensus rather than strong tactics has steadily encouraged dialogue and constructive relationship. Political analysts and experts in conflict resolution believe that despite setbacks, Northern Ireland's tortuous road to peace has left signposts that others could usefully follow. The same could be said about lessons learned about protecting human life and buildings. The list of destroyed buildings, attributed to the 'troubles', is long and all-embracing. From ordinary homes of militants on either side, to shopping malls, hotels, or landmark monuments, they have been carefully selected to inflict maximum material and moral damage. They also have in common the fact that they were destroyed by bomb blasts, often in underground car parks like near the Canary Wharf Tower, or in cars parked nearby, like the Hong Kong Bank and Nat West Tower.

The Europa Hotel in Belfast is said to be the most bombed hotel in Europe. Its rebuilding has become symbolic of people who, believing in a peaceful future, show characteristic resilience. In the constant reconstruction process that has been taking place in Northern Ireland, lessons learned have been applied to new design in order to prevent as much as possible that buildings and their occupants suffer. Many are outlined in Section B.

Nevertheless, all the wealth in the world would not be able to provide 100% safety, and 'fortress'-like measures would undoubtedly prevent normal life to take place. The architectural practice 'Building Design Partnership' has worked for many years in Northern Ireland and one of its executive directors, Roy Adams, has recently been appointed to support the Peace Building in North Belfast initiative. His view sums up the general trend:

> It may seem surprising but the widely held political view in Northern Ireland is that people should be designing buildings with peace in mind. Therefore there is no policy of security beyond the normal Health, Safety and Fire requirements, which enforces the design of buildings in Northern Ireland. For example the new Law Courts buildings close to the river Lagan (the much improved river which flows through the centre of Belfast) has a glazed wall along its entire facade which makes the occupants clearly visible from outside

Whilst the Old Court, a substantial stone building (Fig. 6.5), had to have a 5m blast wall erected in front of it to protect its occupants, the new building (Fig. 6.6) is set back some 20ms from the road and has a glazed facade with special glass and gasket fixings.

Central University Library, Bucharest, Romania
The restoration and structural repair following damage during the 1989 revolution was undertaken by MIRO Group structural engineers.

The building and its structure
One of Bucharest's civic landmarks and part of the main Royal Palace Square (see Fig. 6.9), the Central University Library was designed by Paul Gottereau and built in two stages: first in 1895 and the second between 1911 and 1914 (see Fig. 6.10).

A substantial building of a total floor area of 5850m^2 (7083 including the roof space) 20m high, structurally consisted of:

- plain concrete and brick masonry foundations;
- load bearing brick walls,
- steel girders with concrete encased bottom flanges;
- steel trusses;
- timber floor and roof structures;

Fig. 6.9
Central University Library building,
Bucharest before the revolution.

Fig. 6.10
Central University Library,
Bucharest – plan. © MIRO Group.

- steel frame cupolas with timber elements and reinforced concrete higher central one.

Investigation of the general condition and the extent of the damage

During the Romanian Revolution events of December 1989, the Library building, which was strategically placed relative to the Communist Party

Fig. 6.11
Library building when restoration
work begun. © MIRO Group.

Headquarters and across the square from the Royal Palace, was used
by rebel groups for shelter and as cover during the fierce exchange with
the Ceausecu's guards (see Fig. 6.11). The events, which were watched
'live' on TV by millions around the world, took their toll on the building, which was riddled with bullets damaged by explosions and lost
its main cupola and roofs in the tremendous fire that broke out on
22 December 1989 and which continued to rage because of the thousands
of rare books and priceless manuscripts the building housed. The survey
conducted to establish consolidation needs, found that the building had
already been weakened by an amazing succession of events:

- No less than 10 earthquakes with magnitudes over 6.0 (of which the
  most powerful were those of 1940, $M = 7.4$; and 1977, $M = 7.2$) took
  place since its construction.
- Severe bombing during the last war 1940–1944 hit the library several
  times.
- The fire of 22 December 1989, caused substantial damage:
    - most of the older wing was lost and the beautiful Professors' Hall
      destroyed;
    - the timber roof and floor structures were completely burned;
    - the brick walls had been affected by fire to depths of 10–100 mm on
      most surfaces;
    - the lower parts of concreted steel girders were also affected, as
      were the steel columns;
    - the reinforced concrete central cupola presented numerous radial
      cracks, displacements on the half way circumference and severe
      concave deformations;
    - many walls had become dislodged with cracks in the joining sections;
    - the two smaller cupolas and trusses were severely distorted, espe-
      cially in the front sections;
    - the stone stairways were partly destroyed.

Repairs were undertaken after the two major earthquakes of 1940 and 1977 but they consisted mostly of metal ties and localized repairs. Two more earthquakes took place while the structural consolidation work was in progress! One on 30 May 1990, $M = 6.7$ and another of 31 May 1990, $M = 5.8$.

Non-destructive trials on the existing materials were undertaken and the results did show a maximum strength for the concrete to be Bc 7.5, for bricks C100, and for mortar M10. The brickwork had an average breaking resistance of $60 \, dN/cm^2$ in compression. The ground consisted of a clay layer on sand and gravel with the water level at $-7 \, m$.

Structural analysis

Romanian normative standards of design for seismic resistance (P100–92) place the Library building in the Class I category of importance in respect of its location, setting out a basic acceleration value at $0.2 \, g$ with an amplitude coefficient of 1.4 in seismic conditions.

In calculations, the application of this coefficient is instrumental in defining the recurrence period for an earthquake. For example, a coefficient of 1.4 will indicate a recurrence period of 110 years, which on simple formulae, without a coefficient, would be reduced to 50 years.

The average building's behaviour in earthquake conditions must also be taken into account for calculating the resistance capacity of a building, and the basis of average resistance values has been accepted as appropriate. The structural designers for the consolidation of the Library, opted for a coefficient of 1.75 and average resistance values, which would give a theoretical recurrence period of 500 years (or 110 years without the coefficient).

Consolidation techniques

The main principle for the strengthening method selected was to encase the existing structure with a reinforced concrete skin of 100 mm. The fact that the walls had suffered damage from the fire to a depth of 100 mm made it necessary to hack out to sound fabric, which at the same time gave a good rough surface for adherence of the new skin. Externally, a flat reinforced concrete grid was designed to frame all openings and tie the external walls to the new reinforced concrete floors (see Figs 6.12 and 6.13). The basement was tied into the consolidation framework of the walls and the foundation system was strengthened with ring beams interconnected at the internal walls and tied into the existing foundations. The steel trusses were repaired and strengthened and the smaller cupolas reconstructed with metal elements.

The main central cupola, originally of reinforced concrete, was replaced with a new metal one (see Fig. 6.14). The surviving structural timbers were fireproofed and the fire protection of the metal ones was to follow. To overcome the extensive damp problems in the basement a waterproof, reinforced concrete 'box' was constructed on the entire perimeter of the building with provisions for adequate ventilation of all basement external walls. Concern for the preservation of the historic building features has also been a consideration. The complex geometry and details were

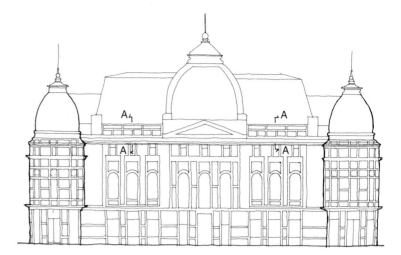

Fig. 6.12
Central University Library, Bucharest:
facade concrete grid consolidation.
© MIRO Group.

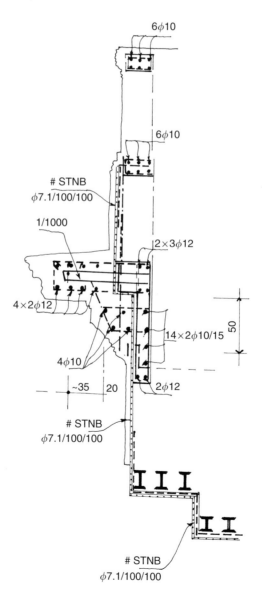

Fig. 6.13
Facade strengthening
detail A-A.
© MIRO Group.

Fig. 6.14
Central University Library, Bucharest:
New roof construction in progress.
© MIRO Group.

Fig. 6.15
Central University Library, Bucharest:
consolidation and restoration work
complete. © MIRO Group.

closely followed and solutions adjusted to suit them. Temporary supports were provided moulds and full size templates executed and progress recorded and compared with photographs.

Observation of building's behaviour

A specific follow-up plan has been devised to observe the following:

- settlement;
- rigidity variations or changes;
- effects of all movement such as measurement of microvibrations;
- periodic data recording after all exceptional events such as earthquakes, strong winds, or large quantities of snow.

Figure 6.15 shows the completed restoration.

World Trade Centre collapse

Minoru Yamasaki (d. 1986) the Architect of the World Trade Centre Building is reported to have said:

> The World Trade Centre is a living symbol of man's dedication to world peace … beyond the compelling need to make this a monument to world peace, The World Trade centre should, because of its importance, become a representation of man's belief in humanity, his need for individual dignity, his beliefs in the co-operation of men, and through co-operation, his ability to find greatness

Terrorism and the reality of what has happened have made a mockery of his vision and the building will now remain in history as the symbol of evil destruction. The tragic events of 11 September 2001 when, at 8:45 AM, New York local time, the North Tower was hit by a hijacked 767 commercial jet aeroplane, loaded with fuel for a trans-continental flight, followed 18 min later, by an other who hit the South Tower, have been at the forefront of international analysis ever since.

Indeed at the time of writing, engineering forensic studies are still in progress trying to establish how and why the towers collapsed and much have already been and will continue to be written on the subject. The purpose of this case study is to establish the main facts and to outline what is thought to have been the cause of the collapse at the time of writing.

The buildings

The site was a 16 acre formerly run-down area of lower Manhattan, and the towers were part of a group arranged around a 5 acre central plaza, they were 110-storeys high, with a $10\,000\,000\,\text{ft}^2$ of rentable space and occupied by about 50 000 people.

Started on 5 August 1966 and inaugurated on 4 April 1973, the Centre was to be a landmark signifying new technology. When initial designs of 80 storey towers fell short by about 2 million square feet of the brief target for rentable space, revolutionary re-thinking and technology were needed to meet the challenge. The problem was that too much floor space was taken by:

(a) the traditional sky scraper structural system;
(b) the number of lifts required if the number of floors was to be raised at 84.

The lift problem was solved by treating the towers as two 40-storey buildings one on top of the other. This meant that fewer shafts were needed and people needing access to the top floors would change to local lifts on the way.

The structural design faced a real challenge from the following factors that had to be considered:

(a) the wind;
(b) maximizing the available rental space;

(c) keeping cost down;

(d) providing resistance to the building being hit by an airplane (following the 1945 Empire State Building incident).

New York winds could reach 100mph with a push force several times stronger than a Los Angeles or Tokyo earthquake. This could 'shake' a structure to pieces by the dynamic motions concentrated in the outer walls. To overcome this, a 'tube structure' design was conceived, with high-strength steel concentrated in the outer walls, 3×30ft columns welded together to form rigid prefab panels and a core of lifts and stairways that allowed considerable open space and saved money, as only half of the steel required by a conventional grid of steel columns and beams was necessary. The design also took into account the fact that the towers would shelter each other. The fast construction (three floors in 2 weeks) also helped save costs.

The disaster (Fig. 6.16)

The building stood the test of time for 23 years without problems until, in 1993, when there was a terrorist attack: a bomb exploded in an underground

(a)

(b)

Fig. 6.16
World Trade Centre collapse.
© Adrian Alexander.

car park, killing 16 people and injuring 1042. The bomb attempted to demolish the base of the North Tower causing it to fall into the South one, bit it did not succeed because it was outside the perimeter skin of the tube structure. Also, the towers acted as giant chimneys aspiring the smoke through the lift shafts and stairways.

The reasons the 11 September 2001 attack was so devastating was: first, because the plane had penetrated the perimeter wall, the building's defence mechanism; and second, because the plane was much larger and carried more fuel than it was envisaged by design.

The building, which was designed to withstand impact from a fully loaded Boeing 707, was hit by a 767. When considering the design, the engineers considered that as a fully loaded 747, crashing into the outer walls, would bring 300 tonnes on impact, the fact that the walls were designed to carry 13 000 tonnes of wind pressure, will mean that impact effects could only be localized. The size and power of the Boeing 767 was substantially more than that envisaged at the design stage. As the engineers have pointed out, the building *did not fall down* on impact! In fact it remained standing for 53 min allowing thousands to escape and took 11 s to collapse. It was, however, stressed well beyond the design calculations.

The causes

Experts are still collecting data and cannot offer yet definitive answers. A preliminary report produced by the FEMA and the American Society of Civil Engineers (ASCE) attributes the collapse to three 'loading' events:

1. The Boeing hitting the building and creating a fireball.
2. The continuing fire, which heated and weakened the structural system which added further stress to the structure.
3. The progressive collapse.

The report calls for further research. At the time of writing, the wide consensus is that the cause of the disaster was the intense heat from the jet fuel fires (estimated in the region of 1000–3000°F), which melted the steel infrastructure, and went past its yield strength and caused the collapse.

Bare steel if heated gets weaker, does not melt straight away. It begins to lose strength and if unprotected, slowly sags. Analysis of the twisted steel columns from the wreckage found them completely clean, even though they were had been covered by sprayed-on fireproofing. Some experts have explained this as having been blown away by the blast, leaving the steel unprotected.

It has also been observed that the immense force was applied at $t = 0$ and there was no actual time for the materials to adapt. Also, that there were certain vulnerable elements in the link construction of the tube frame structure such as the weak floor trusses and floor connections.

The building materials used for the fire protection of the structural elements withstood the fire for 40–60 min, but once they were destroyed, the steel melted and the structure collapsed on the floors below. These floors, in turn, collapsed from the weight of the structure falling from above, resulting in a 'progressive collapse' chain reaction.

The future

While a report on initial forensic investigations is being prepared, apart from finding what happened and why, there are many other questions to be answered, not least what to do with the site.

The parties involved are the tenants who have a 99-year lease since July 2001; the owners of the land, The Port Authority; and the City of New York, each having their own priority. The tenants consider they have the right and obligation to rebuild, but cannot do so without the permission of the owners whose main concern is the reinstatement of the commuter line (estimated to take 2 years) which they seek to integrate with the New York subway. New York City has the task to clear the site of the disaster, and once the site is clear and foundations stabilized, they take a back seat.

There have been several ideas but forward, but at the time of writing, no architects had been appointed. Whatever follows will not only have to be outstanding, but will also have find a number of answers to wider issues concerning how we wish to evolve. The debate continues!

7 Fire

From the earliest days of humankind, fire has been part of life, and striking a fine balance between the benefits it offered and the danger it posed has remained a constant concern. Whether through man's own errors or disregard for its power of destruction, or natural phenomena, fire has claimed countless lives, buildings, forests, and land. From Nero's Rome and London's 1666 great fire, to the World Trade Centre, many of man's finest buildings have been lost to flames.

How does fire occur

Fire is one of the main universal elements, but unlike air, water, or earth fire is not a form of matter but a chemical reaction. It requires three ingredients: fuel, temperature, and oxygen. When a material such as oil, wood, or wax is heated to a certain temperature (flash point) it ignites and the compound molecules break and the atoms recombine with oxygen forming water and carbon dioxide, amongst others. As the burning the material decomposes, some products are released as volatile gases, or smoke. What sets this chemical reaction apart is that it is self-perpetuating, the heat from the flames continuing to create temperatures required for combustion, etc.

Of nature's disasters, forest fires are the most frightening. Giant walls of flames can burn acres of land in a few minutes moving at incredible speeds. Wildland fire is unstoppable and the Australian bush fire in December 2001 has been a terrifying reminder of the near unstoppable destruction it can cause.

It would be well beyond the purpose of this book to attempt considering all aspects of fire hazard in depth. The way it affects buildings alone is complex enough to deserve several books of its own. Consequently, within the context of this subject, information will be restricted to looking at the overall picture, giving some general guidance in respect of areas of concern as well as sources of information.

Types fire (*Statistics source*: infoplease.com/spot/forestfire.html)

Fire disasters affecting wildland and forests

Bush fires – fires affecting low vegetation (less than 6 ft). A constant feature of summers in the south of France and Italy, wildland fires advance with considerable speed and destroy all in their path. Some are caused by careless smokers, others by arsonists eager to make way to land development without any regard to the long-term effect on the environment and ecosystem. When sufficiently fuelled by grass, bush, or saplings in wind-favourable conditions, bush fires can extend to trees and forests.

Forest fires – uncontrolled vegetation fires more than 6 ft in height. This fire can travel at high level through the forest canopy, before affecting the forest floor. The difference of air pressure created causes hot updraughts and firestorms. According to the US National Interagency Fire Centre, in 2002, between January and May, 24 421 fires burned 442 575 acres of wild land and a severe drought has devastated much of the Great Planes, which has left the area susceptible to forest fires. In 2001, 84 079 separate fires destroyed 3 570 911 acres of land and 731 structures. It cost US$ 542 million to fight these fires. In 2000, nearly 123 000 separate fires burned 8.5 million acres of forest and it took 30 000 people and US$ 1.3 billion to fight the fires. It is estimated that two-thirds of forest fires are started accidentally by people, almost a quarter is intentionally set, and about 10% caused by lightning.

Fire prevention

The Australian bush fire in December 2001 has raised awareness of the risk and the need to protect the natural environment without compromising the need for the protection of human life and property.

While burning by Aboriginal people and graziers and the occasional wildfire have been part of the Australian environment and have created its characteristic vegetation patterns and landscape, the common practice of 'hazards reduction burning' has been brought into question by the long-term effect it is having on the natural ecosystem.

The Nature Conservation Council (NCC) in New South Wales has been promoting public education and pursuing strategies for better bush fire risk management since 1984. With the support of legislation such as the Rural Fires Act 1997, it has been working towards enabling the community to participate in management planning with ecologically sustainable policies with emphasis on a cyclical planning process.

Some causes of wild fire are:

• arson;
• campfires;

- discarded lit cigarettes;
- burning debris;
- fireworks;
- prescribed fires.

Some examples of fire fighting methods as used in the United States are:

- *Hotshots*: US fire-fighters building firebreaks around a fire to stop it from spreading.
- *Smokejumpers*: employed by the US Bureau of Land Management and Forest Service with the aim to surpress small fires before they spread. Fire fighters are parachuted in place.
- *Backfires*: these are fires started on the ground in the direction of advancing fires for the purpose of controlled burning of potential fuel for the progressing wildfire.
- *Air tankers*: fire fighting from planes and helicopters dropping water and fire retardants.

Fire disasters affecting humans
Domestic fire risks (statistics FEMA/US National Fire Protection Association)

The US National Fire Protection Association estimates that each year fire kills more Americans than all natural disasters combined. Fire is the third leading cause of accidental death in the American homes and at least 80% of all fire deaths occur in residences, representing about 22% of all fires and 74% of structures burnt.

Fires mostly start in

- the kitchen: 23.5%;
- the bedroom: 12.3%;
- the living room: 7.9%;
- the chimney: 7.1%;
- laundry area: 4.7%.

Fires are often caused by:

- cooking fires, usually due to unattended cooking or human error;
- careless smoking;
- heating;
- arson – the third leading cause after cooking and heating.

Life-saving measures include:

- smoke alarms, but they have to be properly and regularly maintained;
- residential sprinklers;
- fire doors and protected means of escape;
- fire-protected structure to allow sufficient time for the occupants to escape.

Fire in public buildings

There are many causes for fires occurring in public places. Amongst the most common are:

- Inadequate design or fire protection. This, in simple terms concerns:
  - making adequate provisions made to prevent the structure from collapsing for a set time required allowing occupants to leave the building;
  - providing suitable means of escape;
  - preventing the fire from spreading by creating fire-resistant compartments to contain it.
- Poor management, contributed by:
  - allowing fire hazards to accumulate (rubbish, flammable furnishings, and materials, etc.);
  - lack of maintenance: faulty electrical installations or malfunctioning sprinklers, alarms, etc.;
  - carelessness such as work using naked flame or smoking;
  - lack of staff training for fire emergency.
- Arson.
- Human error/negligence.

As with forest fires, carelessness or negligence can cause devastating loss, not only in terms of human life and costs but also in loss of irreplaceable historic heritage. An example of how a careless moment has caused the loss of a unique part of British heritage and involved hundreds of people in years of painstaking re-building work is that of the Windsor Castle fire (see 'Case study').

Fire effects

1. The loss of life – this is caused by the smoke induced asphyxia, collapse of the structural elements, and victims jumping out of windows.
2. The destruction of the building fabric and contents by the flames. The fire will use every available material as fuel: timber structure, furnishings, fabrics, finishes, etc. and consume it in the process.
3. The destruction, alteration, and damage caused to the building elements by the high temperatures, which will cause them to expand, crack, vitrify, plastify, melt, etc.
4. The damage caused to the fabric and contents by the large quantities of water used to put out the fire.
5. The damage caused by the mechanical collapse of structural elements.

Monitoring and prevention strategy

Whether due to negligence, arson, lightning, or accidents, fires are a major threat to humans not only because of life and property loss but also for the long-term effect in the irreversible destruction of the ecosystem. For this reason, the United Nations has included in its International Strategy for Disaster Reduction (ISDR), a separate activity concerning fire: the Global Fire Monitoring Centre. The centre provides documentation, information, and monitoring systems accessible through its website. A worldwide network of institutions and individuals generate the information, which is regularly updated. The data, systematically collected and interpreted, is displayed and archived with products such as:

- early warning of fire danger;
- near-real-time monitoring of fire events;
- interpretation and synthesis of fire information;
- archive of global fire information;
- facilitation of links between institutions involved in fire research, development, and policy development;
- support of local, national, and international initiatives to develop long-term strategies for wildland fire management;
- emergency hotline for assistance and rapid assessment supporting decisions in emergency response.

The World Fire Web is a system for globally mapping fires in vegetation. It uses satellite images acquired by a worldwide network of receiving stations. Each station operates a data processing chain for detecting fires in the satellite imagery (see Fig. 7.1) (NOAA AVHRR). Daily, global fire maps are built up at each station from this regional data by automatically sharing regional fire maps over the Internet. Global fire information is then available on-line, from each station, in near-real-time. Timetable: a pilot network with partial global coverage is in its implementation phase, started in June 1998. By the end of 1999, the network should provide a virtually global coverage of vegetation fire.

The World Fire Web has been chosen as a pilot project to supply fire information to the Global Observation of Forest Cover (GOFC) project.

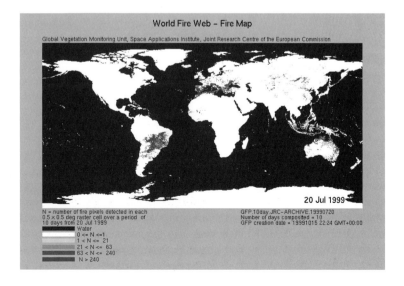

Fig. 7.1
World fire map. © Global Fire Monitoring Center.

The GOFC project (http://www.gofc.org/gofc/projects.html) is coordinating an international research programme designed to produce a comprehensive global forest mapping and monitoring system.

Case study – Windsor Castle

Windsor Castle has been the home of British kings and queens for nearly 900 years. On 20 November 1992, a fire was started in the chapel from a tungsten lamp, which came into contact with curtains screening the altar (see Fig. 7.2). The fire spread rapidly through the roof voids and over 15 h devastated the building destroying 105 rooms of which nine were principal staterooms. The heat and the water from fire extinguishing efforts caused irreparable damage. Many floors had collapsed and others were on the point of collapsing. In the Brunswick Tower, 12 ft of debris covered the main floor. The bay window of the Crimson Drawing Room had been pushed out by the thermal expansion of the steel roof trusses and the wrought iron floor beams in the Prince of Wales Tower had expanded and were distorted. The large quantity of water poured over the burning structure had affected the condition of the salvaged remains and a considerable amount of time was going to be required to allow them to dry out. The built in timbers were likely to have been affected by dampness and it was anticipated that salt damage would affect the carved masonry.

The first decision was to proceed to carefully dismantle remains, using specialist teams suspended in harness above the wreck for safety and to avoid further damage to the surviving fabric. The cost of repairing the damage was estimated at £60 million and the drying out time before applying finishes at 10 years! The water trapped inside the structure was a major problem, as the remedial work had to wait for the moisture contents to drop to acceptable levels.

The first stage of the remedial work concerned the assessment of the damage to materials, which would determine the extent of what could be retained. A great number of samples from the Brunswick Tower rooms were laboratory tested and fire and salt damage danger justified stripping

Fig. 7.2
Windsor Castle on fire. © CINTEC.

out finish from certain parts of the structure to ensure a satisfactory drying out. The stone masonry had also been affected by the fire: the Bath stone had crack openings at mortar joints and general microcracking as was the York stone, which also presented spalling of entire blocks of up to 150mm.

The specialist survey of the ground and walls uncovered a number of voids and concealed flues within the existing structure, which required stabilizing. This was achieved with the use of a proprietary system, the Cintec anchor, consisting of stainless steel anchors enveloped in a woven polyester-based cover. The anchor body, which can be a solid bar, hollow section, or threaded rod, reaching lengths of up to 50m long (at Windsor the longest anchor was 12m) is inserted in the masonry and cementitious grout is pumped at low pressure into the enveloping cover. This realizes a strong masonry/grout/anchor bond and any likely movement is resisted by the low shear stresses between the masonry and grout, into the anchor body. The Cintec system was used around the window at the northeast corner of the St. George's Hall and at the top of the Brunswick Tower where the fire had weakened the crenellated parapet.

Different types of problems were posed by the discovery of earlier mediaeval features under the burned Victorian work, such as the Royal Kitchen and St. George's Hall roof, where new designs were adopted. The remedial work took 5 years and was completed at a cost of £36.5 million and on 17 November 1997, the Queen held a reception in St. George's Hall for all the contractors, craftsmen, and consultants involved in restoring Windsor to its former glory.

8 Disasters resulting from human activities

Classification and impact

The general perception is that disasters are the result of natural phenomena. Historically, this has been predominantly so, but over the past 200 years, the impact of human existence and activities has altered the situation substantially. Human activities *can* lead to disasters when they cause widespread ill health, loss of life, and irreversible destruction of the environment. This can happen in a number of ways, as a result of direct and indirect human action.

Technological advances

The advance of technology has enabled humans to improve many aspects of their existence, develop, and expand their sphere of activity, use natural processes to their advantage. At the same time, there are new challenges to be faced as a consequence.

Relatively new technological processes and materials have not yet had the full test of time, and unlike natural ones, which have been around for thousands of years, they are still to fully manifest themselves. While we know what to expect of stone, timber, or brick, we are only beginning to understand the long-term behaviour and effects of plastics, fibres, or fossil fuel use. We are discovering more and more the negative consequences of human intervention in the natural ecosystem and the effect of man-made materials and their production process. The disastrous effects of technological production can be grouped in the following categories:

(a) The products themselves.
(b) The harmful by-products from the manufacturing process such as:
  • radiation;
  • pollution.
(c) The production, transportation, and technological systems failures.

Excessive exploitation of natural resources and inappropriate land development and building

Global warming and climate changes are probably the world's major challenges at present. They affect our well-being and threaten the survival of the ecosystem. It is widely accepted that the world is warming up more than ever before and that the 1990s have been the hottest decade in the past millennium. The steady rise in temperatures (1–2°C) is accompanied by a rise in sea level (20–80 cm). The consensus is that this is due to 'greenhouse gases', a by-product from the burning of fossil fuel for energy and transport. Carbon dioxide is exchanged naturally through photosynthesis in the living world, oceans and forests by balancing the carbon volume. However, as humans introduce millions of tonnes of carbon artificially as well as clearing or causing the die back of forests, the climatic balance becomes disturbed. Solar radiation becomes trapped by the greenhouse effect created in this way.

The interaction between environment, health, and development has become a major global issue. The destruction of the ecological balance, which occurs through urbanization, deforestation, and desertification, has lead to food shortages, poverty, and famine. Man-made materials and processes requiring high-energy consumption have been shown to affect human health and be a major factor contributing to climate change.

Contamination of the food chain and environment
Throughout the world, people are becoming victims of industrial accidents when hazardous materials are released into the environment. This can occur through the use of chemicals, improper waste management, or unethical manipulation for material gain as in the case of mad cow disease.

Impact
1. *Physical damage* – Damage or destruction of structures and infrastructures can occur through explosions in plant and storage facilities as a result of inadequate safety features and/or maintenence, unsuitable buildings and technological systems, lack of trained staff, or sabotage. Transport accidents damage vehicles and other objects on impact, and are often shown to be the cause of poor vehicles, containers, such as some oil transporting cargo ships which were not found seaworthy. Industrial fires also destroy infrastructures and affect large areas.
2. *Environmental damage* – Dangerous substances suspended in the air such as gases, vapours, and volatile liquids can cause serious health problems, sometimes even death. Direct inhalation of toxic substances and skin contamination are common. Large-scale release of airbourne polluants can spread for hundreds of kilometres. Contamination of the water supply, land, and animal life can also be devastating. Persons or livestock nearest to the scene are most vulnerable, but in certain cases, the damage can reach several countries, such as in the case of the Chernobyl accident in Ukraine or the cyanide spill in Northen Romania. Disrupted ecological systems can cause irreversible damage such as the extinction of some species or long-term damage such as desertification or land and sea shores contamination, which can take generations to clean and reinstate.

The following sections take a brief look at some of those aspects more pertinent to buildings and planning, but the subject of man-made disaster warrants a further and extensive separate study. Sources of information are listed at the end of this book.

Technological production

Listed below are examples of the types of harmful effects arising from technological production, which are causing particular concern.

Manufacture and use of harmful products

Asbestos is a derivative of a group of natural silicate minerals, which can be separated into strong long fibres and can be woven, it is resistant to heat and fire. During the twentieth century, asbestos has been extensively used in a wide range of products with commercial applications, for consumer, industrial, maritime, scientific, and building use. Some of the most common asbestos-containing products have been used to protect against heat and fire, especially in the construction industry. Examples are numerous: pipe-covering, insulating blankets, insulating cement, asbestos cloth, asbestos plaster, gaskets, packing materials, thermal seals, boiler insulation, fireproofing spray, vinyl flooring, ceiling tiles, mastic, adhesives, coatings, acoustic treatment, roofing products such as asbestos cement slates or diamond slates, asbestos rope, insulated electrical wire, brake and clutch assemblies, etc. Figure 8.1 shows where asbestos products can be found in a typical building. It is now known that asbestos is a dangerous substance because of the serious human

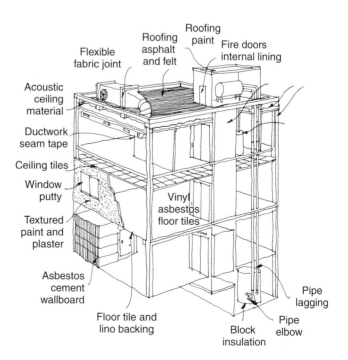

Fig. 8.1
Common building materials containing asbestos.

health hazards caused by the inhalation of asbestos fibres. Controlled by a specific EC directive (87/217/EC) asbestos is no longer used in new construction products, but it is still present in buildings and products of the 1950s and 1960s and therefore can affect people involved with disposal, demolition, and refurbishment of these buildings.

Use of lead produces a cumulative poison affecting mental and physical well-being through ingestion, inhalation, and skin contact. This can occur from the use of lead water pipes and cooking utensils. Lead dust can be released from poly (vinyl chloride) (PVC) products such as certain vinyl blinds as they deteriorate through exposure to sunlight, and certain types of paint.

Synthetic materials used in building construction and furnishings have been found to produce volatile organic compounds that adversely affect human health. Some examples are discussed in the following text.

PVC vinyl – one of the most widely used types of plastic presents a real threat to human health and the environment through its toxic manufacturing process which releases a number of cancerogenic chemicals such as doixins, ethylene dichloride, and vinyl chloride. When PVC is combined with additives such as plasticizers and stabilizers, which are not chemically bound to the polymer, a number of harmful substances are released representing a potential threat of causing asthma, cancer, lead poisoning, immune system damage, etc. PVC vinyl also constitutes a fire hazard, creates toxic fumes and is not easy to dispose of safely: it has to be burned or buried, which can lead to soil and water contamination.

Formaldehyde – a chemical used widely in the manufacture of building materials and household products, it is also a by-product of combustion and other natural processes. Formaldehyde has been found to cause health problems such as: asthma attacks, breathing difficulties, nausea, throat irritations, skin rashes, severe allergic attacks, and it may induce cancer. Formaldehyde is mostly used as part of the adhesive used in the manufacture of pressed wood products such as:

- hardwood plywood panelling, used in decorative panelling, furniture;
- particle boards used as sub-flooring, shelving, furniture;
- medium density fibreboard (MDF) used for drawer fronts, kitchen units, and tabletops. As it contains a higher resin to wood ratio, MDF is recognized as being the highest formaldehyde emitting pressed wood product.

Also used in preservatives in certain paints, cosmetics, and coatings, and certain insulation materials (urea–formaldehyde foam and fibreglass insulation), formaldehyde is released in the air by burning wood, kerosene, or natural gas as well as cigarettes.

The following steps are helpful in reducing exposure to the effects of formaldehyde:

- the use of 'exterior grade' pressed wood products, which are lower emitting because they use phenol resins;
- reducing humidity and temperature levels;
- increasing ventilation.

Harmful by-products and/or processes
Radiation – what is it and how it occurs

Radiation is energy in transit and as such, we encounter it in some form every day as electromagnetic waves when we use light, radio, television, ultraviolet, and microwaves, etc. When radiation-causing energy is high enough, it can interact with atoms causing them to become ionized. Radioactivity is the spontaneous process of transformation or disintegration of an unstable atom and can be defined through the number of nuclear transformations occurring in a given quantity of radioactive material per unit of time, expressed in becquerels (Bq) or curies (Ci).

Certain elements such as uranium, polonium, radon, etc. (nine in total) are naturally radioactive, natural in the sense that radioactive elements are part of nature and we all contain things like radioactive carbon-14, but all radioactive emissions are dangerous to living things. The loss of an electron can induce cell death or genetic mutations and certain particles, whilst having no effect outside the human body, can be very dangerous if eaten or inhaled.

The amount of energy from ionizing radiation deposited in a material mass is known as a *dose*. Doses can be: absorbed expressing the quantity of energy absorbed by any given material for any type of radiation (measured in units of Gray) or effective and equivalent dose which differentiates between different types of tissues and radiation (measured in Sieverts). The unit used to measure absorbed doses is a RAD (radiation absorbed dose) 1 RAD represents the absorption of 100 ergs/g of material. The unit used to derive the equivalent dose relating to human tissue is called a REM (roentgen equivalent man) and it relates the dose absorbed by human tissue to the effective biological damage. 100 REMs equal 1 Sievert. Doses can be: chronic (received over a long period of time) or acute (received over a short period of time). The effects of radiation can be: somatic (seen in an individual receiving the radiation); genetic (seen in the offspring of the individual receiving the radiation before conception) teratogenic (seen in offspring of individual receiving radiation during gestation) stochastic (occurring on a random basis unrelated to dose such as cancer) or non-stochastic (directly related to dose).

Radiation can be lethal to man in circumstances that enable high doses to contaminate his organism, food chain, and environment. This takes place usually in the context of nuclear accidents. There are several types of nuclear accidents:

- nuclear reactors;
- nuclear fuel reprocessing plants;
- nuclear waste storage facilities;
- nuclear weapons;
- radioisotope generator and heating units;
- nuclear weapons tests;
- production and re-processing facility discharges (like Sellafield UK, Hanford, Savannah River, etc.).

The radioactive plume (the concentration profile of an air or waterborne release of material spreading from its source) from nuclear accident results in dry and wet ground deposition. Human exposure to contamination occurs in several ways:

1. external exposure;
2. absorption (dermal deposition);
3. inhalation;
4. ingestion.

The effects of contamination are also related to the time of exposure, which can be:

1. Early – for the length of time that critical exposure is maintained (10 days at Chernobyl).
2. Intermediate – 1 week to 6 months.
3. Late and very long term exposure to biologically significant ground deposition 6 months to over 100 years.

Case study – Chernobyl, Ukraine (Source: Nuclear Energy Agency, NEA, Assessment on Radiation Protection and Public Health, Chernobyl 10 years on)

The Chernobyl case encompasses several of the man-made hazards listed above: the harmful radiation by-product, the inadequate infrastructure, technological systems failure and inadequate safety and emergency provisions. The compounded effect of all these elements resulted in one of the worst peace time disasters the world has suffered in recent times, not only in its immediate effect but also in its long-term implications.

Background

Chernobyl power station was located in a populated area where 2 million people lived, part of Belarus, a former Soviet Union republic with a population of about 11 million, which produced chemicals, engineering products, and electrical goods.

The accident

On 26 April 1986, a major accident at the nuclear power station in Chernobyl, Ukraine, caused the release of large quantities of radioactive substances the effect of which spread across Europe, reaching as far as Canada and Japan. The accident is by far the most devastating in the history of nuclear power.

The number four RBMK reactor (a Russian acronym which translated roughly means 'reactor cooled by water and moderated by graphite) went out of control during a test at low power, leading to an explosion and fire which demolished the reactor building and released large amounts of radiation into the atmosphere. Safety measures were ignored, the uranium fuel in the reactor overheated and melted through the protective barriers. RBMK reactors do not have what is known as a containment structure, a concrete steel dome over the reactor itself, designed to keep radiation inside the plant in the event of such an accident.

The accident happened during a routine maintenance test when inadequate safety precautions combined with a lack of coordination between different sections of staff and the unstable elements in the reactor's design, which made possible a loss of control in operational errors conditions. A number of violent explosions took place resulting in the almost total destruction of the reactor. The fact that the quantity of radioactive material released was extremely large, that it reached high altitude (1 km) and took place over more than a week with changing winds, resulted in a catastrophe of unprecedented proportions which caught emergency services and national authorities completely unprepared (see Fig. 8.2).

The lack of information at the early stages of the disaster and the inadequacy of the intervention procedures in place created confusion among the public, doubt among experts and a general reluctance to act. The most difficult decisions concerned the long-term management of the contaminated areas and the associated relocation and a need for international efforts to harmonize criteria and approaches to emergency management was highlighted. The main issues were the following.

The estimation of radiation dose. Most of the population of the Northern Hemisphere was exposed to varying degrees of radiation from the Chernobyl accident. The main concern is over the effect on the thyroid gland from external irradiation and inhalation of radioactive iodine isotopes and the effects on the whole body from radioactive caesium isotopes.

The *groups concerned.*

- *The evacuees* – over 100 000 persons were evacuated from the 30 km radius area around the accident location during the first few weeks. They received initial significant doses of both types of radiation (from 70 millisieverts, mSv, to 1 Sievert to thyroid and 15 mSv to the body)

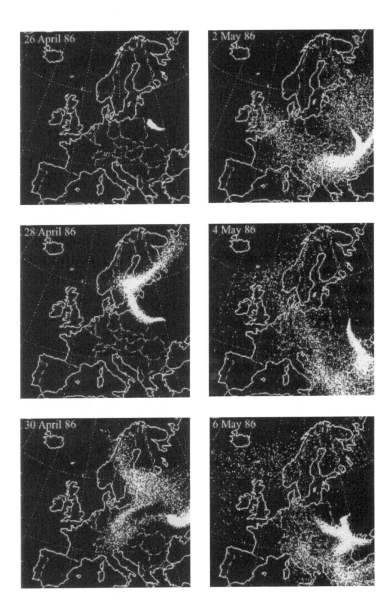

Fig. 8.2
Chernobyl fall out sequence.
© Atmosphere Release Advisory
Centre.

and continued to be exposed, albeit to a lesser degree at their site of relocation.

- *The first on the scene teams, 'the liquidators'* – some 800000 workers, military personnel, firemen, and medical staff involved in the initial emergency action at the time of the accident and the clean-up operation which lasted a few years.
- *The personnel on site at the time of the accident* – about 400 persons suffered very high doses (from a few Grays to 10 Grays) and many developed acute radiation syndrome requiring emergency treatment.
- *People living in contaminated areas of the former Soviet Union* – approximately 270000 people continue to live in contaminated areas,

where protection measures are still needed. Children in the Gomel region of Belarus have received the highest thyroid doses through cow's milk (up to 40 Sieverts). Whole body doses between 1986 and 1989 averaged 40 mSv.

• *People outside the former Soviet Union* – doses received were lower, the upper extreme in some European countries being 1 or 2 mSv, which is the equivalent of an individual annual exposure from natural background radiation.

Impact.

• *Health* – the initial explosion and graphite fire killed 31 people, 140 suffered various degrees of health impairment. According to statistics released by the Ukrainian Government 10 years on, over 5700 'liquidators' also died during the period following the disaster. The Ukrainian Ministry of Health has released a total of 125 000 subsequent deaths, natural or otherwise, since the accident. The observed trend is of an increase of cancer incidence, especially thyroid cancer, the peak not having been reached yet. A widespread psychological stress was suffered by the population in the areas affected, reflected in fears about unknown radiation and mistrust towards officials and experts.

• *Agricultural and environmental* – agriculture and environment were widely affected and food production and environmental aspects in general are still suffering. Large areas of agricultural land are still out of use and are expected to remain so for a long time, as are animal production restrictions. Waterways have been contaminated and a number of forests have suffered from irradiation due to the filter effect of trees, affecting wild life, and forest habitat in general. In some places, the irradiation effect had been so high as to kill trees which then had to be destroyed as radioactive waste. Whilst severe environmental impact was short term, low-level radioactive contamination will persist for decades.

Residual risk. After the accident the remains of the reactor were encased in a massive concrete structure, known as the 'sarcophagus', which was conceived as a provisional protection means until a safe way of disposing of the radioactive materials is found. However, a solution is still to be identified and the long term resistance of the 'sarcophagus', in particular its roof, which presents a number of cracks, raises concerns as do a number of massive structures rendered unstable or damaged by the accident and which could fail causing the collapse of the roof. This in itself would be a major disaster but the fact that Unit 3 of the Chernobyl plant is still in operation poses an added and even bigger threat. The proliferation of waste storage sites constitutes a potential source of contamination of ground water.

Lessons learned. Although the Chernobyl accident was very specific in nature and as such is not a useful reference for future emergency planning elsewhere, it has made clear that a major nuclear accident can affect directly and indirectly other countries, even at a large distance away. This realization has underpinned a concerted effort of international cooperation covering communication, harmonization of emergency management criteria, and coordination of protective action. A decade of assistance to the countries of Central and Eastern Europe and the former Soviet Union focused on identifying the weaknesses in the design and improving design safety of RBMK reactors. Upgrading was performed on all RBMK units to eliminate the design deficiencies which contributed to the Chernobyl accident. The European Commission has launched an extensive collaborative research programme. Sixteen projects have been funded to study health and environmental issues including emergency response procedure and long-term management. One of these projects has led to the publication of an Atlas illustrating the deposition of radioactive material (in particular caesium 137) after the Chernobyl accident. Apart from the severe health consequences of the accident, the physical, industrial, and economic short-term effects there are also long-term consequences of socio-economic disruption, psychological stress, and lack of confidence in nuclear energy.

Pollution

Pollution is one of the major global public health concerns of the twentieth century. In simple terms, pollution is defined as 'any harmful or undesirable change in the physical, chemical, or biological quality of air, water, or soil'. Closely associated with contamination in the context of high concentration of non-characteristic substances in other mediums, pollution can be the result of natural disasters, such as volcanic eruptions or forest fires, but it is predominantly associated with the direct or indirect human introduction of harmful substances in the environment.

Atmospheric pollution can be defined as the presence in the atmosphere of substances or energy in such quantities and of such duration as to be liable to cause harm to life, damage to human-made materials and structures or changes in the weather and climate (*source*: Elsom).

Habitat pollution through the introduction of chemicals in the environmental cycle has had harmful effects on wild life and biodiversity. The main offenders are:

- Chlorine-based poisons such as DDT, PCBs, and dioxin. Widely used to destroy insects, DDT saved millions of lives by killing mosquitoes that spread malaria, but it has lead to contamination of the food chain. Banned in the United States since 1972, it is still being manufactured in Mexico and Asia.
- Organophosphates.
- Nutrient pollution – mainly agricultural run-off and sewage, it reaches bodies of water seeping into the soil. The effect is an alteration of the global nitrogen cycle and the pollution of surface waters with

phosphorus and nitrogen. Amongst other negative effects, nutrient pollution also stimulates the growth of algae in a process called eutrophication, which uses oxygen to the detriment of other marine wildlife, notably fish. The East Coast of United States, The Baltic Sea and the Adriatic have been affected, and the city of Venice is collecting 500 tonnes of algae per day.

• Air pollution and acid rain: acid emissions from fossil-fuel combustion (SO_2, CO_2, and NO) combine with the water in the air to form sulphuric and nitric acids, causing acid rain. This destroys plants and animals as well as man-made structures and it can travel long distances away from the polluting source (see Fig. 8.3).

Pollutants are measured in micrograms per cubic metre of air ($\mu g/m^3$) and affect buildings as:

Wet deposition – this is brought intermittently from high up in the atmosphere and from distant sources by rain or snowfall, polluting substances dissolved in the rain or snow are deposited on the building.
Dry deposition – this takes place more or less continuously involving local pollutants, which react directly with the building fabric causing erosion.

Pollutants affecting the fabric of buildings include:

• Carbon dioxide results naturally from respiration and artificially from fuel combustion. It is capable of dissolving limestones converting them into water-soluble compounds.
• Carbon monoxide.
• Sulphur dioxide.
• Ozone occurs naturally in the upper atmosphere and from man's activities and exhaust fumes. Ozone can cause rapid corrosion of metals

Fig. 8.3
Building in Glasgow showing pollution effect. © ABG.

through its oxidizing action with dramatic effects. Some of the world's best-known monuments like the Taj Mahal or St. Paul's Cathedral have suffered from ozone corrosion attack on exposed iron ties and embedded iron cramps.

- Chlorides.
- Carbon monoxide.

Preventing and mitigating the effects of atmospheric pollution

Legislation: reducing the level of air pollution has been the focus of a number of EC legislative measures and US directives cover the headings of:

- exhaust systems;
- gaseous pollutants;
- industrial plants and large combustion plants;
- lead;
- nitrogen dioxide and ozone depletion;
- sulphur dioxide;
- integrated pollution control;
- air quality assessment.

The European Environment Agency (EEA) has monitored a noticeable fall in SO_2 levels since the introduction of new directives in 1990. This has been explained partly as the result of change from coal to other types of fuel and desulphurization practices. Current strategy adopted by organisations such as the US Environmental Protection Agency (EPA) follows the following principles:

(a) Whenever possible, pollution should be prevented or reduced *at source*.
(b) If prevention is not possible, pollution should be *recycled* in an environmentally safe manner.
(c) If prevention or recycling are not possible, pollution should be *treated*.
(d) Disposal or any other type of release into the environment should only be employed *as a last resort*, and conducted in an environmentally safe manner.

Pollution can also be reduced through better urban and building design and maintenance along the following lines:

(a) Improving plant management and design.
(b) Reducing the use of pollutants through energy-efficient buildings design.
(c) Creating urban pattern design which reduce the need for transport energy.
(d) Provide the use of alternative and renewable energy in design.

(e) Cleaning the external surfaces of buildings to remove soluble salts which cause decay and techniques such as 'dry scrubbing' for the removal of SO_2 with pulverized limestone.

(f) Judicious location of new industries.

Indoor air pollution and the effect of certain synthetic materials have brought on adverse effects on human health. Two different conditions have ensued.

Sick building syndrome (SBS) – usually affecting more than 25% of a building occupants, covers persistent non-specific symptoms (irritation of the eyes any respiratory passages, headaches, chronic fatigue, etc.) which stop when the persons affected leave the building. SBS is often diagnosed based on the exclusion of other identifiable illness. Causes of SBS are yet to be proven. Some research links it to man-made mineral fibres amongst others, and SBS appears more common in buildings which are air tight and have been built in the 1960–1980 period.

Indoor air quality is certainly a factor and number of factors have been identified in respect of basic requirements:

- thermal acceptability;
- normal concentration of respiratory gases;
- dilution and removal of contaminants and pollutants to acceptable levels.

Amongst contaminants considered are: combustion products, chemicals, respirable particulate, radio-nucleates and microbiological agents (indoor bioaerosols).

Building-related illness (BRI) – is the clinically diagnosed disease of building occupants resulting from exposure of indoor air pollutants. BRI persists for a relatively prolonged time after the sufferers leave the building.

Excessive exploitation of natural resources and inappropriate land development

The effects of the climate warming are more and more visible:

- Europe's alpine glaciers are melting and the US Government predicts that by 2030 there will be no more glaciers left in Montana.
- Low-lying lands and islands are threatened by the rising sea levels.
- Heat waves are causing rising death tolls in cities like Chicago, Athens, and New Delhi.
- Wildlife such as coral reefs or North Pacific salmon are dwindling.
- Extreme weather such as super hurricanes like Mitch or Floyd is becoming commonplace.

In 1988, an Intergovernmental Panel on Climate Change was created in Geneva to form national and international polices aimed at reducing energy use in order to have less pollution. The current solution is to call on governments and businesses accounting for large power consumption to take responsibility for a major change in energy use. As around 25% of the world's population living in the industrialized nations consume about 80% of the world's energy, developing nations have been looking to the industrialized ones to take the lead in cutting carbon dioxide, but it is expected that the developing countries will overtake the developed ones in 20–30 years time in energy consumption.

With the Rio Agreement in 1990 and Kyoto in 1995, there has been positive move towards reducing greenhouse gases and a legally binding timetable to make cuts by 2010 has been undertaken by the 'rich' nations. At the same time, scientists have been reluctant to fully underwrite the current theories for the causes behind global warming and climate change on the basis that further analysis and data will be needed. Consequently, introducing effective measures is somewhere between the short-term political agenda of governments who want to be seen to make electoral progress and the long-term agenda of scientists who require sound scientific reasons before deciding on solutions.

Inappropriate land development and building

The current environmental predicament calls for global coordination of the development to redress the ecological balance and changes in the acceptable standards of construction and manufacturing of building materials. Complex legislation at European level as well as international agreements has been focusing on achieving an integrated approach to environmental protection and enhancement.

Sustainable development – The development focusing on meeting the needs and improving the life of the world's population without depleting the natural resources beyond the environment's capacity to supply them – has been identified as an essential consideration. Urban planning, transport, waste energy consumption and water management are important aspect of the sustainable development concept.

Green buildings and materials represent the means to mitigate the current environmental problems and their use an important step in preventing future disasters. Examples of 'green' products are:

- Products made from environmentally helpful materials such as salvaged materials, rapidly renewable, natural or requiring minimal processing.
- Environmentally aware products such as alternatives to ozone depleting products, PVC, preservatives, etc.

- Products that reduce the impact of new construction, demolition, or renovation.
- Equipment facilitating the conservation of energy and water.
- Products that contribute to a safe healthy indoor environment.
- Products that prevent pollution and reduce waste.
- Systems and equipment employing renewable energy.

Contamination of the food chain and environment

Case study – The cyanide spill at Baia Mare, Romania
(Source: The UNEP/OCHA Report on the Cyanide Spill at Baia Mare, Romania compiled by a team of 20 scientists during the period 23 February to 6 March 2000)

The accident

On 30 January 2000, at 22:00 hours, there was a break in a dam encircling a tailings pond at a facility operated by Aurul SA Company in Baia Mare, northwest Romania. The result was a spill of about $100\,000\,m^3$ of liquid and suspended waste containing about 50–100 tonnes of cyanide, as well as copper and other heavy metals.

The break was probably caused by a combination of design defects in the facilities set up by '*Aurul*', unexpected operating conditions and bad weather. The contaminated spill travelled into the rivers Sasar, Lapus, Somes, Tisza, and Danube before reaching the Black Sea about 4 weeks later (see Fig. 8.4).

Some 2000 km of the Danube's water catchment area was affected by the spill. Romanian sources said that, in Romania, the spill caused interruptions to the water supply of 24 municipalities, and costs to sanitation plants and industries, because of interruptions in their production processes. Romania also reported that the amount of dead fish was very small in Romania. Hungary estimated the amount of dead fish in Hungary at 1240 tonnes. Yugoslavian authorities reported large amounts of dead fish in the Yugoslavian branch of the Tisza river and no major fish kills in the Danube river.

On 18 February 2000, a team of international experts were requested to carry out a mission to analyse the damages caused by the spill. The mission, a joint venture of UNEP and OCHA, lasted from 23 February to 6 March undertook sampling, analysis, and discussions with national and local experts, national authorities, affected populations and NGOs. Its findings are summarized below.

Baia Mare and Maramures County

Maramures County, where the town of Baia Mare is located, lies at Romania's northwestern border with Ukraine and Hungary. It has a long history of mining, especially in gold, silver, lead, zinc, copper, manganese, and salt. Waste at the county's seven key mining sites is stored

Spread of the cyanide spill from Baia Mare, Romania

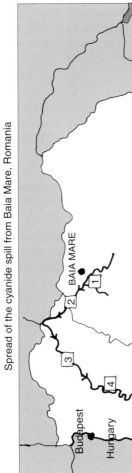

Progress of the spill plume

1 30 January 2000
   Cyanide spill occurs at
   BAIA MARE, Romania

2 1 February
   Spill plume reaches
   Romanian Hungarian border

3 5 February
   Cyanide registers in tests
   at Tiszalok

4 9 February
   Spill plume reaches Szolnok

5 11 February
   It crosses the Hungarian
   Yugoslavian border

6 13 February
   The plume reaches Belgrade
   (Perlez), Yugoslavia

7 15 February
   It meets the Romanian
   border again at ram

8 17 February
   Cyanide shows up in tests
   at Iron Gate, Romania

9 25–28 February
   The plume reaches the
   Danube Delta

Sources: MTI, Ministry for Environmental Protection (Hungary) Environmental Inspectorate, UNEP.

Fig. 8.4
Map of Romania showing spread of cyanide spill. © UNEP.

in ponds and 215 waste ('*tailings*') dams. The county has high levels of chronic ('persistently recurring') soil, water, and air contamination that comes from many pollutants. These were released over decades of past industrial activities that used environmentally unsound technologies which included an old lead smelter, copper smelter, sulphuric acid plant, and the operations of the mining company, Romanian *Compania Nationala a Metalelor Pretioase si Neferoase (Remin)*, established in 1992.

Some Baia Mare residents live within 50 m of highly toxic, chronically leaking, waste sites. The World Health Organization (WHO) identifies Baia Mare as a health risk hotspot, with the population's exposure to lead being among the highest ever recorded. Lead in the blood of some adults averages almost 2.5 times above safety levels. In some children, it averages nearly six times above safety levels. High lead levels in humans are now thought to be associated with impaired learning ability, mental retardation, problems with kidney and neurological functions, hearing loss, blood disorder, hypertension, and death. Baia Mare residents have complained about dust from industrial processes for some time. It is also important to know that the city of Baia Mare's population and urban development are growing, with expansion restricted in some areas by old contaminated tailings ponds.

The company: Aurul SA

Aurul SA is a stock company jointly owned by Esmeralda, Exploration Limited, Australia, and Remin, Romania.

Over a 7-year period, Aurul obtained all of the necessary environmental permits required under Romanian law for its plant in Baia Mare, before beginning operations in May 1999. It was hoped that the Aurul project would meet the needs of both the Romanian authorities and the Australian investors. Aurul would gain profits through its mining operations and local authorities would benefit from Aurul's management and removal of Baia Mare's old contaminated ponds, which blocked further development in the city.

The process and technologies used at the Baia Mare plant for recovering precious metals were completely new to Romania and were expected to be the most modern, safe, and efficient in the region and a major environmental improvement. The Baia Mare plant was designed to process 2.5 million tonnes of tailings per year – to recover about 1.6 tonnes of gold and 9 tonnes of silver per year. The project was to last 10–12 years, although this may increase due to recent business deals made with Romanian companies. The tailings, originating from earlier mining activities and stored next to Baia Mare, contain small amounts of precious metals, especially gold and silver. Aurul's process uses high concentrations of cyanide to remove the precious metals from the tailings. As part of the process, tailings are transported 6.5 km away from Baia Mare to a new dam near Bozanta Mare village. The process was designed to release no waste to the surrounding environment, but it has not been possible to determine how often the plant had been inspected by government authorities before the spill occurred. Soon after operations began in 1999, however, two leaks were reported in Aurul's pipeline system.

Facts on dangerous substances

Cyanide

Cyanide is acutely and almost instantaneously poisonous ('toxic') to living organisms, including humans. Cyanide harms by blocking the ingestion of oxygen by cells. Acute effects include rapid breathing, tremors, effects on the nervous system, and ultimately, death. Chronic effects include weight loss, effects on the thyroid and nerve damage.

Fish are about one thousand times more sensitive to cyanide than humans. If fish do not die from limited exposure, they can still have reduced swimming ability, problems in reproducing (possibly creating deformed babies), and increased vulnerability to predators. Fish are excellent in gauging the presence of cyanide in water – if fish are living after exposure, then no other form of life have been harmed.

Cyanide, however, does not remain in the environment for long and does not accumulate in sediments or organisms (including humans).

Heavy metals

Heavy metals do not break down and are 'bio-accumulative' in plants, animals and the environment. This means that the level of toxins builds up in an organism over time, increasing its toxicity and threat to local ecosystems.

Toxins may also be passed on to other species if a toxic organism is eaten.

Therefore, living organisms face high risks with long-term and chronic exposure to heavy metals.

Among the heavy metals used by mining industries, the most harmful to humans include arsenic, cadmium, lead, nickel, manganese and molybdenum, even at small doses. Zinc, lead, aluminum, boron, chromium, and iron are also all toxic to plant growth.

The acute and chronic effects of copper to humans include stomach and intestinal distress, liver and kidney damage and anemia. Copper is also toxic to most aquatic plants, often contained in river sediments. Copper easily dissolves in water so it is more available for uptake by living things along rivers.

At relatively low levels, health effects from lead can include interference with red blood cell chemistry, delays in normal physical and mental development in babies and young children, chronic exposure to lead has been linked to brain and kidney disease and cancer in humans.

Cause of accident

The breakage in the Aurul dam was partially caused by heavy rains and rapidly melting snow that made the water level in the pond rise. This rise was quicker than the rise of the dam which was intended to 'grow gradually over time' as additional tailings accumulated. The newly engineered dam system therefore failed under the circumstances, and this could have been foreseen.

There were no plans to deal with such a rise in water or to catch overflow wastewater. A completely closed operation with no discharges to the environment was thus not possible under the conditions. Furthermore, the operation was actually open at two points, at the old and the new ponds, which allowed unmonitored amounts of cyanide to be regularly lost into the air and/or groundwater. At the same time, Aurul was operating in line with government permits. Under Romanian law, the plant and ponds, categorized as 'regular' risk, did not require any special emergency planning or monitoring to detect dangerous situations. Accident plans did exist, but were not sufficient. The mission therefore believed that both the company and local authorities had inadequate plans and responses in place for emergencies, considering the large quantities of hazardous materials being used close to human populations and the river system.

Government response

In Romania, about 10h were lost between the time the Baia Mare Environmental Protection Agency received notification of the spill from Aurul and the time the local Romanian Waters Authority was informed. As a result, local residents near the source of the spill were not informed as early as possible.

Once the Romanian Water Authority was informed, however, their regional environment and water authorities immediately checked information about the breach and the spill to determine the degree of pollution, and ordered Aurul to stop activities and close the breakage and timely information exchange and measures taken by the Romanian, Hungarian, and Yugoslavian authorities, including a temporary closure of the Tisza lake dam, reduced the impact of the spill.

Environmental assessment

The assessment of the impacts of the spill on the environment is taken from three main sources: (i) background reports by the affected countries; (ii) monitoring of impacts, by the affected countries, as the cyanide wave travelled downstream; and (iii) information collected by the UNEP/OCHA mission. The methods used to analyse cyanide and heavy metals in each of the three countries produced comparable data according to international standards.

Surface water. In general, the data show that concentrations of cyanide and heavy metals decreased rapidly with increasing distance from the spill. Regarding cyanide, acute effects occurred along long stretches of the river system down to where the Tisza and Danube rivers meet. Water plankton (plant and animal) were completely killed when the cyanide plume passed and fish were killed in the wave or immediately after. Soon after the plume passed, however, plankton and aquatic microorganisms recovered relatively quickly (within a few days) due to unaffected water coming from upstream. As a result, the mission concluded that mud-dwelling organisms in the lower Tisza and middle Tisza regions in Hungary and Yugoslavia were not completely destroyed by the cyanide spill beyond quick recovery.

However, the situation in the upper Tisza (north of Tokaj, Hungary) is more complex. Parts of the Tisza region had been damaged before the cyanide spill by years of chronic pollution (i.e. heavy metals) and dam building. Pollutant safety levels had also often been exceeded. The region has many poorly maintained and operated industrial plants and ponds containing cyanide and/or heavy metals, many of which are leaking continuously. Chronic pollution is also high from sewage and agriculture. Pollution of surface water, groundwater, and soils is thus likely to re-occur.

In comparison to surface water, the data show a less negative impact on the ecosystem from sediment pollution. The spill drastically increased the existing heavy metal contamination (especially copper, lead, and zinc) of sediments in WHO guidelines available on acceptable standards of cyanide. However, heavy metal contamination then dropped rapidly with increased distance from the source. Therefore, the resulting toxic effects on the aquatic ecosystem may not have moved far downstream. At the same time, many river areas downstream were found to have concentrations of heavy metals in their sediments, including some tributaries that were not even affected by the spill. This was especially true in the Baia Mare area but also further downstream in Hungary. These hotspots were probably caused by past industrial, sewage, and agricultural activities over a long period of time. The result is that sediment quality is already at a stage where adverse toxic effects on the aquatic ecosystem may occur.

Drinking water. In Romania, the village of Bozanta Mare near the Aurul plant has private wells that are shallow and connected with the river. They are thus highly vulnerable, especially to pollution from the Aurul pond, which is in the water catchment area of the wells. The wells were affected by the spill with cyanide levels nearly 80 times over permissible limits on 10 February. By 26 February, cyanide concentrations fell below limits but the concentrations of cadmium, copper, manganese, and iron were higher than admissible Romanian values. Also, the mission found ongoing pollution from human waste and an excessive use of agricultural fertilizers.

Further downstream from Bozanta Mare, along the river Somes, the drinking water does not appear to be at risk. Nevertheless, most wells are also shallow and vulnerable to surface pollution. Consequently, in Romania, immediate human health risk seems to be minimal from the spill, although chronic health impacts due to long-term pollution by heavy metals are possible. Also, there is usually no water monitoring of private wells in Bozanta Mare, or groundwater monitoring downstream of Bozanta Mare, except in Satu Mare.

In Hungary, contaminated drinking water is not expected to be a long-term effect of the mining accident. Neither cyanide nor heavy metals were found in the water of Hungary's deep wells, which are well protected against surface pollution, with probably no connection between the river Tisza and deep groundwater. Hungarian public water supply systems were also not endangered by the cyanide pollution.

In Yugoslavia, the Becej public water supply system and two assessed private wells were not affected by the spill.

Lessons learned

The following recommendations from the UNEP/OCHA report were intended to mobilize and assist local governments and the people in the affected areas in their efforts to reduce the negative effects of the industries around them.

1. *Information* – There is a great need for more objective and reliable information, especially from local authorities and the media. The spill and mission showed that the level of public knowledge of toxic chemicals, and future risks from mining and related industrial processes, is very low. At the same time, people in the Baia Mare area were well aware that soil and groundwater had been polluted before, and that pipes transporting tailings had broken on several occasions, spilling water containing cyanide outside of industrial areas.
2. *Communications* – Communication between local authorities, NGOs and the public, concerning preparations for emergencies and damage prevention options, is poor. Communications channels should be improved and NGOs and other interest groups should help to inform the population.
3. *Health* – The long-term effects of mining activities on public health, especially by cyanide and heavy metals, is a key concern, especially in Bozanta Mare and Baia Mare, as are dust problems in the summer.
4. *Assessments* – At Aurul SA, a full risk assessment of operations should be done to make them safer. An emergency plan for the improved system should also be produced and made fully accessible to workers and local stakeholders. The organisational responsibilities off-site for dealing with a future dam breakage should be clear and dependable early warning systems should be established, especially for Baia Mare.

5. *Sediment analysis* – Further analysis of the heavy metals in river sediments is urged in all three countries (especially at Aurul SA), to make a reliable assessment of the long-term risks of the spill and chronic pollution. Sediment quality was already found threatening to many local aquatic ecosystems.

6. *Drinking water* – Improvements should include surveys to plan and develop new water resources (Baia Mare and along Somes river) and new monitoring systems for groundwater and private wells by local authorities. An inventory of current private wells (Romania, Hungary, Yugoslavia) and an inventory of polluted areas that endanger groundwater, surface, and drinking water (entire river basin) should be created. Emergency water supplies should be available to the region, a health survey of the population in affected areas should be drawn up and proper monitoring of diseases caused by water pollution should be established. Finally, the drinking water supply systems for private households in Maramures County should be changed to public collective systems along with required sewage treatment facilities.

7. *Biodiversity* – Multinational monitoring of the long-term ecological effects of the spill on the region's biodiversity, especially birds, mammals, and water vegetation, is urged.

8. *Regional industries* – An inventory and risk assessment study of all mining and related industries in Baia Mare and the entire Maramures region, including abandoned sites, should be made. Dams containing toxic waste or other liquids should have retention systems for overflow or accidents resulting from breaks in dams. Plants using cyanide should pay special attention to preparing for emergencies, public communication, and special monitoring and inspection by authorities.

9. *Local economies* – The longer-term economic implications of the spill and other polluting activities in the region need to be assessed. Maramures County, rich in mining and related industries, is of key economic importance to Romania. But it can create environmental problems downstream in areas dependent on the environment for fishing, tourism, agriculture, and other economic activities. Many workers and businesses in the area are concerned about a loss of markets, as the image of products from the region has greatly suffered as a result of the spill (i.e. consumer fear of contaminated food).

10. *Regional plans* – There is a strong need for a broad, longer-term environmental management and sustainable development strategy for both Maramures County and the entire water catchment area of the Tisza river. This should address mining and related industries, other economic activities, cross-border economic development, biodiversity, social needs, and increased international cooperation and support.

11. *International objectives* – Romania should sign the international *UN/ECE Convention on the Trans-boundary Effects of Industrial*

Accidents, and there should be an international system for addressing the issues of liability and compensation related to such spills and their consequences. Moreover, there is a need for intensive and ongoing dialogue between members of the mining industry and governments to come to more secure and safe management practices in mining. This is especially so among those industries dealing with reservoirs containing hazardous and highly toxic substances such as cyanide.

9 Historic buildings destruction

Earthquakes, storms, or hurricanes do not discriminate between famous landmarks or bus shelters, centuries old masterpieces or commercial hoarding. They have no regard for history, family heirlooms, or national treasures. While the death toll and material loss caused by a disaster are immediately apparent, the long-term effect of losing the historical frame work of our lives and culture is perhaps the most difficult loss to come to terms with in the aftermath of a disaster. When disaster strikes the first priority is to survive, but having done so, the destruction of familiar landscape and landmarks put our predicament into perspective.

Natural disasters such as the major storms, which hit northern France in December 1999, have completely changed its landscape. Winds of over 100 mph, lashed out at The Notre Dame Cathedral, Palace of Versailles, and the Mont St. Michel Abbey, which lost some of their former glory, but these paled into insignificance compared to the effect on the landscape of 300 million trees being felled by the storms! Some were young and some were hundreds of years old, 12 ft in circumference, weighing 10 tonnes, they were all pulled out and thrown about like matchsticks.

An entire building with all its contents, art objects, and royal treasures part of our national that were identity were lost in the fire at Windsor Castle. The loss is irreversible, despite the magnificent rebuilding and restoration.

Man's intervention can be equally destructive. Wars, greedy property development, demolition, vandalism, and neglect have been the cause of losing more historic buildings than many earthquakes and hurricanes put together. The problem is vast and it has been the subject of continuous international concern for a long time.

Here, we can only attempt to identify some of the general issues and establish guidelines for the protection of historic buildings from the threat of natural and man-made disasters.

General issues

Vulnerability

Many historic buildings that have survived natural and man-made calamities over the years, are considered 'safe' simply because they are still there. To a certain extent, this is supported by the fact that local vernacular and craftsmanship have adapted over the years to meet the specific local conditions (wind, rain, snow, earthquake, etc.) as efficiently as possible. However, a number of aspects should be considered:

- Old buildings become weakened by each experience and if not protected they eventually collapse.
- Similarly, if conditions change, for example, water tables have moved, trees have been cut, surrounding areas built on, the reaction of the ground and of the old structure will differ.
- Some of these buildings are converted and 'modernized' in ways which can weaken or alter their structural equilibrium or introduce new dangers (electrical faults, gas explosions, etc.).
- Change of use can also alter the dead weight of the building (furniture, office equipment, etc.) which will alter the building's reaction to stresses such as earthquake.
- Some building materials suffer irreversible morphological changes in time and this will alter the way in which the structure responds to strain.

Specific type of damage

Old buildings are subjected to the same stresses as new ones, but they can react differently not only because of their age but also because of the way they have been constructed. Areas of particular concern are highlighted below.

Earthquake damage

Vibration damage – some old buildings are not securely fastened to the ground or the structural frame and can be literally be shaken to pieces, pulled off the ground, or slide off their foundations.

Foundation failure – result this may in partial or total collapse due to ground displacements, or liquefaction will affect those old buildings whose original foundations have been eroded or become inadequate due to changing circumstances.

Failure of non-reinforced masonry – this happens because of poor resistance to side to side motions. This usually occurs as a result of insufficient connections between floors and roofs, floors, and walls which causes walls to deflect and collapse. The lack of steel or other reinforcement in the walls causes them to crack diagonally and buckle. Old lime mortar which has lost its bonding strength can also contribute to failure.

Failure due to an irregular shape – old buildings often have asymmetrical plan shapes as a result of diverse transformations and additions that took place over the years. This induces different inertia loads, which can have catastrophic effects in an earthquake.

Storm, hurricane, tornado damage

Roof damage – this is a common occurrence when old buildings are hit by strong winds. Depending on the strength of the storm, the suction effect can range from roof tiles being stripped off to an entire roof being lifted. This is usually the result of poor maintenance and weak ties to the structure.

The effect of pressure – the difference between a sudden drop in outside pressure and the higher one inside, can cause the higher pressure inside to effectively 'explode' the building, with spectacular effects, especially if the building is of light timber frame and boarding construction.

Flood damage

Water, mud and dampness – these will cause irreversible damage to historic objects and property located below flood lines. Floods and burst pipes being somewhat more predictable than other phenomena such as earthquakes or hurricanes, sensible storage and preventive organization can make all the difference.

Mechanical damage – this will be caused by sudden bursts of water hitting all in its path. This will easily shatter old structures and can dislodge and carry away whole parts of buildings as well as any projecting decorative features.

Objects and substances carried by the water – these may also cause damage. Debris, spilled heating oil, or chemicals can destroy vulnerable historic objects such as manuscripts, fabric, watercolours, etc.

Salt damage – seawater brought by wind surges and high tides pose the added problem of *salt damage* to the building fabric and the danger of permanent dampness.

Fire damage

Historic buildings frequently contain added fire risks such as:

Combustible materials – the structural elements are often constructed of highly combustible materials. Old, dry timber frames and staircases burn easily and much of the irreplaceable contents catch fire rapidly. Floor wax polish or wall fabrics enable flames to spread almost instantaneously. The Windsor Castle fire was started by a heated light placed too close to curtains.

Antiquated services and fittings – factors such as electrical wiring, cooking ranges or heating appliances, open fires, and unswept chimneys, all add to the fire danger.

Lack of fire compartmentation – in old buildings, the lack of fire compartmentation facilitates the rapid spread of fires from one room to the rest of the building.

Neglect, vandalism, and theft

Man's indifference and abuse of historic buildings closely rivals natural disasters in numbers lost. The process is gradual and therefore, its extent is more difficult to detect. Lack of maintenance and funds, delays or failure by authorities and owners to intervene in time allow degradation to escalate. Neglected buildings are vulnerable to break in by 'architectural salvage' operators. First to go are the lead roofing, decorative fittings, fire surrounds, ironmongery, then panelling, doors, windows, etc. Once the rainwater can make its way in, the whole fabric becomes damp, mortar disintegrates, frost dislodges masonry, and progressive collapse sets in.

Homeless people may take shelter overnight, light a fire which spreads to the roof and floor timbers and what was a historic place becomes a ruin.

The Eltham Orangery case study below, illustrates an all too common example of how such a process can lead to near loss of a unique building, giving an idea of the high cost and painstaking effort involved in restoring such a building, all of which could have been avoided with reasonable preventive maintenance and monitoring.

Vandalism and neglect

Case study – Eltham Orangery (Contributors: Rena Pitsilli-Graham, Caroe & Partners, and Freeman Historic Properties)
History and description of the building

The Eltham Orangery is an early seventeenth century structure that was originally part of Eltham House. It is believed that the Orangery was built by Colonel Petit, who after a distinguished army career, retired to Eltham. The house was situated on what is now Eltham High Street, in the London Borough of Greenwich. The Orangery was built against the rear garden wall facing south. The early seventeenth century was a period of horticultural interest and experimentation and there is evidence to suggest that Colonel Petit and his circle were keen followers of developments in this field.

The Orangery may be the work of the architect John James, architect to St. George's Church, Hanover Square, where similarities with the Orangery can be seen in the architectural details. John James is also reported to have taken a keen interest in horticulture and garden design, and to have translated French gardening books.

The Orangery is a handsome building with impressive architectural features (see Fig. 9.1); The main South elevation is faced with fine-gauged brickwork, with Portland stone dressings, which bear military decorations, evidence of Colonel Petit's career. The rear elevation, which formed the original garden boundary wall and the flank walls, are constructed with ordinary stock brickwork (see Fig. 9.2).

Case history

The building has lain derelict since the house was demolished. There are reports that it lost its parapets early on, with oral history suggesting that

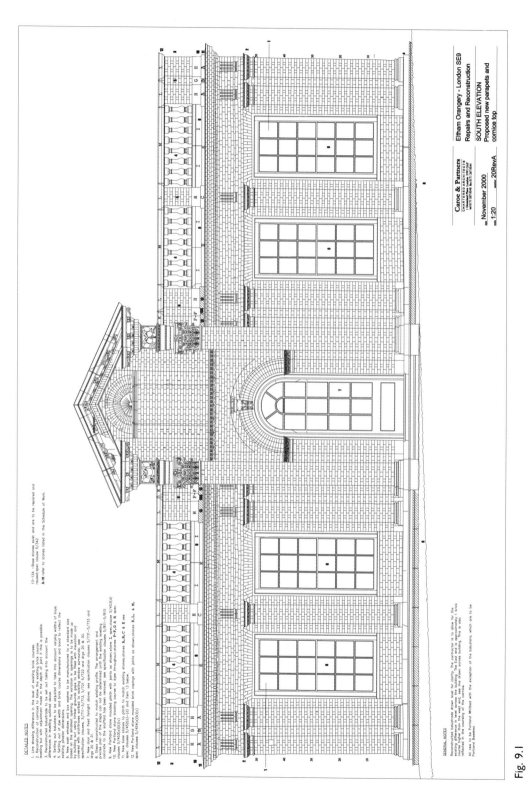

Fig. 9.1
Eltham Orangery – South elevation. © Caroe & Partners.

Fig. 9.2
Eltham Orangery – before
restoration. © English Heritage.

they were taken down for use in someone's garden. In the 1970s, it was
taken over by the local authority, the London Borough of Greenwich and
there have been several unsuccessful attempts to find a use for it. The
building is listed grade II*.

Over the recent years, it has suffered from mindless vandalism and
neglect, with increasing intensity. A fire set inside the building in 1978,
by vandals burned the roof down and charred the windows (later replace-
ments) but also the original, carefully detailed panelling on the reveals on

the central doorway. A prospective developer was allowed by the authorities administering the listed building control legislation to take up the stone floor of the Orangery, on the basis of investigations into the footings of the building; a completely unnecessary and destructive operation as trial holes in limited areas would have been sufficient for the purpose. In this case, ignorance and lack of understanding of the value of the historic fabric, contributed to the erosion of the integrity of the building.

During its ownership of the building, the local authority has been reluctant to expend any money on securing or repairing the building, the only exception being the introduction of a scaffold supporting a temporary roof, to protect the building after the fire. Without the restraint afforded by the roof timbers, the walls of the building were now in danger of spreading, outwards. The scaffold provided a brace for the rear and front walls and allowed protective polythene sheeting to be wrapped around the building (see Fig. 9.3). A timber hoarding was also erected around the site but this proved ineffective against intruders.

In 1995, encouraged by English Heritage, Freeman Historic Properties expressed an interest in acquiring the building, undertaking its repair with a view to finding a use for the building. Caroe & Partners were appointed by Freeman Historic Properties to survey the building, prepare a schedule of work for its repair and produce drawings for extending the building. Planning permission was given in early 2000 for small extensions on either side of the building and for office use. An estimate of cost for the repair of the building, excluding the cost of the extension was prepared and English Heritage offered a grant of 93.75%. Negotiations for the transfer of the building to Freeman Historic

Fig. 9.3
Eltham Orangery – scaffold.
© Rena Pitsilli-Graham.

Properties proved lengthy and the building remained in the local authority ownership until the middle of summer 2000.

Vandalism by local youths and vagrants seeking refuge inside the building, under the shelter of the temporary roof continued. The thin brickwork walls below the windowsills were kicked in, after Caroe & Partners had initially surveyed the building in 1996. Major damage was caused by the collapse of the West flank wall possibly a year or so after the demolition of the window aprons. This wall was weakened by decayed horizontal bonding timbers above the original door opening. The absence of header bricks between the facing and core brickwork of this wall and the lack of ties to the rear and front walls made the wall very vulnerable to collapse. The cause was thoughtless, malicious damage, and at the same time, there was deliberate disturbance to the remaining base stones of the balustrade, that still remained on top of the walls.

The main damage to the West wall was discovered during a visit to site by the architect, in the early summer of 2000. A structural engineer's advice was sought immediately. The local authority officers responsible for the building were reminded that demolition under a dangerous structure notice should not be contemplated without listed building approval. Freeman Historic Properties undertook the emergency propping of the partly collapsed West wall. Further security measures were undertaken with the introduction of corrugated iron sheeting screwed to the outside scaffold and barbed wire nailed on top, in an effort to stop all unauthorized access inside the building (see Fig. 9.3). These security measures proved to be effective.

A specification and drawings were prepared for the repair of the building and tenders were sought in the spring of 2001. The lowest tender was considerably higher than anticipated and there followed a period of uncertainly, while English Heritage applied to the Department of Media Culture and Sport for the increase in funds required for the project to proceed. In the interim, Caroe & Partners urged English Heritage to consider emergency repairs to reinstate the collapsed part of the West wall. This would have reinstated the stability of the building and enabled it to better withstand any possible further delays, should funding not be forthcoming.

Instructions were issued to the appointed contractor for the rebuilding of the West elevation, on the basis of an emergency grant. Through pure human error, the mason on site took down the remaining part of the West elevation still adjoining the rear wall, approximately 30% of the overall area of the wall. Although the incident was traumatic for everyone in the team working for the rescue of the building, including the mason himself, it is not certain that it would have been possible to save this section of brickwork. As illustrated above, it was poorly constructed and not tied to the rear wall.

Fig. 9.4
Eltham Orangery – new brickwork.
© Rena Pitsilli-Graham.

Fig. 9.5
Eltham Orangery – section showing
repairs and reconstruction details.
© Rena Pitsilli-Graham.

Shortly after instructions for emergency works were issued, approval was given for an increase in the state funding of the project. A contract was placed with the contractor for undertaking the entire project in September 2001. Delays in the mobilization of the contractor and further delays in the supply of hand-made bricks resulted in the first bricks beginning to be laid in February 2002 (see Figs 9.4 and 9.5). Work is currently continuing and the West elevation is well on the way to being rebuilt, using original bricks salvaged from the demolition and new hand-made bricks to match.

A new slated roof with lead parapet gutters will be built (see Fig. 9.6). Photographs of the burned out roof, showing the charred timbers still in position, and the rafter sockets still evident on the inside face of the South wall were used to produce the drawings for the new roof. The sash windows will be reinstated to details historically correct for the date of the building and the new central doorway and reveal panelling will be remade using the evidence of the damaged timbers on site. The gauged brickwork of the front elevation is being carefully repaired including the rebuilding of the cornices using existing sound bricks and new moulded bricks to match (Figs 9.4 and 9.5).

The central niche, below the pediment will be carefully repaired by conservators, who will also clean the stone carvings (see Figs 9.7 and 9.8). A new, Portland stone, bottle balustrade has been designed based on the evidence of the base stones that had survived. The moulded stone steps to the front of the building will be uncovered when the scaffold is struck and completed where damaged or missing. The octagon and square pattern stone floor has now been transferred from the local authority's warehouse to site; sound and partially damaged stones will be reinstated, inside the building. If funds permit new stones will be cut to complete the floor. Completion of the works is due at the end of August 2002.

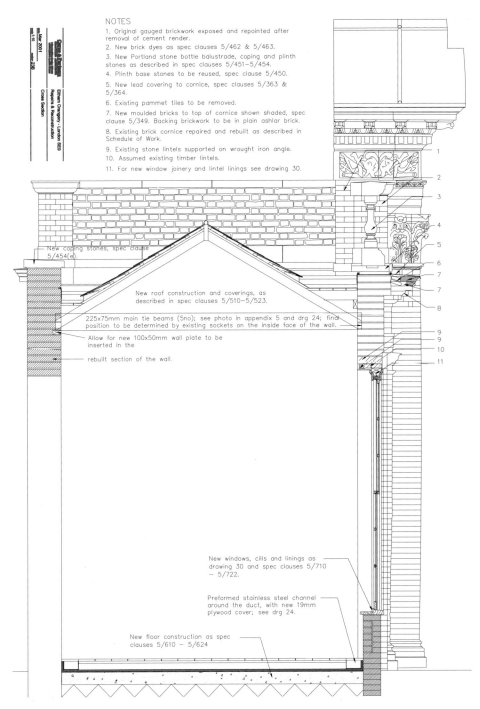

NOTES

1. Original gauged brickwork exposed and repointed after removal of cement render.
2. New brick dyes as spec clauses 5/462 & 5/463.
3. New Portland stone bottle balustrade, coping and plinth stones as described in spec clauses 5/451–5/454.
4. Plinth base stones to be reused, spec clause 5/450.
5. New lead covering to cornice, spec clauses 5/363 & 5/364.
6. Existing pammet tiles to be removed.
7. New moulded bricks to top of cornice shown shaded, spec clause 5/349. Backing brickwork to be in plain ashlar brick.
8. Existing brick cornice repaired and rebuilt as described in Schedule of Work.
9. Existing stone lintels supported on wrought iron angle.
10. Assumed existing timber lintels.
11. For new window joinery and lintel linings see drawing 30.

New coping stones, spec clause 5/454(e).

New roof construction and coverings, as described in spec clauses 5/510–5/523.

225x75mm main tie beams (5no); see photo in appendix 5 and drg 24; final position to be determined by existing sockets on the inside face of the wall.

Allow for new 100x50mm wall plate to be inserted in the

rebuilt section of the wall.

New windows, cills and linings as drawing 30 and spec clauses 5/710 – 5/722.

Preformed stainless steel channel around the duct, with new 19mm plywood cover; see drg 24.

New floor construction as spec clauses 5/610 – 5/624

Fig. 9.6
Eltham Orangery – section showing repairs and reconstruction details. © Caroe & Partners.

Fig. 9.7
Eltham Orangery – new brickwork
corner detail. © Rena Pitsilli-Graham.

Fig. 9.8
Eltham Orangery – deatil of Central
Pediment looking West © Rena
Pitsilli-Graham.

Development demolition

Case study – 'THE HOUSE OF THE PEOPLE', Bucharest, Romania

Occasionally, we come across destruction of epic proportion such as the one in Bucharest, Romania where one of the city's oldest areas, representing approximately one-sixth of the city (see Fig. 9.9) was raised to the ground to make way for the Civic Centre development which includes amongst others the 'Casa Poporului' (People's House) and a kilometre long boulevard of the 'Victory of Socialism' (see Fig. 9.10).

Seventy thousand people were forced out of their homes, 26 churches and two synagogues were bulldozed and the Vacaresti Monastery, built on the South bank of the river Dimbovitza in 1718 was completely destroyed. Its thick walls were so difficult to demolish that controlled explosion techniques had to be employed to remove it. The neighbouring sixteenth Prince Mihai Monastery was moved 279 m east, to a small wasteland area, between high-rise block of flats.

Ceausescu, the deposed Romanian leader initiated the development in the early 1980s, in the aftermath of a powerful earthquake, which caused extensive damage in Bucharest in March 1977.

Fig. 9.9
Bucharest, demolished old district.

The site for the gargantuan 'Casa Poporului', which has the largest footprint in the world after the Pentagon, was chosen because the district's elevated location is reputed to have anti-seismic properties, supported by the fact that it had escaped relatively unscathed from two major earthquakes in the last century.

The structural engineer's brief was to ensure that the building survives future earthquakes for at least the next 500 years! (see Vrancea case study, Chapter 2).

Having escaped sustained bombing during the Second World War, this largely residential district, unique in its character with a blend of traditional features and oriental influence, has been replaced by overbearing, characterless blocks of flats, which sadly abound in this country (Fig. 9.11).

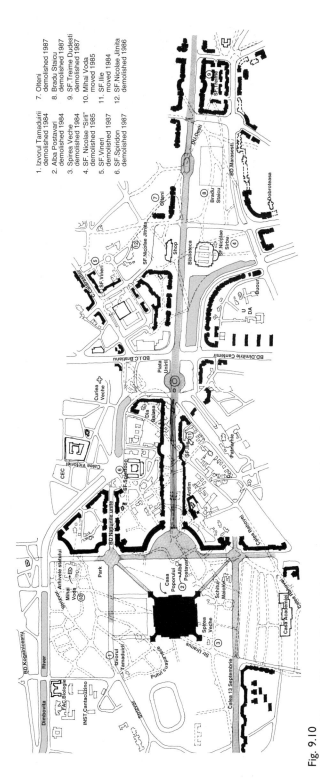

Fig. 9.10
Bucharest, Victory of Socialism Boulevard plan superimposed on the old town plan.

Fig. 9.11
Victory of Socialism Boulevard.

Historic buildings protection in disaster conditions

Preparedness

Lessons learned from past natural disaster's effect on historic buildings should form the basis for general recommendations.

- If well maintained, historic structures and their surroundings have more chance of survival. A regular programme of repairs and monitoring of the fabric condition will make it possible to save and preserve old buildings. It has been shown that of the historic buildings lost, those already in poor condition before the disaster outnumber those in good repair, which survived with comparatively little damage.
- Availability of a written action plan when a disaster strikes, setting priority tasks specific to the historic building in question, will be invaluable in preventing the occurrence of irreversible damage and loss. It will also provide valuable guidance for the 'first on the scene' interventions and building and engineering teams, inexperienced with the historic aspects.
- Availability of measured surveys, records, photographs, and inventories are essential for loss assessment, repairs, and restoration. A network of public and private sources of information regarding the monument and its contents must be identified to guide funding of repairs and insurance claims.
- Strengthening (retrofitting) of old buildings reduces their vulnerability to specific hazards identified for their location. This can include:

  - underpinning foundations;
  - improving the quality of tying the roof and floor structures and to walls;
  - fireproofing and strapping together structural timbers;

– strapping timber frames to foundations;
– adding expanded metal reinforcement to traditional timber panels;
– reinforcing masonry by drilling and grouting reinforcement steel;
– thickening walls.

Mitigation

• *Immediate intervention*: in a disaster situation there is shock, panic, and confusion. First priority is given to saving lives and general emergency action will be concerned with putting out fires, evacuating people to safety, and preventing looting. In these conditions, looting and indiscriminate demolition are the biggest threats to historic buildings and their contents. The military, volunteers, and disaster relief agencies will need guidance to ensure they can be effective in protecting cultural property.

• *Emergency inspections* must be made; dangerous sections made safe and damage assessed. Specialist expertise will be necessary to diagnose historic structures and identify specific problems and solutions. When surveying the condition of buildings, a system of colour coding of the damage extent is widely recognized and employed:

green = usable grades 1, 2, and 3: superficial damage from almost intact to light structural;

yellow = temporarily unusable grades 1 and 2: structural damage from components to load-bearing walls;

red = Unusable grades 1, 2 and 3: severe structural damage, partial or total collapse.

• Emergency protection: it is important that this is provided as soon as possible and of as good a quality as possible, as it may be some time before repair work can start. Valuable property must be labelled and stored at a previously designated safe location. A conservation architect should be consulted to avoid unnecessary demolition as specialists available could be reluctant to take responsibility for keeping a partially collapse building. There are a number of international volunteer organizations such as *Architectes sans Frontières* or *Architectes de L'Urgence* in France who aim to provide immediate help in disaster conditions.

Management

• Legislation and the implementation of comprehensive systems for the prevention and mitigation of future disasters would be principal concerns. The following aspects are:
– raising public awareness;
– introducing building control standards adapted to enable old buildings to cope with specific disaster threats;
– providing the means to enable cooperation and coordination of the different 'first at the scene' intervention teams.

• Ensuring that appropriate skills and materials are available before commencing repairs is an important consideration before embarking on repairs

- Instituting financial incentives and funding aimed specifically at covering the additional costs involved in pre-disaster consolidating of historic buildings or post-disaster repairs
- Incorporating historic buildings considerations in local and national emergency procedures.

Appendices

Emergency action checklists and fact sheets

Earthquake emergency checklist
(*Source*: FEMA fact sheet)

1. *Find out if your property is at risk from earthquake.* Check with your local building official, city engineer, or planning department. They can tell you whether you are in an earthquake hazard area and give you further advice about how to protect yourself and your house and property from earthquakes.
2. *Take steps to provide the necessary protection.* Earthquake protection can involve a variety of changes to your house and property varying in complexity and cost.
    (a) Large-scale structural alterations or consolidation work, which must be carried out only by a specialist building contractor under the supervision of a professional such as a structural engineer or architect.
    (b) Small-scale measures to improve safety such as:
    - secure tall and heavy furniture such as bookcases to the walls to prevent them topple over;
    - distribute heavy or dangerous substances at lower levels in fastened cupboards;
    - secure water heaters, gas and oil containers;
    - keep gas pipes and electrical wiring in good repair as they are a potential source of fire.
3. *Establish safety procedure.*
    (a) Identify safe places inside your building and outdoors:
    - inside the building: under sturdy furniture, away from where glass could shatter, against an inside wall doorframe;
    - outside: away from buildings, trees, overhead roads, and cables.
    (b) Work out a basic family action plan:
    - make sure everybody knows how to call emergency services, switch off gas, electricity, etc.;
    - have disaster kit prepared (torch, first-aid kit, emergency food and water, dust mask, battery radio, etc.);
    - work out how to communicate if event happens while the family dispersed at work, school, etc.;
    - have a 'contact' (friend, relative) in a safer area to call for news and keep in touch.

4. *What to do during an earthquake*
    (a) *Inside*: take cover under a sturdy piece of furniture such as a heavy desk or against an inside wall and avoid leaving the building during the shaking when the danger of heavy objects or masonry falling on you is high.
    (b) *Outside*: move away from buildings, overhead structures, cables, etc. and stay in the open until the shaking stops.

5. *What to do after an earthquake*
    (a) Beware of aftershocks, secondary tremors, which may bring weakened structures down; they can occur soon after the earthquake, but also days or even months later, so avoid damaged buildings.
    (b) Help people in need or injured, but do not move those seriously injured, call for help.
    (c) Listen for emergency information to find out when it safe to return home.

Flood emergency checklist (Fact sheet: Floods and flash floods; *Source*: http://www.fema.gov/library/floodf.htm)

Mitigation pays. It includes any activity that prevents an emergency, reduces the chance of an emergency happening, or lessens the damaging effects of unavoidable emergencies. Investing in mitigation steps now, such as constructing barriers such as levees and purchasing flood insurance will help reduce the amount of structural damage to your home and financial loss from building and crop damage should a flood or flash flood occur.

Before

1. Find out if you live in a flood-prone area from your local emergency management office or Red Cross chapter.
2. Ask whether your property is above or below the flood stage water level and learn about the history of flooding for your region.
3. Learn flood-warning signs and your community alerts signals.
4. Request information on preparing for floods and flash floods.
5. If you live in a frequently flooded area, stockpile emergency building materials.
6. These include plywood, plastic sheeting, lumber nails, hammer and saw, pry bar, shovels, and sandbags.
7. Have check valves installed in building sewer traps to prevent floodwaters from backing up in sewer drains. As a last resort, use large corks or stoppers to plug showers, tubs, or basins.
8. Plan and practise an evacuation route.
9. Contact the local emergency management office or local American Red Cross chapter for a copy of the community flood evacuation plan. This plan should include information on the safest routes to shelters. Individuals living in flash flood areas should have several alternative routes.
10. Have disaster supplies on hand.
    - flashlights and extra batteries;
    - portable, battery-operated radio and extra batteries;
    - first-aid kit and manual;
    - emergency food and water;
    - non-electric can opener;
    - essential medicines;
    - cash and credit cards;
    - sturdy shoes.
11. Develop an emergency communication plan.
12. In case family members are separated from one another during floods or flash floods (a real possibility during the day when adults are at work and children are at school), have a plan for getting back together.
13. Ask an out-of-state relative or friend to serve as the 'family contact'. After a disaster, it is often easier to call long distance. Make sure everyone in the family knows the name, address, and phone number of the contact person.

14. Make sure that all family members know how to respond after a flood or flash flood.
15. Teach all family members how and when to turn off gas, electricity, and water.
16. Teach children how and when to call 9-1-1, police, fire department, and which radio station to tune to for emergency information.
17. Learn about the National Flood Insurance Program.
18. Ask your insurance agent about flood insurance. Homeowners' policies do not cover flood damage.

During a flood watch

- Listen to a batter-operated radio for the latest storm information.
- Fill bathtubs, sinks, and jugs with clean water in case water becomes contaminated.
- Bring outdoor belongings, such as patio furniture, indoors.
- Move valuable household possessions to the upper floors or to safe ground if time permits.
- If you are instructed to do so by local authorities, turn off all utilities at the main switch and close the main gas valve.
- Be prepared to evacuate.

During a flood

1. If indoors:
   - Turn on battery-operated radio or television to get the latest emergency information.
   - Get your pre-assembled emergency supplies.
   - If told to leave, do so immediately.
2. If outdoors:
   - Climb to high ground and stay there.
   - Avoid walking through any floodwaters. If it is moving swiftly, even water 6 inches deep can sweep you off your feet.
3. If in a car:
   - If you come to a flooded area, turn around and go another way.
   - If your car stalls, abandon it immediately and climb to higher ground. Many deaths have resulted from attempts to move stalled vehicles.

During an evacuation

- If advised to evacuate, do so immediately.
- Evacuation is much simpler and safer before floodwaters become too deep for ordinary vehicles to drive through.
- Listen to a battery-operated radio for evacuation instructions.
- Follow recommended evacuation routes – shortcuts may be blocked.
- Leave early enough to avoid being marooned by flooded roads.

After

1. Flood dangers do not end when the water begins to recede. Listen to a radio or television and do not return home until authorities indicate it is safe to do so.

2. Remember to help your neighbours who may require special assistance – infants, elderly people, and people with disabilities.
3. Inspect foundations for cracks or other damage.
4. Stay out of buildings if floodwaters remain around the building.
5. When entering buildings, use extreme caution.
   - Wear sturdy shoes and use battery-powered lanterns or flashlights when examining buildings.
   - Examine walls, floors, doors, and windows to make sure that the building is not in danger of collapsing.
   - Watch out for animals, especially poisonous snakes that may have come into your home with the floodwaters. Use a stick to poke through debris.
   - Watch for loose plaster and ceilings that could fall.
   - Take pictures of the damage – both to the house and to its contents – for insurance claims.
6. Look for fire hazards.
   - Broken or leaking gas lines.
   - Flooded electrical circuits.
   - Submerged furnaces or electrical appliances.
   - Flammable or explosive materials coming from upstream.
7. Throw away food – including canned goods – that has come in contact with floodwaters.
8. Pump out flooded basements gradually (about one-third of the water per day) to avoid structural damage.
9. Service damaged septic tanks, cesspools, pits, and leaching systems as soon as possible. Damaged sewage systems are health hazards.

Inspecting utilities in a damaged home
1. Check for gas leaks – if you smell gas or hear blowing or hissing noise, open a window and quickly leave the building. Turn off the gas at the outside main valve if you can and call the gas company from a neighbour's home. If you turn off the gas for any reason, it must be turned back on by a professional.
2. Look for electrical system damage – if you see sparks or broken or frayed wires, or if you smell hot insulation, turn off the electricity at the main fuse box or circuit breaker. If you have to step in water to get to the fuse box or circuit breaker, call an electrician for advice.
3. Check for sewage and water lines damage – if you suspect sewage lines are damaged avoid using the toilets and call a plumber. If water pipes are damaged, contact the water company and avoid the water from the tap. You can obtain safe water by melting ice cubes.

Fact sheet: hurricanes and tornadoes (*Source:* http://www.fema.gov/library/hurricaf.htm)

Hurricanes can be dangerous killers. Learning the hurricane warning messages and planning ahead can reduce the chances of injury or major property damage.

Before
1. Plan an evacuation route.
2. Contact the local emergency management office or American Red Cross chapter, and ask for the community hurricane preparedness plan. This plan should include information on the safest evacuation routes and nearby shelters.
3. Learn safe routes inland.
4. Be ready to drive 20–50 miles inland to locate a safe place.
5. Have disaster supplies on hand.
   - flashlight and extra batteries;
   - portable, battery-operated radio and extra batteries;
   - first-aid kit and manual;
   - emergency food and water;
   - non-electric can opener;
   - essential medicines;
   - cash and credit cards;
   - sturdy shoes.
6. Make arrangements for pets. Pets may not be allowed into emergency shelters for health and space reasons. Contact your local humane society for information on local animal shelters.
7. Make sure that all family members know how to respond after a hurricane.
8. Teach family members how and when to turn off gas, electricity, and water.
9. Teach children how and when to call 9-1-1, police, or fire department and which radio station to tune to for emergency information.
10. Protect your windows. Permanent shutters are the best protection. A lower-cost approach is to put up plywood panels. Use 0.5 in. plywood – marine plywood is best – cut to fit each window. Remember to mark which board fits which window. Pre-drill holes every 18 in. for screws. Do this long before the storm.
11. Trim back dead or weak branches from trees.
12. Check into flood insurance. You can find out about the National Flood Insurance Program through your local insurance agent or emergency management office. There is normally a 30-day waiting period before a new policy becomes effective. Homeowners polices do not cover damage from the flooding that accompanies a hurricane.
13. Develop an emergency communication plan.
14. In case family members are separated from one another during a disaster (a real possibility during the day when adults are at work and children are at school), have a plan for getting back together.

15. Ask an out-of-state relative or friend to serve as the 'family contact'. After a disaster, it is often easier to call long distance. Make sure everyone in the family knows the name, address, and phone number of the contact person.

Hurricane watches and warnings

A hurricane watch is issued when there is a threat of hurricane conditions within 24–36 h. A hurricane warning is issued when hurricane conditions (winds of 74 mph or greater or dangerously high water and rough seas) are expected in 24 h or less.

During a hurricane watch

- Listen to a battery-operated radio or television for hurricane progress reports.
- Check emergency supplies.
- Fuel car.
- Bring in outdoor objects such as lawn furniture, toys, and garden tools and anchor objects that cannot be brought inside.
- Secure buildings by closing and boarding up windows. Remove outside antennas.
- Turn refrigerator and freezer to coldest settings. Open only when absolutely necessary and close quickly.
- Store drinking water in clean bathtubs, jugs, bottles, and cooking utensils.
- Review evacuation plan.
- Moor boats securely or move them to a designated safe place. Use ropes or chain to secure boat to trailer. Use tiedowns to anchor trailer to the ground or house.

During a hurricane warning

- Listen constantly to a battery-operated radio or television for official instructions.
- If in a mobile home, check tiedowns and evacuate immediately.
- Store valuables and personal papers in a waterproof container on the highest level of your home.
- Avoid elevators.

If at home:

- Stay inside, away from windows, skylights, and glass doors.
- Keep a supply of flashlights and extra batteries handy. Avoid open flames, such as candles and kerosene lamps, as a source of light.
- If power is lost, turn off major appliances to reduce power 'surge' when electricity is restored.

If officials indicate evacuation is necessary:

- Leave as soon as possible. Avoid flooded roads and watch for washed-out bridges.

- Secure your home by unplugging appliances and turning off electricity and the main water valve.
- Tell someone outside of the storm area where you are going.
- If time permits, and you live in an identified surge zone, elevate furniture to protect it from flooding or better yet, move it to a higher floor.
- Bring pre-assembled emergency supplies and warm protective clothing.
- Take blankets and sleeping bags to shelter.
- Lock up home and leave.

After

1. Stay tuned to local radio for information.
2. Help injured or trapped persons.
   - Give first aid where appropriate.
   - Do not move seriously injured persons unless they are in immediate danger of further injury. Call for help.
3. Return home only after authorities advise that it is safe to do so.
   - Avoid loose or dangling power lines and report them immediately to the power company, police, or fire department.
   - Enter your home with caution.
   - Beware of snakes, insects, and animals driven to higher ground by floodwater.
   - Open windows and doors to ventilate and dry your home.
   - Check refrigerated foods for spoilage.
   - Take pictures of the damage – both to the house and to its contents – for insurance claims.
4. Drive only if absolutely necessary and avoid flooded roads and washed-out bridges.
5. Use telephone only for emergency calls.

Tornado watches and warnings

When a tornado is coming, you have only a short amount of time to make life-or-death decisions. Advance planning and quick response are the keys to surviving a tornado. A *tornado watch* is issued by the National Weather Service when tornadoes are possible in your area. Remain alert for approaching storms. This is the time to remind family members where the safest places within your home are located, and listen to the radio or television for further developments. A *tornado warning* is issued when a tornado has been sighted or indicated by weather radar.

Mobile homes

Mobile homes are particularly vulnerable. A mobile home can overturn very easily even if precautions have been taken to tie down the unit. When a tornado warning is issued, take shelter in a building with a strong foundation. If shelter is not available, lie in ditch or low-lying area a safe distance away from the unit.

Tornado danger signs

Learn these tornado danger signs:

- An approaching cloud of debris can mark the location of a tornado even if a funnel is not visible.
- Before a tornado hits, the wind may die down and the air may become very still.
- Tornadoes generally occur near the trailing edge of a thunderstorm. It is not uncommon to see clear, sunlit skies behind a tornado.

During

1. If at home:
   - Go at once to a windowless, interior room; storm cellar; basement; or lowest level of the building.
   - If there is no basement, go to an inner hallway or a smaller inner room without windows, such as a bathroom or closet.
   - Get away from the windows.
   - Go to the centre of the room. Stay away from corners because they tend to attract debris.
   - Get under a piece of sturdy furniture such as a workbench or heavy table or desk and hold on to it.
   - Use arms to protect head and neck.
   - If in a mobile home, get out and find shelter elsewhere.
2. If at work or school:
   - Go to the basement or to an inside hallway at the lowest level.
   - Avoid places with wide-span roofs such as auditoriums, cafeterias, large hallways, or shopping malls.
   - Get under a piece of sturdy furniture such as a workbench or heavy table or desk and hold on to it.
   - Use arms to protect head and neck.
3. If outdoors:
   - If possible, get inside a building.
   - If shelter is not available or there is no time to get indoors, lie in a ditch or low-lying area or crouch near a strong building. Be aware of the potential for flooding.
   - Use arms to protect head and neck.
4. If in a car:
   - Never try to out drive a tornado in a car or truck. Tornadoes can change direction quickly and can lift up a car or truck and toss it through the air.
   - Get out of the car immediately and take shelter in a nearby building.
   - If there is no time to get indoors, get out of the car and lie in a ditch or low-lying area away from the vehicle. Be aware of the potential for flooding.

After

- Help injured or trapped persons.
- Give first aid when appropriate.

- Do not try to move the seriously injured unless they are in immediate danger of further injury.
- Call for help.
- Turn on radio or television to get the latest emergency information.
- Stay out of damaged buildings. Return home only when authorities say it is safe.
- Use the telephone only for emergency calls.
- Clean up spilled medicines, bleaches, or gasoline or other flammable liquids immediately. Leave the buildings if you smell gas or chemical fumes.
- Take pictures of the damage – both to the house and to its contents – for insurance purposes.
- Remember to help your neighbours who may require special assistance – infants, the elderly, and people with disabilities.

Fujita – Pearson Tornado Scale

F-0: 40–72 mph, chimney damage, tree branches broken.

F-1: 73–112 mph, mobile homes pushed off foundation or overturned.

F-2: 113–157 mph, considerable damage, mobile homes demolished, trees uprooted.

F-3: 158–205 mph, roofs and walls torn down, trains overturned, cars thrown.

F-4: 207–260 mph, well-constructed walls levelled.

F-5: 261–318 mph, homes lifted off foundation and carried considerable distances, autos thrown as far as 100 m.

Inspecting utilities in a damaged home

1. Check for gas leaks – if you smell gas or hear blowing or hissing noise, open a window and quickly leave the building. Turn off the gas at the outside main valve if you can and call the gas company from a neighbour's home. If you turn off the gas for any reason, it must be turned back on by a professional.
2. Look for electrical system damage – if you see sparks or broken or frayed wires, or if you smell hot insulation, turn off the electricity at the main fuse box or circuit breaker. If you have to step in water to get to the fuse box or circuit breaker, call an electrician first for advice.
3. Check for sewage and water lines damage – if you suspect sewage lines are damaged avoid using the toilets and call a plumber. If water pipes are damaged, contact the water company and avoid the water from the tap. You can obtain safe water by melting ice cubes.

Mitigation

Mitigation includes any activities that prevent an emergency, reduce the chance of an emergency happening, or lessen the damaging effects of unavoidable emergencies. Investing in preventive mitigation steps now such as strengthening non reinforced masonry to withstand wind and flooding and installing shutters on every window will help reduce the impact of hurricanes in the future.

Fact sheet: extreme heat (*Source*: FEMA)

Doing too much on a hot day, spending too much time in the sun or staying too long in an overheated place can cause heat-related illnesses. Know the symptoms of heat disorders and overexposure to the sun, and be ready to give first aid treatment.

Before

- Contact your local emergency management office or Red Cross for information on extreme heat.
- Install window air conditioners snugly.
- Close any floor heat registers nearby.
- Insulate spaces around air conditioners for a tighter fit.
- Use a circulating or box fan to spread the cool air.

Keep heat outside and cool air inside.

- Install temporary reflectors, such as aluminium foil covered cardboard, to reflect any heat back outside. Keep the cool air inside by weather-stripping doors and windowsills.
- Consider keeping storm windows up all year. Storm windows can keep the heat of a house in the summer the same way they keep the cold out in the winter.
- Check air-conditioning ducts for proper insulation.

During

- Protect windows. Hang shades, draperies, awnings, or louvers on windows that receive morning or afternoon sun. Outdoor awnings or louvers can reduce the heat entering the house by as much as 80%. Conserve electricity.
- During periods of extreme heat, people tend to use a lot more power for air conditioning, which can lead to a power shortage or outage. Stay indoors as much as possible. If air conditioning is not available, stay on the lowest floor out of the sunshine. Remember that electric fans do not cool, they just blow hot air around.
- Eat well-balanced, light meals.
- Drink plenty of water regularly. Persons who have epilepsy or heart, kidney, or liver disease; are on fluid-restrictive diets; or have a problem with fluid retention should consult a doctor before increasing liquid intake.
- Limit intake of alcoholic beverages. Although beer and alcohol beverages appear to satisfy thirst, they actually cause further body dehydration.
- Dress in loose-fitting clothes that cover as much skin as possible. Lightweight, light-coloured clothing that reflects heat and sunlight and helps maintain normal body temperature.
- Protect face and head by wearing a wide-brimmed hat.
- Allow your body to get acclimated to hot temperatures for the first 2 or 3 days of a heat wave.

- Avoid too much sunshine. Sunburn slows the skin's ability to cool itself. Use a sunscreen lotion with a high sun protection factor (SPF) rating.
- Avoid extreme temperature changes. A cool shower immediately after coming in from hot temperatures can result in hypothermia, particularly for elderly and very young people.
- Slow down. Reduce, eliminate, or reschedule strenuous activities. High-risk individuals should stay in cool places. Get plenty of rest to allow your natural 'cooling system' to work.
- Take salt tablets only if specified by your physician. Persons on salt-restrictive diets should check with a physician before increasing salt intake.
- Vacuum air conditioner filters weekly during periods of high use.
- Learn the symptoms of heat disorders and know how to give first aid.

During a drought
- Lower water use. Watering the lawn and washing the car waste water. Whenever possible, re-use water.
- Place a brick or other large, solid object in the flush tank of the toilet to reduce the water used to flush.
- Farmers should contact the county Farm Service Agency for disaster assistance information.

Heat disorders
Sunburn
Symptoms: skin redness and pain, possible swelling, blisters, fever, headaches.

First aid: take a shower, using soap, to remove oils that may block pores preventing the body from cooling naturally. If blisters occur, apply dry, sterile dressings and get medical attention.

Heat cramps
Symptoms: painful spasms usually in leg and abdominal muscles, heavy sweating.

First aid: firm pressure on cramping muscles or gentle massage to relieve spasm. Give sips of water. If nausea occurs, discontinue.

Heat exhaustion
Symptoms: heavy sweating, weakness, skin cold, pale and clammy, weak pulse, normal temperature, possible fainting, vomiting.

First aid: get victim to lie down in a cool place. Loosen clothing. Apply cool, wet cloths. Fan or move victim to air-conditioned place. Give sips of water. If nausea occurs, discontinue. If vomiting occurs, seek immediate medical attention.

Heat stroke (sun stroke)

Symptoms: high body temperature (106+), hot, dry skin, rapid, strong pulse, and possible unconsciousness. Victim will likely not sweat.

First aid: heat stroke is a severe medical emergency. Call 9-1-1 or emergency medical services or get the victim to a hospital immediately. Delay can be fatal. Move victim to a cooler environment. Try a cool bath or sponging to reduce body temperature. Use extreme caution. Remove clothing. Use fans and/or air conditioners. *Do not give fluids.*

Fact sheet: landslides and mudflows
(*Source*: http://www.fema.gov/library/landslif.htm)

Landslide and mudflows usually strike without warning. The force of rocks, soil, or other debris moving down a slope can devastate anything in its path. Take the following steps to be ready.

Before

1. Get a ground assessment of your property.
2. Your county geologist or county planning department may have specific information on areas vulnerable to landsliding. Consult a professional geo-technical expert for opinions and advice on land-slide problems and on corrective measures you can take.
3. Minimize home hazards:
   - Plant ground cover on slopes and build retaining walls.
   - In mudflow areas, build channels or deflection walls to direct the flow around buildings.
   - Remember: if you build walls to divert debris flow and the flow lands on a neighbour's property, you may be liable for damages.
4. Learn to recognize the landslide warning signs:
   - Doors or windows stick or jam for the first time.
   - New cracks appear in plaster, tile, brick, or foundations.
   - Outside walls, walks, or stairs begin pulling away from the building.
     - Slowly developing, widening cracks appear on the ground or on paved areas such as streets or driveways.
     - Underground utility lines break.
     - Bulging ground appears at the base of a slope.
     - Water breaks through the ground surface in new locations.
     - Fences, retaining walls, utility poles, or trees tilt or move.
     - You hear a faint rumbling sound that increases in volume as the landslide nears. The ground slopes downward in one specific direction and may begin shifting in that direction under your feet.
5. Make evacuation plans.
6. Plan at least two evacuation routes since roads may become blocked or closed.
7. Develop an emergency communication plan.
8. In case family members are separated from one another during a landslide or mudflow this is (a real possibility during the day when adults are at work and children are at school), have a plan for getting back together.
9. Ask an out-of-state relative or friend to serve as the 'family contact'. After a disaster, it is often easier to call long distance. Make sure everyone knows the name, address, and phone number of the contact person.
10. Insurance.

During

If inside a building:

- Stay inside.
- Take cover under a desk, table, or other piece of sturdy furniture.

If outdoors:

- Try and get out of the path of the landslide or mudflow.
- Run to the nearest high ground in a direction away from the path.
- If rocks and other debris are approaching, run for the nearest shelter such as a group of trees or a building.
- If escape is not possible, curl into a tight ball and protect your head.

Sinkholes

A sinkhole occurs when groundwater dissolves a vulnerable land surface such as limestone, causing the land surface to collapse from a lack of support. In June 1993, a 100-foot wide, 25-foot deep sinkhole formed under a hotel parking lot in Atlanta, killing two people and engulfing numerous cars.

After

1. Stay away from the slide area.
2. There may be danger of additional slides.
3. Check for injured and trapped persons near the slide area.
4. Give first aid if trained.
5. Remember to help your neighbours who may require special assistance – infants, elderly people, and people with disabilities.
6. Listen to a battery-operated radio or television for the latest emergency information.
7. Remember that flooding may occur after a mudflow or a landslide.
8. Check for damaged utility lines.
9. Report any damage to the utility company.
10. Check the building foundation, chimney, and surrounding land for damage.
11. Replant damaged ground as soon as possible since erosion caused by loss of ground cover can lead to flash flooding.
12. Seek the advice of geo-technical expert for evaluating land-slide hazards or designing corrective techniques to reduce landslide risk.

Mitigation

Mitigation includes any activities that prevent an emergency, reduce the chance of an emergency happening, or lessen the damaging effects of unavoidable emergencies. Investing in preventive mitigation steps now such as planting ground cover (low-growing plants) on slopes, or installing flexible pipe fitting to avoid gas or water leaks, will help reduce the impact of landslides and mudflows in the future. For more information on mitigation, contact your local emergency management office.

Fact sheet: terrorism (prepared by FEMA in the United States)

Before

Learn about the nature of terrorism.

- Terrorists look for visible targets where they can avoid detection before or after an attack such as international airports, large cities, major international events, resorts, and high-profile landmarks.

Learn about the different types of terrorist weapons including explosives, kidnappings, hijackings, arson, and shootings. Prepare to deal with a terrorist incident by adapting many of the same techniques used to prepare for other crises.

- Be alert and aware of the surrounding area. The very nature of terrorism suggests that there may be little or no warning.
- Take precautions when travelling. Be aware of conspicuous or unusual behaviour. Do not accept packages from strangers. Do not leave luggage unattended.
- Learn where emergency exits are located. Think ahead about how to evacuate a building, subway or congested public area in a hurry. Learn where staircases are located.
- Notice your immediate surroundings. Be aware of heavy or breakable objects that could move, fall or break in an explosion.

Preparing for a building explosion

The use of explosives by terrorists can result in collapsed buildings and fires. People who live or work in a multilevel building can do the following:

- Review emergency evacuation procedures. Know where fire exits are located.
- Keep fire extinguishers in working order. Know where they are located, and how to use them. Learn first aid. Contact the local chapter of the American Red Cross for additional information.
- Keep the following items in a designated place on each floor of the building:
  - portable, battery-operated radio and extra batteries;
  - several flashlights and extra batteries;
  - first-aid kit and manual;
  - several hard hats;
  - fluorescent tape to rope off dangerous areas.

Bomb threats

If you receive a bomb threat, get as much information from the caller as possible. Keep the caller on the line and record everything that is said. Notify the police and the building management. After you have been notified of a bomb threat, do not touch any suspicious packages. Clear the area around the suspicious package and notify the police immediately.

In evacuating a building, avoid standing in front of windows or other potentially hazardous areas. Do not restrict sidewalk or streets to be used by emergency officials.

During
1. In a building explosion, get out of the building as quickly and calmly as possible.
2. If items are falling off of bookshelves or from the ceiling, get under a sturdy table or desk.
3. If there is a fire:
   - Stay low to the floor and exit the building as quickly as possible.
   - Cover nose and mouth with a wet cloth.
   - When approaching a closed door, use the palm of your hand and forearm to feel the lower, middle and upper parts of the door. If it is not hot, brace yourself against the door and open it slowly. If it is hot to the touch, do not open the door – seek an alternate escape route.
   - Heavy smoke and poisonous gases collect first along the ceiling. Stay below the smoke at all times.

After
If you are trapped in debris:

- Use a flashlight.
- Stay in your area so that you do not kick up dust. Cover your mouth with a handkerchief or clothing.
- Tap on a pipe or wall so that rescuers can hear where you are. Use a whistle if one is available. Shout only as a last resort – shouting can cause a person to inhale dangerous amounts of dust.

Assisting victims

- Untrained persons should not attempt to rescue people who are inside a collapsed building. Wait for emergency personnel to arrive.

Chemical agents
Chemical agents are poisonous gases, liquids or solids that have toxic effects on people, animals or plants. Most chemical agents cause serious injuries or death. Severity of injuries depends on the type and amount of the chemical agent used, and the duration of exposure. Were a chemical agent attack to occur, authorities would instruct citizens to either seek shelter where they are and seal the premises or evacuate immediately. Exposure to chemical agents can be fatal. Leaving the shelter to rescue or assist victims can be a deadly decision. There is no assistance that the untrained can offer that would likely be of any value to the victims of chemical agents.

Biological agents
Biological agents are organisms or toxins that have illness-producing effects on people, livestock, and crops. Because biological agents cannot necessarily be detected and may take time to grow and cause a disease, it is almost impossible to know that a biological attack has occurred. If government

officials become aware of a biological attack through an informant or warning by terrorists, they would most likely instruct citizens to either seek shelter where they are and seal the premises or evacuate immediately.

A person affected by a biological agent requires the immediate attention of professional medical personnel. Some agents are contagious, and victims may need to be quarantined. Also, some medical facilities may not receive victims for fear of contaminating the hospital population.

More information on bio-terrorism preparedness and response is available online from the Department of Health and Human Services Centre for Disease Control.

Wildfire emergency checklist (*Source*: FEMA)

- Learn and teach safe fire practices.
- Build fires away from nearby trees or bushes always have a way to extinguish a fire, never leave a fire unattended.
- Obtain local building codes and weeds abatement ordinances for buildings near wooded areas.
- Use fire-resistant materials when building, renovating, or retrofitting structures.
- Create a safety zone to separate home from combustible plants and vegetables.
- Install electrical lines underground, if possible.
- Prune all branches around residence to a height of 8–10 ft.
- Keep trees adjacent to buildings free of dead or dying wood and moss.
- Remove all dead limbs, needles, and debris from rain gutters.
- Store combustible/flammable materials in approved safety containers and keep away from home.
- Keep chimney clean.
- Avoid open burning, especially during dry season. Install smoke detectors on every level of your home.
- Make evacuation plans from home and neighbourhood and have back-up plans.
- Avoid using wooden shakes and shingles for roofing.
- Use only thick, tempered safety glass in large windows and doors.
- Have disaster supplies on hand (flashlights, extra batteries, portable radios, first-aid kits, emergency food and water, non-electric can opener, essential medicines, cash and credit cards, and sturdy shoes).
- Develop an emergency communication plan in case of separation.
- Ask an out-of-state relative to serve as the 'family contact'.

If trapped in a wildfire, you *cannot* outrun it:

- Crouch in a pond or river and cover head and upper body with wet clothing.
- If a body of water is unavailable, look for shelter in a cleared area or among a bed of rocks and lie flat and cover body with wet clothing or soil.
- Listen to radio for emergency information.
- Remove combustible items (outdoor furniture, umbrellas, tarp coverings, and firewood) from around the home.
- Take down flammable drapes and curtains and close all venetian blinds or non-combustible window coverings.
- Close all doors and windows inside home to prevent draft.
- Close gas valves and turn off pilot light.
- Turn on a light in each room for visibility in heavy smoke.
- Place valuables that will not be damaged by water, in a pool or pond.

- If hoses and adequate water are available, leave sprinklers on roofs and anything that might be damaged by fire.
- Be ready to evacuate all family members and pets when fire nears or when instructed to do so by local officials.
- Be cautious when re-entering a burned wildland area – hot spots can flare up without warning.
- Check the roof immediately and extinguish any sparks or embers and the attic for hidden burning sparks.
- Re-check for smoke and sparks throughout the home for several hours afterward.
- Breathe the air close to the ground through a wet cloth to avoid scorching lungs or inhaling smoke.

Nuclear accident mitigation

In the event of a nuclear accident, the most intense levels of contamination are associated with rain and snowfall events. Monitoring the weather information will be essential in implementing emergency plans.

Information about the contamination, ground deposition, and ingestion pathway is unlikely to be available for several months after the accident takes place. This is because of the time consuming type of analysis required, which must be undertaken in a laboratory setting.

In any nuclear accident there are two courses of action: evacuation and sheltering.

Evacuation

This is the only viable option for people living in the vicinity of a nuclear facility at the time of an accident because information about the amount of the contamination and the direction of the plume passage is very vague at the initial stages and this is not a straightforward operation. (At Chernobyl, population moved some 200 km away from the immediate area of the accident, actually entered areas with *greater* amounts of ground contamination because of the weather pattern.)

Emergency evacuation will require safety procedures as follows:

- Access control into the contaminated area.
- Control/sheltering of livestock and animals not evacuated.
- Food and water control.
- Decontamination efforts.
- Relocation plan.

Sheltering

Except in situations where people are certain to be in close proximity and downwind from a major nuclear accident, immediate sheltering is the safest option in avoiding the most intense short-lived activity in the passing plume.

The main priority is to avoid inhalation and ingestion through contaminated foods. The following precautions are recommended.

- If no stocked fallout shelter is available, the best option is to remain indoors in one's own residence, keeping windows and doors closed and blocking all other apertures to minimize inhalation of the passing plume.
- Livestock and pets must also be sheltered and only uncontaminated feeds used.
- If unable to find shelter, or if forced to go outside during the plume passage, a simple dust mask would be an essential first-line protection against inhaling radioactive particles.

- Surface water and rainwater supplies should be avoided.
- Contaminated clothing and footwear should be removed from the immediate vicinity of occupation.
- Certain types of food should be avoided, namely, leafy vegetables with foliar contamination , fruits difficult to wash as raspberries for example, food subject to rapid animal ingestion such as cow's or goat's milk, and cheese.
- Filtering and/or diluting will make most sources of public drinking water safe.
- Garden ground should be covered with tarpaulins if possible to prevent absorption into the soil.

Contributors

Prof. Ing. Alexandru Cismigiu

Born in Romania in a family of researchers, Alexandru Cismigiu has established a distinguished academic career teaching theory of structures and materials and engineering. He taught for 15 years at the Technical Construction University and 35 years at the School of Architecture and Town Planning in Bucharest, his professional life combining a personal style of teaching, design, and research.

Amongst the many buildings he has been responsible for designing the structure, are: The Parliament House, The Palace Hall, The National Theatre, all in Bucharest, the first tall buildings in Skoplije after the 1963 earthquake.

An internationally valued expert in seismic matters in the Balkans, Prof. Cismigiu was designated UNESCO expert when a major earthquake hit Skopje, a town he is now an honorary citizen of. After the 4 March 1977 earthquake in Bucharest, Prof. Cismigiu has taken part in a large number of expert consolidations of Romanian historic monuments, some of which were on the point of collapse, developing his own concept for structural strengthening. His experience of the Romanian earthquakes has been the subject of a number of conferences he gave on seismic matters in Tokyo 1960, Santiago 1962, and New Delhi 1977.

He continues to take an active part co-authoring with his daughter, also a structural engineer, a number of specialist presentations to international conferences such as:

- WCEE – Acapulco 1996: *The seismic pathology of religion related buildings in Romania and their treatment.*
- The 6th World Conference on Composite Materials in Los Angeles: *Mixed structures of composite materials in front of the 20th century.*

In recognition for his professional achievements, The National Association of Romanian Builders has elected Prof. Alexandru Cismigiu 'Constructor of the twentieth century'.

Bertrand Penneron

A French architect graduate of the Paris-La Villete Architectural School since 1987, Bertrand Penneron has also completed further studies at the Versailles Architectural School, the Chaillot School of History and Conservation of Historic Monuments. In 1994, he also gained a degree in landscape studies.

He has established his own practice in Tours, Central France since 1988, and works with three other colleagues: an architect graduate of the Chaillot School (the French equivalent of postgraduate studies on the conservation of historic buildings), a designer draftsman, and a quantity surveyor.

His work is multifaceted with a prevalence of historic buildings and landscaping projects, many of which are on the banks of the Loire river.

Miro Group

Miro Group is a Franco-Romanian group of structural engineers created in 1993, working in central Europe, especially in Romania and France. The group specializes in structural design of new buildings, consolidation and restoration of historic buildings, and the consolidation and rehabilitation of civil and industrial buildings.

The group (working at the time part of the design consortium S.C. Carpati Proiect S.A) have been responsible for the restoration and structural consolidation of the Central University Library in Bucharest, Romania. The following engineers were involved.

Group Director: Mircea Mironescu – Structural Engineer Group Director, Vice- President of the Romanian Commission for Seismic Risk Reduction; Member of the Romanian Historic Monuments Engineering Committee; President of the Association of Romanian Construction Engineers (AICR); Consultant Structural Engineer for projects in Romania, Bucharest such as: The Industrial Export Centre, The World Trade Centre, Financial Plaza, etc.

Group members

- based in Romania: Andrei Bortnowschi, Virgil Sava, Teodor Brotea, Adrian Stanescu, structural engineers.
- based in France: Bogdan Goilav founder member of AICR and Everest Engineering France, member of American Concrete Institute (ACI), The French Association of Seismic Engineers, and French Association of Civil Engineers.

Jonathan P. Kumin, AIA

American Institute of Architects, Alaska Chapter (including past Chapter President)

Construction Specifications Institute

National Council of Architectural Registration Boards Certificate

As Principal-In-Charge at Kumin Associates since 1978, Jon Kumin has directed the successful design of new construction and renovations of a diverse range of project type. Assignments range from science laboratories at the geographic South Pole for the National Science Foundation to a complete, self-contained community in Yuzhno-Sakhalinsk, Russia.

Jon Kumin has been involved with technical investigations of existing structures for both major public and private clients, and has helped develop appropriate standards for buildings in Alaska and other northern regions. He is particularly interested in the integration of the architectural, engineering and construction efforts. He is a frequent lecturer on appropriate design for cold climates, at venues such as the University of Alaska and numerous professional conferences.

Projects designed under Jon Kumin's guidance have won national recognition as outstanding examples of their type from organisations as diverse as the Council of Educational Facility Planners, American Association of School Administrators, and the US Department of Defence. Public service includes serving on the Board of Governors for the University of Michigan architecture school.

Christine Theodoropoulos, Anne Deutsch, Josh Glavin, and Boora Architects, Inc.

Christine Theodoropoulos is an Associate Professor at the University of Oregon – BS Civil Engineering (1979) Princeton, Master of Architecture (1985) Yale, reg. Civil Engineer, California, reg. architect, California. In her research and professional work, Prof. Theodoropoulos addresses the intersection between the disciplines of structure and architecture. Her professional activities involve research and consulting work in the fields of seismic design and historic structures. She has served as a consultant to AIA Research on projects and educational programmes related to seismic design. Her involvement with historic structures has included work with HABS/HAER, the directorship of the Neutra Research House in Los Angeles and research regarding historic bridges in Los Angeles, California and Portland, Oregon. Professor Theodoropoulos teaches courses in seismic design, structures and architectural design studios.

Anne Deutsch is a graduate student in the Master of Architecture program at the University of Oregon. She has an undergraduate degree, BS in Architectural Studies, from the University of Illinois at Urbana-Champaign (1993) and has several years of professional office experience.

Josh Glavin is also a graduate student in the Master of Architecture programme at the University of Oregon. He has an undergraduate degree, BS in Architecture from the University of Idaho (2000).

Deutsch and Glavin have been preparing studio projects for the new school in The Dalles, Oregon for their Masters thesis project.

Boora Architects, Inc. have designed the new school, which is now under construction. AMEC Earth & Environmental, Inc. conducted the Geo technical Engineering Investigation for the Dalles Middle School site in 2001.

Rena Pitsilli-Graham, Freeman Historic Properties, and Caroe & Partners

Rena Pitsilli-Graham is an architect, trained in England and specialised in the repair and conservation of historic buildings. She has worked with Feilden & Mawson on the repair of Marlborough House and with Caroe & Partners on the repair and representation of the White Tower and other buildings in the Tower of London, on Rochester Cathedral, the British Museum, and several churches.

Freeman Historic Properties Limited undertakes the repair of problem listed buildings. An earlier project was the restoration of Wothorpe Grandstand (Grade II*) near Stamford, a derelict eighteenth century racecourse grandstand, which was adapted for residential use. Dr. Jenny Freeman, Chairman has the AA Diploma in Building Conservation and has written a book on the Edwardian architect, W.D. Caroe the founder of Caroe & Partners.

Caroe & Partners was founded in 1884 by W.D. Caroe (1857–1938), and through four generations of architects bearing the family name, the practice has been associated with the care of historic buildings of great significance, from cathedrals to National Trust Houses, from monuments of international significance to humble parish churches.

Information sources

Disaster websites (Source: Cambridge scientific abstracts)

1. Asian Disaster Preparedness Center
   (Asian Institute of Technology, PO Box 4, Klong Luang, Pathumthani, 12120, Thailand)
   http://www.adpc.ait.ac.th/default.html
2. Australian Emergency Management Information Centre
   (Emergency Management Australia)
   http://www.ema.gov.au/libraryf.htm
3. City of Seattle Emergency Management
   (Seattle Public Access Network, Seattle, WA, USA)
   http://www.ci.seattle.wa.us/eoc/default.htm
4. Disaster Emergency Response and Management Systems
   (Caribbean Disaster Emergency Response Agency, The Garrison, St. Micheal, Barbados)
   http://www.cdera.org/derms.htm
5. Disaster Relief
   (American Red Cross, 1621 N. Kent Street, Arlington, VA 22209)
   http://www.disasterrelief.org/
6. Disaster Services
   (Alberta Transportation and Utilities, Alberta, Canada)
   http://www.tu.gov.ab.ca/DIS000.HTM
7. Disaster/Humanitarian Assistance
   (Pan American Health Organization)
   http://www.paho.org/english/ped/pedhome.htm
8. Emergency and Disaster Planning Information
   (Teleport Internet Services)
   http://www.teleport.com/~alany/uscg/ready.html
9. Emergency Preparedness Information Exchange
   (Search and Rescue Society of British Columbia, P.O. Box 187, British Columbia, V8W 2M6 Canada)
   http://sarbc.org/sar-dis.html
10. Epidemic louse-borne typhus fever
    (World Health Organization, Geneva, Switzerland)
    http://www.who.int/inf-fs/en/fact162.html
11. EQE Earthquake Home Preparedness Guide
    (EQE International, 1111 Broadway, 10th Floor, Oakland, CA 94607, USA)
    http://www.eqe.com/publications/homeprep/
12. Global Emergency Management Disaster Counselling Support Network
    (University of Plymouth, Drake Circus, Plymouth, Devon PL4 8AA, UK)
    http://tin.ssc.plym.ac.uk/gemc.html

13. Hazards Literature Database
    (Natural Hazards Research and Applications Information Center, Natural Hazards Center, Campus Box 482, University of Colorado, Boulder, CO 80309-0482)
    http://www.colorado.edu/hazards/litbase/litindex.htm

14. Illinois Disaster Resources
    (University of Illinois at Urbana-Champaign, Champaign, IL, USA)
    http://www.ag.uiuc.edu/~disaster/about.html

15. Integrated Natural Hazard Mitigation in Rhode Island
    (Coastal Resources, University of Rhode Island, Narragansett Bay Campus, Narragansett, RI 02882, USA)
    http://brooktrout.gso.uri.edu/field/us/HazardMit/index.html

16. Mitigating the Impacts of Natural Hazards in the US Virgin Islands
    (Island Resources Foundation, 6296 Estate Nazareth No. 11, St. Thomas, VI 00802-1104)
    http://www.irf.org/irhazmit.htm

17. Natural Disaster Management
    (United Nations, Department of Humanitarian Affairs)
    http://www.ndm.co.uk/

18. Natural Disaster Reduction: From Improved Forecasts to Effective Mitigation
    (National Oceanic and Atmospheric Administration, Department of Commerce, 14th Street & Constitution Avenue NW, Room 6013, Washington, DC 20230, USA)
    http://www.noaa.gov/baker/agu1996.htm

19. Natural Disasters – The Virtual Past
    (Charles Sturt University, Australia)
    http://life.csu.edu.au/virtpast/Disasters.html

20. Natural Hazards Center – Information on Human Adaptation to Disaster
    (The National Hazards Center, University of Colorado, Boulder, Colorado, USA)
    http://www.colorado.edu/hazards/

21. Natural Hazards Mitigation Group
    (Department of Mineralogy, University of Geneva, 13, Rue des Maraichers, CH 1211 Geneva 4, Switzerland)
    http://www.unige.ch:80/hazards/

22. Natural Hazards Research and Applications Center
    (Natural Hazards Research, Applications and Information Center)
    http://adder.colorado.edu/~hazctr/Home.html

23. North American Emergency Management
    (P.O. Box 420731, San Francisco, CA 94142, USA)
    http://www.naem.com/eqk/html/eqk.html

24. Population at Risk from Natural Hazards
    (NOAA, National Ocean Service, 1305 East–West Highway, 9th Fl., Silver Spring, MD 20910-3281, USA)
    http://state_of_coast.noaa.gov/bulletins/html/par_02/par.html

25. Preparedness Training and Exercises
    (Federal Emergency Management Agency, 500 C Street SW, Washington, DC 20472, USA)
    http://www.fema.gov/pte/prep.htm
26. Reducing Risk Through Mitigation
    (Federal Emergency Management Agency)
    http://166.112.200.140:80/mit/
27. Report on Disaster Relief Programme
    (The Internet Society, 12020 Sunrise Valley Drive, Suite 210, Reston, VA 20191-3429, USA)
    http://www.isoc.org/ftp/isoc/bodies/trustees/documents/94-326.txt
28. Self Organization in Disaster Response
    (University of Colorado Natural Hazards Program)
    http://www.colorado.edu/hazards/qr/qr78.html
29. Transition from Response to Recovery: A Look at the Lancaster, Texas Tornado
    (University of Colorado at Boulder, Boulder, CO, USA)
    http://www.colorado.edu/hazards/qr/qr79.html
30. A World Safe from Natural Disasters
    (Pan American Health Organization)
    http://www.paho.org/english/ped/peddisen.htm

Earthquake websites and organizations

http://www.georisk.com/terminol/termeq.shtml#Fault:

Weather information and organizations websites

1. Radar Information
   metsys.weathersa.co.za/RadarInfo.htm
2. Earth Systems Education Real Time Information of the Earth
   earthsys.ag.ohio-state.edu/earth_today.html
3. Met Office: Homepage
   www.met-office.gov.uk/
4. BBC – Weather Centre – Home Page
   www.bbc.co.uk/weather/
5. Meteorology Department Home Page
   www.met.rdg.ac.uk/

Fire monitoring and information websites

1. Wildland Fire Information
   http://www.nifc.gov/National Interagency Fire Center
   http://www.or.blm.gov/nwfire/Northwest Fire Prevention/Education Fire Restrictions and Closures Information
   http://www.fs.fed.us/r6/w-w/firecenter/Northeast Oregon Interagency Fire Center (NOC)
   http://www.fs.fed.us/r6/uma/PICC/Pendleton Interagency Communication Center (PIC)

http://www.fs.fed.us/r6/centraloregon/index_rac.htmlRedmondAirCenter
http://www.nv.blm.gov/wgbccWestern Great Basin Coordination Center
http://www.rfl.psw.fs.fed.us/Riverside Fire Lab
http://www.fire.org/Fire.org
http://www.fs.fed.us/fire/planning/nist/Forest Service Fire Applications Support

2. International Fire Management Sites
   http://www.anu.edu.au/Forestry/fire/firenet.htmlInternational Fire Info Network
   http://www.nofc.forestry.ca/fire/Canadian Fire Management
   http://earthobservatory.nasa.gov/Observatory/Datasets/fires.trmm.html
   http://earthobservatory.nasa.gov/Observatory/Datasets/fires.trmm.htmlGlobal Fire Monitoring
   http://www.gis.umn.edu/Department of Forest Resources (GIS)
   http://www.fire.ca.gov/California Department of Forestry & Fire Protection
   http://flame.doacs.state.fl.us/Florida Fire Home Page
   http://www.wsfire.com/WesternStates Fire Information Resource

3. Recommended Link (Favorite) Sites
   http://wildlandfirefighter.com/links.htmlWildland Firefighters Link Page
   http://thomas.loc.gov/Thomas: US Congress
   http://www.firstgov.gov/

4. Global Forest Watch
   http://www.globalforestwatch.org/

5. Interactive Health Ecology Access Links (IHEAL)
   http://mole.utsa.edu/~matserv/iheal/

6. United Nations System: Sustainable Development Country Archives
   http://www.un.org/esa/agenda21/natlinfo/countinf.htm

7. United Nations System-Wide Earthwatch
   http://www.unep.ch/earthw.html

8. World Rainforest Movement (WRM)
   http://www.wrm.org.uy/

9. World Resources Institute (WRI)
   http://www.wri.org/

United Nations Environment Programme (UNEP)
Regional Office for Europe, 15, Chemin des Anémones
1219 Chátelaine, Geneva, Switzerland,
Tel: (41–22) 917–8111; Fax: (41–22) 917–8024;
Email: roe@unep.ch; http://www.unep.ch

Office for the Coordination of Humanitarian Affairs (OCHA)
United Nations Palais des Nations,
1211 Geneva 10, Switzerland,
Tel: (41–22) 917–1142; Fax: (41–22) 917–0247;
Email: ochagva@un.org; http://www.reliefweb.int/ocha_01

Bibliography

Ashcroft, Frances. *Life at the Extremes: The Science of Survival*. Harper Collins (2000), Flamingo (2001).

Cherouette Patrick, *Construction en zone sismique: les enseignements a tirer du drame turc,* Les Cahiers Techniques du Batiment No. 203, 2000; *Pathologie Les erreurs de conception à corriger en zone sismique,* Les Cahiers Techniques du Batiment No. 219, 2001.

Cismigiu, Alexandru (1977). *Dupa 4 martie 1977* Arhitectura nr. 4.

Cismigiu, Alexandru (1981). Dogaru Lucian *Prezente Romanesti in inginerie seismica*, Arhitectura nr.1.

Comerio, Mary C. (1988). *Disaster Hits Home – New Policy for Urban Housing Recovery.* University of California Press.

Dion, R. *Histoire des levées de la Loire.*

Dowrick, D.J. (1977). *Earthquake Resistant Design – A Manual for Engineers and Architects.* John Wiley, London.

Environment Agency (2002). *The Thames Barrier.*

Feilden, Bernard M. (2001). *Conservation of Historic Buildings.* Architectural Press.

Fisk, Dorothy (1940). *Weather in the Making.* The Scientific Book Club.

Gordon, J.E. (1991). *Structures or Why Things don't Fall Down.* Penguin.

Jalil, Wolfgang, *L'avis d'expert,* Les Cahiers Techniques du Batiment No. 203, 2000, No. 219, 2001.

King, Harold. Revised by Derek Osbourn *Mitchell's Building – Components.*

Koenigberger, O.H., Ingersoll, T.G., Mayhew, A., Szokolay, S.V. (1978). *Manual of Tropical Housing and Building.* Longman Group Ltd.

Levitt, Allan M. (1997). *Disaster Planning and Recovery.* John Wiley.

Nelson, Carl. L (1991). *Protecting the Past from Natural Disasters.* The Preservation Press, National Trust for Historic Preservation in the United States.

Roaf Sue, Manuel Fuentes and Stephanie Thoms (2002). *Ecohouse a Design Guide.* Architectural Press.

Smith, Anthony. (2002). *The Weather: What is happening to Our Climate?* Arrow Books.

Stroud Foster Jack (1973). *Mitchell's Building Building Construction – Part 1 Structure and Fabric.* Batsford Academic and Educational London.

Strud, Foster and Raymond Harrington. *Mitchell's Building Series, Structure and fabric Part 2*. Batsford Academic and Educational London.

The Institution of Structural Engineers (1995). *The Structural Engineer's Response to Explosion Damage*.

Toigo, John (2000). *Disaster Recovery Planning*. Prentice Hall.

UNESCO (1985). *Building Construction under Seismic Conditions in the Balkan Region and Post Earthquake Damage Evaluation*. United Nations Development Programme, Vienna.

Glossary

Earthquake terms

Acceleration   rate of increase of velocity per time unit.

Aftershock   seismic event occurring after an earthquake, usually within days. Although often smaller in intensity can be quite destructive as buildings and structures have already been weakened.

Axial loading   compressive force acting along the vertical axis of a structural element.

Base shear   probable maximum value of the force required to maintain equilibrium when a system is vibrating laterally in response to a chaotic disturbance.

Braced frames   frames stiffened against lateral buckling.

Damping   slowing down or preventing of oscillations caused dissipation of kinetic energy. Critical damping represents the minimum amount of damping which would stop movement.

Epicentre   the point on the Earth's surface directly above the focus of an earthquake.

Fault   plane surface of fracture in a rock body, caused by brittle failure, along which relative displacements between adjacent blocks can be observed.

Focus   the location, usually within the Earth of the first motion of an earthquake is estimated to have occurred.

Hypocentre   an alternative word for focus.

Liquefaction   in soils, temporary transformation to a fluid state due to sudden decrease in shear resistance associated with the collapse of the surrounding structure as a result of an increase in fluid pressure.

Lithosphere   the upper layer of the solid Earth, comprising blocks known as tectonic plates. If subjected to stresses of the order of 100 Mpa, it deforms by brittle failure.

Loading   term for the forces acting on a building.

Mode   shape of oscillation taking place in a system of components and masses. Normal mode is the first or fundamental mode where displacements from the base are observed.

Moment   measure of the effect of a force about a point of rotation, expressed in units of force and distance, for example, Newton metres (Nm).

Pancaking   falling apart of a building, collapsing vertically rather than falling over, in earthquake conditions.

Period   the time a system takes to pass through the mean position twice, travelling in the same direction. The fundamental period is that of the normal mode.

Plate tectonics   the movement of rigid units in the Earth's lithosphere, each of which has a separate motion from the other plates.

Seiches   a disturbance within a closed body of water.

Seismograph   instrument measuring timing and nature of ground motion at locations remote from the station.

Seismometer   device detecting seismic waves originating from earthquakes and measuring the effect of ground disturbance on particular systems of a given period and damping.

Shear   effect on material resisting a sliding force, which causes its successive layers to be shifted laterally over each other. The maximum value of the force responding to a disturbance of the design system is known as Base Shear.

Spectrum   the relationship between the response of a system (acceleration, velocity, displacement) and the period values of damping.

Subduction zone   zone, at an angle to the surface of the Earth, down which a lithospheric plate descends.

Torsion   effect of a force on a structural member causing it to twist.

Tsunami   giant seismic wave occurring as a result of a sub-ocean earthquake. Its velocity is related to the depth of the water. At sea the tsunami is hardly noticeable, but when reaching shallow waters they build up heights of more than 30 metres, causing severe damage to coastal areas.

Volcanoes

Lava   molten rock. Its behaviour depends on its viscosity, which depends on the silica content, temperature and dissolved gases. The less viscous the lava the faster it flows, the more viscous the lava the greater the tendency towards explosive eruption.

Magma   supposed fluid strata under the solid crust of the Earth.

Eruption   the release of lava and gas from the Earth's interior to the Earth's surface and into the atmosphere.

Pyroclastic   literally 'fire-broken', applied to volcanic rocks consisting of fragmented particles, generally produced by explosive action.

Flood

Flash floods   a brief but powerful surge of water, either over a surface ('sheet flood') or down a normally dry stream channel ('stream flood'), usually caused by heavy rainfall of short duration, typical of arid environment.

Flood plain   part of a river valley, made of unconsolidated sediment and periodically flooded.

Dry-proofing measures taken to keep water out of the building.

Wet proofing measures taken to improve the ability to withstand the effects of flooding once the water has entered the building.

Surge level height reached by water surge.

Valve a flap or other constriction that can close to ensure that a fluid flows in only one direction.

Levée raised embankment of a river sloping away from the channel resulting from periodic over bank flooding.

Weather

Anabatic wind wind that blows up a warm gentle slope.

Cyclone- system of winds rotating around a centre of minimum barometric pressure.

Cyclogenesis formation and strengthening of cyclonic air circulation tending to form or deepen depressions.

Firn snow that has survived a summer melting season, an intermediate material in converting snow to glacial ice.

Gradient rate of change of a function in meteorology, such as pressure or temperature, at right angles to the isolines.

Heat conduction the transfer of heat from a warmer to a colder region in the same substance without mass transfer, depending on the thermal conductivity of the material.

Katabatic wind wind that occurs when cold dense air chilled by radiation cooling moves gravitationally beneath less dense air.

Mean radiant temperature indicates the effect of surface temperature of surrounding objects on human comfort.

Prevailing wind the wind direction that is most frequent over time in a particular location.

Streamers column of light of objects on the surface of the earth responding a strong electric field such as that of an electric storm.

Thermal mass mass of building expressed in volume of heated space.

Thermal movement movement due to expansion or contraction caused by temperature changes.

Wind loading effect of wind force acting on a building.

Wind suction upward suction caused by wind passing over a roof, tending to raise the roof and its structure.

Mass movement

Solifluction downhill movement of unconsolidated weathered material saturated with water.

Landslide mass movement consisting of transfer of earth material down hillslopes.

Subsidence sinking or settling of the ground surface due to natural or anthropogenic causes.

Man-made disasters

Anthropogenic   resulting from human activities or of human origin.

Greenhouse effect   The effect of heat retention in the lower atmosphere as a result of absorption and re-radiation by clouds and gases.

Grey water   household generated wastewater from shower, bath, sink and laundry waste, excluding toilet wastes.

CRUD   acronym for 'Chalk River Unidentified Deposits' – black, highly radioactive substances from inside piping and components of Chalk River nuclear reactor.

Curie   measurement of radioactivity: the amount of radioactive material relative to disintegrations per second.

Plume   the concentration profile of an airborne or waterborne release of material as it spreads from its source.

Radioactivity   spontaneous decay of nucleus of an atom by emission of particles, usually accompanied by electromagnetic radiation. Also defined as the mean number of nuclear transformations occurring in a given quantity of radioactive material per unit of time.

VOC   Volatile Organic Compounds – generic name for a variety of toxic chemicals used in reprocessing spent nuclear fuel and other industrial applications concerning weapons production.

Index